These Strange German Ways and the Whys of the Ways

A CULTURAL GUIDE
TO THE GERMANS
AND THEIR CUSTOMS

For the Curious,
Such as Businesspeople,
Accompanying Spouses,
Students, Tourists
and Armchair Travelers

Susan Stern

ILLUSTRATED BY HANS TRAXLER

Atlantik-Brücke Board of Directors
Dr. Arend Oetker, *Chairman*
Dr. Beate Lindemann, *Executive Vice Chairman*
Max Warburg, *Treasurer*

A publication of Atlantik-Brücke e.V.
Magnus-Haus, Am Kupfergraben 7
D-10117 Berlin, Germany
Tel.: (+49 30) 20 39 83 0
Fax.: (+49 30) 20 39 83 20
Email: info@atlantik-bruecke.org

ISBN 3-925744-09-6

Creative design: Dede Cummings
Printed by: Transcontinental Printing, Québec, Canada.

10 9 8 7 6 5 4 3 2 1

Printed in Canada on acid-free paper

ATLANTIK

BRÜCKE

DEDICATION AND ACKNOWLEDGEMENTS

To ANJA, MY BELOVED DAUGHTER. You missed out on having Dad's unfinished last book dedicated to you, and if one day you finish it for him, you won't be able to dedicate it to yourself, so this one is all for you.

I'M PRETTY HARD TO TAKE at the best of times, but I can become fairly impossible when I'm wrapped up in a project such as writing a book. I can't say that I've been working on this one for two years without a break, but even during the sometimes long pauses between bouts of creativity, *These Strange German Ways* has been on my mind. My long-suffering daughter finally escaped to the United States, but wasn't spared even there because I kept bugging her to tell me about her cross-cultural experiences. She appears every so often in the coming pages because she is unquestionably the German I am closest to and know best! My special friend Igor Reichlin was phenomenally patient with me and not only provided invaluable help with the business section of the book, but also came to my rescue every time my computer played up (often). Irmgard Burmeister, creator of the original *These Strange German Ways*, continued to support her creation by giving me very wise and affectionate advice and lots of encouragement. Deirdre McKay, my best friend who alas! now lives in Australia, offered to check the book over the final weekend—thank heaven for e-mail. I could go on and on. For two years, I got on everybody's nerves as I checked out all the strange German, American and all the other ways I could think of. So to all of you, named and unnamed—thank you!

Finally, a word of gratitude to Inter Nationes, an organization which provides valuable background material on all aspects of contemporary Germany, for letting me use some of my own material which originally appeared in different form in their Basic Information series.

CONTENTS

SECTION TWO: **THE WAYS**

PART ONE: DOING BUSINESS WITH THE GERMANS

FOREWORD

THE BOOK IS TRANSFORMED but the title remains. *These Strange German Ways* is so much part of the Atlantik-Brücke—its creator and first author, Irmgard Burmeister, introduced it into our repertoire in 1964—that we cannot bring ourselves to change the name. It has become an integral part of us. It continues to be our runaway best seller, read and appreciated throughout the world. However, as the readership changes—from members of the American forces stationed in Germany, to today's completely diverse global travelers—so does the book. And the entirely new book introduced by Susan Stern in 1994 is once again, in 2000, an entirely new book, albeit still by Susan. But this time around, the subtitle announces a metamorphosis, a new incarnation. *These Strange German Ways* has become a comprehensive guide not just to the ways but also to the whys-of-the-ways of 21st century Germans!

Traditionally, I have used the Foreword to say a few words about the Atlantik-Brücke. Founded as a private, non-profit organization in the early 1950s, its sole purpose is to promote greater interaction and understanding between Germany and its North American partners, the United States and Canada. To this end, the Atlantik-Brücke arranges a wide variety of trans-Atlantic programs for such diverse groups as Young Leaders to 11th graders, and from members of Congress and the German parliament to business leaders. It works together with many organizations in North America, from the American Council on Germany to the American Jewish Committee, to portray Germany as it has become over the past half-century: a country with a past and a legacy, but also with a present and a future. It provides valuable resources to journalists. Together with the Armonk Institute of New York, the Atlantik-Brücke works with U.S. state boards of education to give social science teachers a more personal relationship to the country they present in their classes. And, of course, the Atlantik-Brücke has a number of publications which follow the same goal: better cross-cultural understanding. Which brings us back full-circle to this brand new *These Strange German Ways*. It's funny, it's informative, it's provocative—not necessarily in that order. It is as much for the businessperson who wants to know about cross-cultural negotiations as for the exchange student who wants to know about dating habits. It's for anyone looking for interesting, amusing perspectives on Germany! Susan Stern imparts her knowledge, insights and views in a lively, personal conversation with each one of us. Once again, on behalf of the Atlantik-Brücke I would like to congratulate her and thank her for yet another excellent book.

And to the readers of this book—as always, I wish you pleasant reading.

BEATE LINDEMANN
Executive Vice Chairman
Atlantik-Brücke e.V.

PROLOGUE TO THE 1994 NEW BOOK

ONCE UPON A TIME some thirty-odd years ago, a marvelous book came into being. Called *These Strange German Ways*, it rapidly became an indispensable, everything-you-need-to-know-about-Germany handbook for American visitors to the land of the *Oktoberfest* and mad drivers. Over the years it was printed, reprinted, revised and updated to meet the demand of an insatiable public who wanted to be initiated into the mysteries of German customs, foibles and habits. When the 16th edition was just about exhausted, an equally exhausted author and editor, Irmgard Burmeister, put out an SOS. After three decades, she said, it was high time that somebody else took over *These Strange German Ways* so that she herself could find the time to take care of the strange German plants that she was cultivating in her Hamburg garden.

And so it was that I was asked to come up with a new version of *These Strange German Ways*. Not just a new edition, but a brand-new book reflecting the Post-Wall Germany we are now living in or with. The task—to match a book which had sold in the hundreds of thousands throughout the world and had become an institution—was daunting. But since Irmgard promised to give me advice and comfort, what else could I do? I accepted the challenge.

THE STRANGENESS OF WAYS

In this age of political correctness, talking about the "strange" ways of the Germans, or of anyone else, has become a sensitive business, as I rediscovered just the other night. "And what's so strange about the way we do things?" asked the German sitting next to me at a dinner party. His tone was not exactly frosty, but it wasn't very amused either. I hastened to explain. An hour or so later, after hearing me hold forth on comparative cultures, he was probably sorry that he'd ever asked, but I think he'd accepted that I'd used "strange" to mean unfamiliar rather than weird, and that no ethnic slur had been intended. We parted amicably or so I could assume from the way he raised my hand to his lips and blew on it gently as we said goodbye.

Indeed, whether they are blowing kisses on female hands or touching chimney sweeps to bring good luck, the Germans, like everybody else, go about the Business of Living in their own sweet way. They are first and foremost individuals. But beyond that, they think as Germans, behave as Germans, inhabit their homes as Germans, conduct their working life as Germans, socialize and travel as Germans, celebrate holidays as Germans. Many of them are supremely unaware that they go about things in a way that could be called characteristically their own—but then, I guess we all tend to harbor the delusion that our own particular attitudes and behavior are internationally standard. "But everybody hangs their bedclothes out of the window to air," wailed my German mother-in-law recently, wondering for the umpteenth time at my unwillingness to do so. She comes from southern Germany and after almost a quarter of a century of knowing me, she still can't fathom my strange foreign ways.

Well, when you've lived here in Germany for as long as I have—over two decades—you become pretty familiar with German Ways, even if you sometimes refuse to conform and risk soot and worse on your bedclothes. What once struck you as strange now seems the rule. You find yourself expecting a certain formality and distance in your relationships with people you don't know well and you reciprocate in kind. You come to appreciate the importance of time in everyday German life and you make great efforts to keep appointments and arrive on time. You learn never to breathe down people's necks and crowd their personal space. You stop being surprised that doors are closed wherever you go and you even end up closing them yourself.

It takes a while to get to know a people and their ways, and you can't learn everything from a book. Still, I hope that the pages to come will prepare you for some of what awaits you when you get to Germany, and take the edge off any culture shock you might experience. Happy reading, happy travels.

PROLOGUE TO THE ENTIRELY NEW
2000 BOOK

AFTER *These Strange German Ways—The New Book* appeared six years ago, some of my best German friends called me up the next day. "You rat," they cried, "we thought that after all these years you'd become a bona fide, honorary almost-German, and instead, you've stabbed us in the back. You've exposed our fears and foibles, ridiculed our values, hung out our squeaky-clean bed clothes, mocked the very rules and regulations by which we live. Shame on you." I was mortified. "You've got it all wrong," I said, and tried to explain what I'd set out to do. In vain. My friends hung up in a huff, and refused to talk to me for the rest of the afternoon.

Well, that was a few years ago. Lots of people have read the book in the meantime, and most of the Germans among them—in the end, probably not all that many; for indeed, why would any Germans read a book about themselves by a foreigner in English?—anyway, most of those few Germans have been polite enough not to let on if they were upset by my well-intentioned remarks. But the initial phone calls have continued to rankle. Perhaps none of my German readers understands me, I often think despondently before going to bed at night. Perhaps they will always take my Anglo-Saxon humor as sarcasm, irony and even outright criticism. And I have asked myself how I could bring them to view themselves as others do without their taking offense.

So now, with the fourth edition of the book running out and a large U.S. company beating on the Atlantik-Brücke's doors to acquire distribution rights, it is definitely time to set the record straight. Instead of simply *describing* how the Germans tick, I have gone a major step further and tried to explain *why* they tick the way they do. To this end, I've divided the book into two distinct sections, with most of the *Whys* in section one, and most of the *Ways* in section two. My explanations are anything but revolutionary, I should hasten to add. Lots of people have lots to say about different cultures, how they can be quantified and qualified and compared to each other, how they communicate, or fail to communicate, with each other. Intercultural or cross-cultural studies are the rage these days, particularly since increasing mobility in the business world has made it imperative for people around the globe to recognize that "the way we do things back home" is not necessarily the way others elsewhere do things, and a successful cross-cultural joint venture of any kind—from a personal friendship to a multi-national co-operation—must be based on the understanding of, and tolerance for, the differences in thinking and behavior of the parties involved. Cultures can be measured on a variety of scales, and cultural behavior can be analyzed and even predicted. And so it's perfectly politically correct in culture-speak to talk about "the" Germans as opposed to "the" French or "the" Saudi Arabians, and such categorization is entirely meaningful, even allowing for often huge regional differences.

The whys and wherefores of German behavior (as well as the behavior itself) have fascinated me ever since I arrived in Germany in the early 1970s as the greenest horn in the world, and discovered fast that if I wanted to function and feel comfortable in my new cultural environment, I had a lot to learn. Cultural studies hadn't really been invented then, so I had to discover everything the hard way: through personal experience, whatever books I could find, and, as I mentioned in the introduction to the 1994 book included above, my mother-in-law. Two decades later, at around the time of German unification, I contributed an article called "Germanity" to one of two books (*Meet United Germany, Volume 1, Perspectives*) which I produced for the Atlantik-Brücke and the Frankfurter Allgemeine Zeitung Information Services. *Germanity* (my word) is a popularized socio-cultural mini-guide to the Germans. I borrowed—rather freely I admit, but with due credit—from one of America's foremost socio-cultural gurus, Robert T. Hall, and came up with a communication aid for foreigners which has proven to be quite useful.

No doubt, if I were to re-write "Germanity" today, I would tamper quite a bit with the early 1990s model. Instead of borrowing primarily from Robert T. Hall, I would extend my pilfering to other socio-cultural gurus, in particular to Geert Hofstede and Alfons Trompenaas, both Dutch researchers and practitioners in cross-cultural communication. Then I'd put all the experts in a jar, add a few of my own ideas, shake furiously, and produce a "new" paradigm. Such procedure is called scholarly research. This is in fact what I've done in the many cultural awareness seminars and workshops for international business people and their accompanying partners that I've conducted over the years. It seems to work pretty well.

And this too is what I've done in this newly written version of *These Strange German Ways* It contains elements of the 1994 "New Book," although I've added and subtracted a number of items, and updated wherever necessary. Much of this revised earlier material can be found in the last two parts of the second section of the book, *Practicalities: Everything (Else) You Need To Know* and *Totally Miscellaneous Strange German Ways*. But the rest—the bulk—of the book is very different from its predecessor. And I can only hope that the Germanity explanations will be so convincing that my German friends will once again send me Valentines and regret ever calling me a rat.

PREAMBLE
AND FRIENDLY USER'S GUIDE

THE BOOK YOU ARE ABOUT TO READ was supposed to be a compendium. After I'd written it—and looked up the word compendium—I realized that it wasn't, because it is neither a summary nor an abstract "containing the essential information in a brief form." It does contain information which I hope is essential, but the word "the" bothers me, because it implies that nothing has been omitted. Much has. Moreover, nobody has ever accused me of being brief.

On the contrary, this book is in parts long-winded and often repetitive. The long-windedness comes from my being a teacher—I can't help it. The repetition is intentional—well, more or less—because the book is not designed to be read from cover to cover, and certainly not at one sitting. In fact, I highly recommend that you delve into it selectively after you have gone through the table of contents and figured out what might interest you. This is what I had in mind while I was writing, and so I have deliberately (cross my heart) repeated some items in different places—with a different slant, of course, and in different words. Wherever possible, I have cross-referenced, so "see page x" appears frequently.

I decided to divide the book into *The Whys* and *The Ways*, but it turned out that some topics or items were hard to pigeon-hole into one or other of the categories. Does a German bedroom tell you anything about why Germans are the way they are? Are German attitudes to sex and state interference (two separate items) whys or ways? Such questions caused me sleepless nights, but The Whys and The Ways still made sense to me.

From the start, my biggest headache was the style of the book. It careens without warning from the completely serious (on cultural diversity; the relationship between church and state; the handicapped; the legacy of war etc., etc.), to the somewhat tongue-in-cheek (on the German love for order; *Angst*; German homes and gardens; etc., etc.). I tried, I really tried, to find a harmonious, unified form for the whole book, but I was not very successful. More reason, then, to read different parts of the book at different times. Nevertheless: the information I have included, expressed seriously or humorously, is absolutely true. To the best of my knowledge.

So here's the *User's Guide*: Read as much as you can of *Section One*. It's a bit theoretical at times, but contains some light relief—and it tells you what you need to know to appreciate or better understand not just the Germans, but other cultures, too. It thus provides the basis for *Section Two*. That section is easier to read, and I've designed the different parts for different interest groups—business people, accompanying spouses, students, and so on—so you can skip whole chunks. At the risk of missing some pearls of wisdom, of course.

At school in England, I learned that the first person "I" should be avoided at all costs in any piece of writing that was supposed to be taken seriously. What can I say? I do want *These Strange German Ways* to be taken seriously. However, I do not claim that everything I say in the book is impartial or unbiased, and by using "I" at times, I am simply taking responsibility for my often very personal opinions.

I hope you will enjoy this book.

THE
WHYS

The Relativity of Reality

SEARCHING FOR GERMANITY

Nowhere (else) in the world is the question of national identity raised more frequently and with more concern. What appears to be arrogance is as often as not an expression of lack of self-confidence and self-assurance.

Werner Holzer: "The Eternal German Riddle"
(in *Meet United Germany*, ed. Susan Stern)

IDENTITY PROBLEMS

Oh! those Germans. Who and what are they? Only just over a decade ago, rich, bothered and divided (the title of an excellent pre-unification book about West Germany by British author David Marsh). Today, at the start of the 21st century, more or less rich—some more, some less—every bit as bothered, and still very divided, although no longer into two separate countries.

Which does not answer the question as to who they are, these people whose country occupies a significant chunk—albeit smaller than Montana—of the European continent. Indeed, there are more Germans in Europe, around 82 million, than there are Brits or French, less than 60 million of each. Add the roughly 60 million Americans of German ancestry in the United States alone, plus quite a few million more ethnic Germans in the countries which used to be behind the Iron Curtain, and the numbers mount up. In other words, there's a large contingent of bloodline Germans in our global population, so you'd think it would be easy to say who they are.

Well, ethnic jokes aside, it isn't. If you yourself are one of them, you may think you have an inkling of your Germanic essence, but—no offense—you probably don't. For how many people know themselves well, not merely as individuals—difficult enough—but as part of a collective, as members of a nation? Especially when that nation is Germany, and self-knowledge is greatly hampered by the Germanic

trait of agonizing over everything, otherwise known as "worry-wartism," as well as by romantic self-delusion. Why, the Germans claim to see themselves as a bunch of melancholic, broody thinkers and poetic philosophers, whereas everybody else sees them as down-to-earth, hands-on, practical do-ers—that is, no-nonsense people who get things done. Add to that confusion the terrible legacy of war and worse which second-half 20th century Germans have been left to deal with and which still continues to wreak havoc on German self-image—no, if you're German, it's not easy to know yourself. And then again, how many people of any nationality, thinking they know themselves pretty well, are able to put that knowledge into words? How many can put their finger on that elusive "something" that makes them collectively what they are, and distinguishes them from others? So even if you are German to the core, you probably don't have a clear, communicable idea, let alone a reasonably accurate one, who the Germans are, and you might need someone—maybe even a non-German—to tell you. And if you think that is pure chutzpah, I apologize!

STEREOTYPES AND CLICHÉS . . .

... and it often occurs to me that nothing identifies a German so much as (his) search for his identity.

John Ardagh: *Germany and the Germans*

Non-Germans—the Brits and the French in particular—take a particularly fiendish delight in telling the Germans and the world who they think the Germans are and what makes them tick. So-called experts write volumes on the subject, and just about everybody else seems to have some wisdom to contribute, more often than not unflattering. Misunderstood maybe, the Germans are definitely much-maligned. Which of us has not heard at some time or other that the Germans are . . . aggressive, pedantic, assertive, stiff, unapproachable, unfriendly, humorless—and so on? Even normally positive attributes such as "efficient" and "punctual" can quiver with negative vibes when applied by the rest of the world to the Germans. A good number of the clichés in circulation can be written off to fear or envy—or both, and in view of the aforementioned bellicose history of the first part of the 20th century, and the perceived almost indecent prosperity of West Germany in the second part, this is not too surprising. But—and now we come to the really tricky part—can we simply write off the clichés as completely unfounded, ignorant nonsense? Or is there something about "the Germans" which could lead the least prejudiced, most positively inclined observer to admit that the epithets might indeed contain some germinal truth and reflect traits or characteristics that many people of German extraction seem to share?

Clichés are by definition trite, and in our politically correct world, they've become unacceptable, even in attempts at humor. However, we shouldn't simply dismiss them. The reason they exist at all is because enough people over enough time have repeated much the same sentiments, and do this not because everybody chooses to perpetuate the same biased nonsense, but because these sentiments reflect some kind of perceived reality—that is, the way we see things. Moreover, the way we see things is itself a reflection of own psychic baggage—our vision may be clouded by our own feelings of insecurity or envy, for example. The Brits have never really forgiven the Germans for losing the war and then turning defeat into an economic miracle. In other words: ethnic stereotyping is essentially the boiling-down of enormously complex perceived reality to a few conventional notions which are then applied uncritically and indiscriminately to anybody belonging to the species. Hell, according to one version of an old, tired joke, is a place where the cooks are all British, the policemen all Italian, the lovers all German, and the mechanics all French. And heaven? Just reshuffle the stereotypes.

. . . AND BEYOND

Back to square one. In our quest to figure out who and what the Germans are, we can't escape whatever-it-is that leads to the clichés, stereotypes and lousy jokes. On the contrary—it's precisely that whatever-it-is, the elusive something I referred to above, that we need to capture in order to come up with a practical, useful description of the nation and its people—the quintessential Germans. We need to figure out just what makes the Germans tick. Above all, we need to determine what distinguishes them from everybody else and makes them Germans rather than Brits or Mexicans or Turks. In short, we're looking for the German core—something I call "Germanity."

But does Germanity exist? Is it possible to lump all Germans together and make global statements about them? The best answer is probably the German *jein*—a mixture of *ja* (yes) and *nein* (no). To start with the latter: although Germany is neither a melting pot of different cultures and ethnic groups like the United States, nor a composite of groups arbitrarily united by political boundaries like the Soviet Union of the past, or—possibly—the Europe of the future, it still does not have a homogeneous population. This is hardly surprising given the fact that what we today call Germany has always been a collection of states: in the past, kingdoms, dukedoms, principalities and the like; in more recent times, federal states. The revised 1987 edition of the *Random House Dictionary of the English Language* begins its definition of Germany with, "A former country in the middle of Europe . . . ," and much as that entry may have caused confusion, it was, at the time, technically correct. There was a Federal Republic of Germany and a German Democratic Republic, but no "Germany." I'm not about to delve deep into history here, but the psycho-socio-political vicissitudes (read: wars and their aftermath) of the amorphous middle European area often incorrectly referred to over the centuries as "Germany" has done nothing to help form and cement a firm German identity in its people. Particularly when abroad, the

Germans, unlike the Brits, the French, the Americans—and most other nationalities for that matter—tend not to consider themselves *first and foremost* as nationals of their country, but rather, as burghers of their communities: they define themselves more readily and happily as native sons and daughters of local states or cities. A Saxon or Bavarian, a Hamburger, Frankfurter or Berliner—these are primary identities, whereas (even) a New Yorker, I suspect, will subordinate his metropolitan to his national sense of self.

So—the Germans don't go around waving the German flag either literally or figuratively, and they themselves emphatically refuse to entertain the thought that they have much in common with each other. Certainly, there is much to the widespread belief that northern and southern Germans differ in everything from temperament to taste, religion to politics, garb to gab, and that eastern (ex-German Democratic Republic) and western Germans have scarcely more in common than their language. Indeed, some wags have it that not even this is the case. That most German of words *Heimat*, literally translated as native place, home town, is absolutely loaded with closed community connotations, the notion that cultural belonging extends no further than the village boundary. The Germans? A disparate folk if there ever was one.

German Day, U.S.-Style

Where in the world are Germans most likely to proclaim their heritage with the greatest pride? From my own experience, I would say: in the American Midwest. On October 3, 1993, I was invited to give a keynote speech at the University of Indianapolis on the occasion of the third birthday of United Germany. This was my first trip to Indiana, and I knew the state was home to a lot of German Americans. Nothing, however, had prepared me for the huge turnout to the birthday festivities, or for the enthusiasm of the audience, decked out in short leather pants and dirndls, the men with red, black and gold striped ties and all waving the German flag. This was German Day, in pure July Fourth tradition. For me, coming from the home country where flag-waving is normally acceptable only at sports events, and where national festivities are celebrated with a maximum of dignity and unpretentiousness, the uninhibited and boisterous acknowledgement, "German-and-proud-of-it," came as a surprise, almost a shock. Here in Germany, we are just not used to it. And this in itself, however understandable, is sad.

2 SOFTWARE OF THE MIND

The culture of a country—or other category of people—is not a combination of properties of the "average citizen," nor a "modal personality." It is, among other things, a set of likely reactions of citizens with a common mental programming.

Geert Hofstede: *Cultures and Organizations*

What follows is a necessary excursus. In order to make the Germans more understandable, to move beyond the cliché and stereotyping and get to the nitty-gritty of Germanity, I need to talk a bit in general terms about cultural programming. This is the key to everything that follows in this book, the key to the "what makes a German a German" conundrum, the key to all those strange German ways. So stick with me for just a while . . .

VIVE LA DIFFÉRENCE

That said, and in full awareness of the dangers of generalizations, I still assert: Germanity—that elusive something that makes Germans into Germans—does exist. Quite simply, the Germans, however heterogeneous, do somehow differ from the Egyptians, the Chinese or the Italians, and on a level that has nothing to do with physical appearance. Something shared makes them all, however diverse they are, or think they are, into Germans—and, of course, the Egyptians into Egyptians, the Chinese into Chinese, etc.—and distinguishes them from the others. And, I maintain, it is entirely possible to make intelligent comments about so-called "typical" German characteristics, even taking into account regional differences, without falling back on clichés, stereotypes and prejudice. Germanity is simply the sum of all that Germans share: common values and behavior patterns acquired in an on-going learning process which starts at birth and may continue throughout a person's life. I'm talking about cultural programming—what a wise Dutchman, Geert Hofstede, calls the "software of the mind."

CULTURAL DIFFERENCES

The view that "people are people and very similar the world over" may appear both egalitarian and politically correct, but frankly, I don't think it makes any sense when applied to anything but the human anatomy. The way we—humankind—think and act is not purely innate or instinctive, but is very much determined by our particular culture: the totality of our environment and education, which varies in nature and kind from nation to nation, region to region, ethnic group to ethnic group. I don't mean to minimize the role of heredity in making each of us what we are; our genes are certainly responsible not just for our appearance, but also for other important aspects of our psycho-physical make-up. Nor am I discounting our individuality—our personal genetic cocktail in our particular cultural environment ensures that each of us is unique. However, we are not uniquely unique. There's a whole dimension of our being which we share with people who were brought up the way we were. The way we perceive the world—our unshakable beliefs, our fundamental values, the "accepted" way we go about the major and minor rites and rituals in life—this *Weltanschauung* which is not ours alone, but common to our group, is the received wisdom of our forefathers and foremothers. It is passed on to us after birth. In short, it is all learned.

This learned behavior is our collective culture—not Culture with a capital "C" (music, literature, fine arts), but a far broader culture with a small "c," Hofstede's mental software. And while the idea that we start being culturally programmed from the moment we are born may be upsetting and unsettling, it goes a long way to explain how and why different groups grow up with, and take for granted, not just superficial behavior patterns, but less obvious deep values and notions. What one culture may denounce as evil, bad or corrupt—nepotism and favoring family members and friends over strangers, bribery, even cheating—another may consider acceptable or even praiseworthy and good. What is extremely important to one culture—face-saving, for example, or honor, or trust or punctuality—may be irrelevant to another. There are cultures which value and reward individualism and personal initiative, and others which abhor "the protruding nail" and regard conformity as a great virtue. There are cultures which thrive on rules and regulations, and always go by the book, and others which consider what rules they have as mere guidelines, and prefer to go with their guts. Family life, business, leisure: there is no aspect of our life which is not significantly culture-shaped. We may not be exactly what we eat, but we are what we culturally digest.

Are we aware how and to what degree we are culturally programmed? Again, *jein*—yes and no. The more we are exposed to other cultures, the more we become conscious of our own. Occasionally even self-conscious—as if we were to catch sight of ourselves in a mirror, only to find ourselves vaguely ridiculous. We all know that the Romans do things differently, and that should we ever happen to be in Rome, doing things the Roman way is recommended, politically-acceptable behavior. But we don't really know how the Romans do things—and what "things" are we talking about anyway? So we probably continue doing "things" our own way, and figure—if we ever give it a moment's thought—that the Romans are nice, friendly people who will tolerate our strange, foreign behavior.

A MATTER OF TIME

How, you may be wondering, does cultural programming work? Well, let's take the notion of time. Whereas one Mom—statistically rarely Dad—feeds her baby by the clock, another feeds her baby whenever it cries. The first Mom strictly toilet-trains her baby, the second one lets her child find its own rhythm. Mom One puts her offspring to bed at the same time every night—and, in fact, as the child grows up, Mom imposes fairly rigid schedules for meals, play, visits to the doctor and most other activities. Mom Two puts her kid to bed whenever it is convenient, continues to feed on demand, takes her kid to the doctor when the kid is sick, and generally has very few scheduled activities. Both Moms are loving, warm and caring. Both children thrive.

The Moms above are not acting alone or idiosyncratically. They are products of their own cultures. Mom One comes from a time-oriented culture, Mom Two doesn't. Mom One is obliged to respect fixed times and schedules, otherwise both she and poor kiddo would be at serious odds with their environment. Mom Two would be doing her offspring no service by organizing their lives according to a clock, and has other priorities: obligations to friends and relatives, debts of honor, spontaneous whims. Needless to say, the two children are likely to grow up with very different attitudes towards time, reflecting the attitudes of their respective Moms, and strongly reinforced by the values and organization of the society in which they live. Neither children (and later adults) are aware that they have been time-conditioned—until they meet and try to interact with each other. Then the sparks fly.

Mom One could easily be German. In terms of the cultural importance attributed to time, the Germans appear to be world champs, beaten only—perhaps—by the Swiss. This is not to say that other cultures are not time-conscious—indeed, all western industrialized cultures are. We are talking degree and priorities here. The Germans walk a tight chronological time-line, which means that they tend to organize their lives around the clock, perform one task after another, and ascribe right and wrong times to most of their activities. Notions of being on time, in time, or punctual are all-important, and are experienced as positive values in themselves. Those who disregard the dictates of time are considered by the Germans to be un-serious, unprofessional and outright pests when, through their un-punctuality, they cause Germans to waste time. The Germans tend to live by precise schedules, timetables and programs which often stretch far into the future, and they do not welcome unexpected interruptions, postponements or cancellations. Spontaneity does not come naturally—and when Germans do decide to act spontaneously, they often feel like little kids doing something forbidden. Because of their tight time budgeting, they are not usually available at short notice, and even if they were, they could not readily admit it. After all, a person with free time is highly suspect.

Mom Two could be Spanish (Latin American, Arab . . .). Time as such is not very important, but people are. Appointments may be made, but are not taken seriously—they can be broken without notice if a friend drops by, or something else unexpectedly crops up. Since the very notions of punctuality, being in or on time, don't really exist, they can't be violated—punctuality simply isn't an issue. Except, of course, if a Spaniard happens to be dealing with a person from a time-conscious culture . . .

SPACE TO CALL ONE'S OWN

Just as our notion of time is instilled into us from birth, so too is our notion of space—the physical and psychological space we need to surround ourselves with to feel at ease. Say a child grows up in an environment in which families are normally nuclear or even one-parent, in which each family member has his/her own room, however tiny, in a one-family unit, and where individual privacy, both physical and psychological, is valued and territory respected. That child is likely to need a lot more personal space throughout life than the child born into an extended family in a communal village, or palace for that matter, without walls or doors, either literally or figuratively. The children are neither advantaged nor disadvantaged—they will simply grow up with different spatial needs. And by extension, their adult orientation towards territory, privacy, ownership and possession is also likely to be very different.

Our early time-and-space programming is a vitally important part of our mental software, and puts an indelible cultural stamp on us. Our orientation to time and space more or less dictates how we go about our daily tasks, whether we are tolerant of delay and distraction, where we set our priorities, how we cope with the unexpected, and so on. It is inevitably frustrating for a person from a time-conscious culture to have business dealings involving appointments, schedules and deadlines—all of which, of course, translate into money—with a person from a time-careless culture, because the first person's world can only function around linear time, and no amount of cultural understanding will change that. The second person's world, on the other hand, is more likely to revolve around people and relationships—and no amount of cultural understanding will change that either. The two worlds are incompatible, and despite efforts made on both sides, interaction between the two people can be tough.

The American sociologist Edward T. Hall calls time-bound cultures monochronic (M-cultures) and non-time-bound cultures polychronic (P-cultures). His explanation for why some cultures are more monochronic than others goes back to the industrial revolution; the more industrialized and efficient a culture became, the more it became time-oriented. I am not doing Hall justice here, but the notions monochronic and

The dictates of Time

polychronic are very helpful in understanding why cultures tick the way they do. So too is another Hall notion, that of "contexting."

SPACE AND CONTEXT

Context is the information that surrounds an event; the shared information (knowledge, background and experience) which people possess and which enables them to interpret whatever is going on. Identical twins, two peas with the same genes in the same pod, share so much information that they can often communicate without words. Child One and Child Two above, with no common genes and raised in entirely different pods, share so little background information that everything has to be explained and put into context before they can interact with each other. The identical twins are in what Hall calls a high context situation, the offspring of Mom One and Mom Two in a low context one.

Just as there are high and low context people, there are also high and low context cultures. To start with the low: this is a culture where people live in relative isolation (for example, in their own rooms behind closed doors), where personal space and privacy is respected and lives are highly compartmentalized . . . need I go on? Information does not flow freely in these cultures, because there are too many psychological and physical barriers. When people interact, they impart the information relevant to whatever they are doing on a need-to-know basis. This is often done grudgingly, as if they were giving part of themselves away, relinquishing power. For in low context cultures, knowledge is a precious commodity. In a high context culture, where people live on top of each other so to speak, and constantly share information through intricate networking and personal connections, there is so much shared knowledge, background and experience that little or nothing has to be spelled out in any given interaction. Knowledge is in the public domain, free and plentiful. High context people find low context people slow, boring and pedantic; low context people find high context people unmethodical, unconcentrated, and often unwise for "giving everything away."

There are very high and very low context cultures, and all shades in between. P-cultures are generally on the high end of the scale, M-cultures on the low. The Germans are extremely low context because their physical and psychological space needs leave them isolated, unaware what is going on around them unless they are specifically briefed. Since they don't mingle in the metaphorical marketplace, they are relatively unexposed to gossip and grapevine information. Doors to individual rooms at home and at work are normally kept closed. Their offices are private sanctuaries, and those at the higher levels of the corporate hierarchy are often protected by a secretary whose sole function is to keep the world (unwelcome visitors, phone calls—in a word, information), at bay. The Germans are essentially private people who are not quick to allow strangers into their lives, at least not as friends. They are not physically touchy, back-slapping people, they do not encourage familiarity or address acquaintances or even workmates by their first names. Nor do Germans mix the different spheres of their lives—family and colleagues rarely come together. Indeed, the Germans are compartmentalized in almost everything they do, and this, of course, impacts on information flow, which is predictably slow. Knowledge-sharing activities such as brainstorming go against the grain. And so on—I shall have a lot more to say about these propensities throughout this book.

ANGST AND AMBIGUITY

Our orientation to time and space are only two of the elements of our core mental programming, but they are vital ones. As I have already suggested, they determine much of the behavior which others—usually those different from ourselves—see as "typical." There are, of course, many other important elements, some of which are more easily explainable than others. Why is it, we may wonder, that some cultures appear relatively care- and stress-free, while others come across as *Angst*-ridden? There is no doubt that some individuals are genetically more disposed to experience anxiety than others—and Freud has a lot to say about early programming factors that are gender- and sex- rather than culture-related. But angst is also a cultural feature, and infants can be programmed early to feel worry and free-floating anxiety. Moms and Pops who freely express their concerns and fears about all of the awful things that could happen and constantly warn their offspring about the dangers that surround them are more likely to produce anxious children than parents who seem—and often are—oblivious to the dangers of the world and rarely warn their kids about anything. Again, there is no "right" or "wrong" way of going about these things—most children survive willy-nilly, prepared for the worst or not—but there are definitely cultural ways.

The Germans are famed for their propensity to worry, in fact, it was they (or was it the Austrians?) who came up with the word *Angst*, now part of the standard vocabulary of other languages such as English. It would appear that worrying is a Germanic way of warding off whatever is being worried about, a sort of magic talisman—certainly, *not* worrying would cause the worst to happen. And while they worry about more or less everything, they worry most about anything which is unpredictable or beyond their control. The unknown is, almost by definition, frightening. The future, being by its very nature unknown, is viewed at best with suspicion. And so, in an attempt to control the environment, prevent chaos and anarchy and impose some sort of reliable order on life itself—in other words, to reduce angst—the Germans resort to inflexible rules, regulations and laws. And these they have in abundance, for all possible eventualities.

Germans in general do not usually see themselves as such worriers. Rather, they consider themselves cautious, well-prepared for any unexpected occurrence, security-minded—but certainly not consumed by angst. However, as we will see later (p. 121), there is such a notion as angst management in German business. When Germans do admit to worrying, they are quick to point out that the worry is justified. Parents who do not give their children precautionary advice are completely irresponsible. And so on. As a worrier myself, I know what they mean. But the fact is that worry is not just an individual, but also a cultural mind-set.

People who suffer from chronic angst are unlikely to be tolerant of ambiguity or to be enthusiastic risk-takers. The Germans have traditionally been true to form. A nation of *Juristen*, people who have studied law but are not necessarily lawyers, they cross every "t" and dot every "i" to make sure that no ambiguity could possibly haunt them and raise their angst levels. Situations are supposed to be crystal clear—and just to make sure, they keeping asking for confirmation: *"alles klar?"* With regard to risk—well, they are normally very careful indeed (except when they are behind the wheel of their car, but that's another story, see pp. 194–5). It is not surprising that German business has a reputation for being solid and conservative, that Germans long resisted venture capital, playing the stock market and so on. Only in very recent years, with their backs up against the wall in an increasingly competitive world, are the ever-pragmatic Germans learning not so much how to embrace risk, but how to redefine it and make it appear less risky. Still, I wonder what will happen to their love-affair with the stock market, a fairly steady winner so far, when the first serious downslide occurs. For much more on this, see the *Business* chapter (p. 105 on).

LOCAL YOKELS IN A GLOBAL WORLD?

Ha! you may be thinking. All this stuff about cultural differences—the woman sounds as if she lived in the 19th century. Doesn't she watch CNN? Doesn't she ever travel and stay at the Hiltons and Sheratons of this world? Hasn't she heard of the global village, cellular phones, plastic money, blue-jeans culture and the colonization of the Third World? We're all citizens of the planet, not local yokels. Cultures are converging . . .

Jein—yes and no! Although global village oases are on the increase, we continue to live in a world of distinct cultures. We need only to observe a bunch of identically-dressed, notebook-toting yuppie businesspeople from different parts of the world gathered together in a conference room. They all speak reasonable English, the accepted lingua franca. They are there to negotiate some kind of deal. And what invariably happens? Not even the ones with MBAs from top U.S. or European business schools will be so free of their cultural heritage that they can avoid running into intercultural communication problems. I know of no international company which would dispute that, and there is a thriving niche market—intercultural business consulting—which exists to facilitate these cross-cultural encounters and sort out the mess when things go wrong. We live in an international cooperation and merger-mad world, and the success or failure of these mega-deals is highly dependent on cultural understanding. Culture at this sophisticated point becomes further complicated by the fact that it exists on so many levels: individual, ethnic, national, religious, professional (the specific culture of a particular profession) and corporate (the specific culture of a particular organization). So we try as best we can to compromise and adapt culturally in order to achieve a desired goal. And after the final bowing and hand-shaking is over, we retire to our homes and revert to our familiar patterns.

Or do we? Is it not a possibility that we are experiencing cultural convergence at a rate that was hitherto unthinkable? Perhaps in the course of our lives our original mental software is so constantly and so thoroughly updated through confrontation with other mental software that in some cases, much of our original start-up programming, once ineradicable, is being modified—or even lost, buried and forgotten? This leads me to the following musings:

THE FRUIT AND THE TREE

What if cultural programming is undergoing a revolution?

I have suggested that we are culturally programmed from the earliest possible age, and that we carry our cultural baggage around with us for the rest of our lives. I have argued that cultural programming is passed down from generation to generation and that it becomes so much part of our identity that it is remarkably change-resistant. However cosmopolitan we may later become, we remain to a perhaps alarming extent the cultural creatures we were as infants, and our guts, if not our heads, react accordingly. A monochronic person will instinctively move backward when a polychronic person moves in too close and breathes down the monochrone's neck. A high context person will feel involuntary irritation at the perceived pedantry of a low context person, no matter how much cultural understanding both parties may bring to the situation. And so on. Rational acceptance of another person's behavior is one thing. Changing knee-jerk reactions, basic orientations, or a learned, deep-structure value system is another.

And yet, and yet. It may have been true throughout the ages that the fruit did not fall far from the tree, and that children, once they had gone through rebellious puberty and adolescence, usually ended up accepting much the same basic values as their parents, community, society—and those that didn't were branded the black sheep, the eccentrics, the exceptions. By the time those children themselves produced children, they unconsciously passed on their originally received wisdom—and if they didn't do a good job, there were often grandparents around to act as a corrective. I do not maintain that this received wisdom was ever completely identical to the wisdom the new parents had themselves received as tots, but it was close enough to perpetuate cultural continuity. And so it was. Only now, it may not be quite as simple.

MEANINGFUL COMMUNICATION

We live in a global world, so we are constantly told. Certainly, communication technology has developed in leaps and bounds. Not only can we travel the world with the greatest of ease in our flying machines—we've been able to do that for some time now—but we can now do it without flying machines. All it takes is a computer and the

World Wide Web. Willy-nilly, we've acquired a World Wide Language—the language of the Internet, which is English, now accessible to some degree, I understand, to a billion people. And not to any old billion—to the privileged ones who are dictating the pace. We have a global economy, global financial markets, global institutions. All of this planetary oneness requires effective global communication of a sort we could not have conceived of only a few decades ago. Millions of people all over the world have to communicate with each other meaningfully, because their livelihoods, and through the knock-on effect, the livelihoods of further millions, depend on the outcome of their meaningful communication. In the old days when we had CNN but not the Internet, we received the rest of the world passively on our screens and most of us had no need to communicate, let alone meaningfully. When we traveled the world, we traveled mainly as tourists—and had no need to communicate meaningfully. Now we are forced to work on a daily basis, cell phone-to-cell phone, screen-to-screen with people around the earth—and to communicate so meaningfully that we can keep our global, interconnected world spinning and produce value-added. Evermore of us (and the figures are impressive) work in multinational companies, foreign subsidiaries, companies dependent on foreign trade and international institutions that may even require us to use English as a lingua franca in our home offices—on our own turf and far from the Anglo-Saxon world—and conduct mega-negotiations in that language via video. The European Central Bank, located in Frankfurt, Germany, conducts all of its business in English, although England to date has not even joined Euroland, and is present at the bank only as an observer. Representatives of the Euroland countries, as culturally far apart as Spain and Finland, must of absolute necessity communicate with each other so effectively that the economic well-being of the European Union—and by extension, of the rest of the world, for Euroland is as mighty and weighty as Dollarland—is assured. Dollarland, of course, has it much easier: it is culturally relatively homogeneous and it communicates within its borders in its own tongue.

The world, then, is becoming more of an economic melting pot, and since we all know that money makes the world go round, it has become a huge incentive for people to go to often great lengths to communicate meaningfully with entirely foreign cultures in a mutually beneficial enterprise to enrich themselves. In other words, the will and determination to communicate effectively is there—and that, I suggest, is relatively new on such a global scale. To communicate effectively you have to understand your partners. This necessity in turn leads to an increased willingness to overcome received prejudices—a willingness not to judge too quickly, and even, it sometimes happens, to question oneself and one's own received wisdom. Add to this self-interested disposition the ongoing technological revolution, which enables all these people from different cultures to gain ever-easier and ever-faster access to each other's thinking and ways, and it is entirely possible that our cultures are on a convergence course.

HARMONIZED AND HOMOGENIZED

I don't much like the word "convergence" when applied to the kind of mental-software culture I am talking about, but I cannot wish it away. Things are changing in the way our newborns are being culturally programmed. Certainly, they are being imbued with much of the received wisdom of their parents—but their parents have often moved much further away from their original programming than was the case in previous generations. A turbo mechanism has set in. The changes in passed-on culture which were once infinitesimal over centuries and millennia have been vastly speeded up. We continue to receive—be programmed with—our "old" ethnic, national, local culture, but these days, with a heavy overlay of what might be called a common or convergent culture.

Where does this thought take us? Hasn't this convergence already taken place in the United States? Here we have a hodgepodge of ethnic groups and new and former-generation immigrants who have accepted and freely adopted an overlay culture, the "American Way of Life," and are first and foremost Americans. But Americanization did not happen overnight, and due to the passing down of received wisdom, recent generations have not yet entirely lost all of the characteristics of their roots. This is most dramatically the case with the Amish population, but Native Americans, Afro-Americans, blacks and whites from the southern states as opposed to the northern ones, midwesterners of German ancestry, Jews of German origin as opposed to Eastern European origin (and so on)—all these groups, no matter how American they are to the core, remain somehow distinct—or at least, they like to think so. The melting pot metaphor has been replaced by the salad bowl, but this doesn't change anything.

Is this not convergence? And if it has already happened in the United States, will it not happen in Europe, and infinitely faster because of the turbo-times we live in? Will we not end up with a

"European Way of Life" analogous to the "American Way of Life," with all the ethnic and national "ways" subordinated to it? In other words: Will we soon have a European Union made up of what some Euroskeptics are already calling "Europuddings," a harmonized, homogenized population communicating in English? And will we soon hear people proudly proclaim, "I'm a European Spaniard," or "I'm a European Swede?" Never! shout the diehard French and Brits and indeed, almost all the present Europeans, with the possible exception of the Germans. And these nation-staters pound the convergence theory on the head.

EUROPUDDINGS AND REGIONALISTS

European identity, the diehards claim, can be defined only through the multiplicity and diversity of its cultures. Precisely because globalization is leading to the demise of the economic rivalries which have led over the ages to disastrous national wars, regional (that is, ethnic, local, but also national) cultures are now able to flourish as never before. And so, as Europe grows together in an economic, and to some extent social and political union, its component parts will become freer than ever to accentuate their differences. Indeed, nations may split up into smaller component parts—witness the devolution of Scotland—and new common-interest alliances such as Bavaria and Austria may come into being. On a global level, the same argument is applicable: the world has no reason to fear across-the-planet Americanization, because the very process itself will lead every last community to (re)discover and assert its own uniqueness. We will all, down to the very last Mohican, be able to preserve our individual culture, and the global economic (etc.) interconnection of interests will, for the first time, act as a guarantee rather than as a threat.

A Europe of regions. . . . Confident as they like to sound, the regionalists are quaking in their boots. They perceive that the old finishing-school type of educational exchange programs that give our young a "taste" of exotic cultures but not an enduring appetite for them can too easily turn into serious, longer-term study programs abroad, and turn our future generations into Europuddings or worse. They see lots of Young Leaders, bright young people who are selected early by the existing ruling class to take over politics and industry—and Young Leaders exist in all the countries I know—being groomed to be citizens of the world in elite education facilities throughout the world, where the language of instruction is, of course,

English, and the culture is at best, international, and at worst, Anglo-Saxon. Now this is not new, it's been going on for ages. Oldies such as Bill Clinton spent a year at Oxford, and I'll bet that there are no more than a handful of Third World leaders who were not educated abroad, many in hallowed Anglo-Saxon halls in Britain or the United States. What is newer, however, and what changes the picture, is the sheer number of European students able to study abroad, thanks in part to such popular (read: for the populace) EU study programs as Erasmus/Socrates. Inter-European education is no longer exclusively for the upper-elite. New too is the type of convergence education these students are receiving: it's become closer to total immersion, with the foreign/visiting students having to plunge in with the locals. And amazingly, they find they are speaking much the same language—a kind of universal student-speak.

DIVERSITY LIVES!

What is my point? As far as Europe is concerned, we may be witnessing a cultural revolution. Our traditional programming may not be as ontologically fixed as it used to be. We will continue to be culturally determined from the earliest possible moment of our lives, but the software may be very new and changing rapidly, so that future generations will no longer end up with a close approximation of the cultural make-up of their own immediate (national) cultural ancestors, but instead with a far more hybrid—Europudding—culture.

It's a possible, plausible and seductive scenario. Do I subscribe to it? I'm honestly not sure. I look around myself here at home (Frankfurt), and I continue to see young people I recognize as distinctly German. They have not suddenly or even gradually become Europeans or Global Citizens. My current students are certainly better traveled than previous generations: many of them have spent at least a year abroad. But the Germans among them—there are plenty of non-Germans—remain Germans, with their Germanity (core values) pretty intact. In Frankfurt, a city which, thanks to its guest-worker population as well as its banking community, is one of the most cosmopolitan in the country, I have no difficulty distinguishing the "natives" from the foreigners. Nor, incidentally, do they. The sizeable Turkish population, resident in Frankfurt for decades, remains essentially Turkish and largely unintegrated. Even in the yuppie international banking community (every seventh Frankfurt resident is a banker, and around 500 foreign banks are represented) the different national cultural groups stick together outside the workplace, and we have an extremely lively expatriate scene, each nation-culture for itself, with separate watering holes, social clubs and other hang-outs. Indeed, what social interaction there is among the different foreign nationals in Frankfurt is often occasioned by the need for united support groups to reduce the culture shock of living in Germany. Exceptions abound, of course, but don't they prove the rule?

In other words: I continue to think that we remain in cultural essence the creatures our society—be it national or ethnic—made us, rather than cross-border, inter-regional or even global creatures. This situation may be changing to some extent, but not, I believe, so significantly that we need concern ourselves with Europuddings. Yet. The babies are not old enough to tell another tale.

The Art of Being German

A GERMAN DEFINED

Q: What do you feel makes you German as opposed to French, Italian or English?

A: Well in the first instance I was born here and I grew up here. If I had been born in France, I would have a different way of behaving, I would be a different sort of person. I have certain characteristics as I see them. If you like, discipline, a penchant for perfection.
From an interview in Alan Watson's *The Germans: Who Are They Now?*

GERMANY—HISTORY AND GEOGRAPHY

Germany is a nation of very diverse regions. This may at first seem strange, because the country is far more ethnically homogeneous than the United States, for example. Leaving aside the large number of foreigners living in Germany (see pp.87–93), the Germans themselves have been around for ages, and from some perspectives, they can be considered as one people. As we will see below, bloodline is, or at least has been until very recently, of prime importance in determining who is German, and this in itself assumes the existence of a specific ethnic heritage.

On the other hand, Germany itself doesn't have a long history of being one country. During the Middle Ages, the German Empire kept expanding and shrinking as the various parts of it were won and lost; the Holy Roman Empire of the German Nation was little more than a loose conglomeration of separate feudal (and feuding) states. When the new German Empire came into being in 1871, it was proclaimed as a federal state; the different parts of it were brought together in law and in name but not in character. Thereafter, the vicissitudes of history led to territorial chunks being added and subtracted and the remainder divided; in other words, the borders have continued to change. In the most recent geopolitical rearrangement, the unification of Germany in 1990 turned the country once again into a single political entity, but it is still very much a patchwork of regions, a truly federal republic.

History inevitably leaves its mark. The different parts of Germany have remained a collection of more or less distinct areas, each with a recognizable local culture in terms of architecture, customs, traditions, food and the like, with a local center, and very often, a strong sense of rivalry. Unlike its European neighbors, Germany has no single "number one" city to match London, Paris or Rome. Instead, it has 14 half-million-plus cities, four of them with over a million inhabitants: Berlin, by far the largest with over 3.5 million, followed by Hamburg (1.7 million), Munich (1.4 million) and Cologne (1 million—just). Now that Berlin is once again the seat of the federal government (since 1999) as well as the federal capital (since 1990), it is beginning to have big ideas about itself; but since the financial capital of Germany is likely to remain Frankfurt; the media capital, Cologne; the fashion capital, Düsseldorf; the IT and biotechnology capital, Munich . . . Berlin may have to resign itself to being one capital among others. (Just as an indication of how fiercely proud the residents of German cities can be, the previous sentence has caused outrage among some of my German friends. The media capital is Hamburg, say some; the IT capital is now Stuttgart according to others. Sorry—I just wanted to make a point.)

So—Germany is the sum of its regions, and its native population, still relatively homogeneous from an ethnic (bloodline) perspective, is not quite as straightforwardly homogeneous from an ethnological (cultural) perspective. Eastern Germans or *Ossis* and western Germans or *Wessis* are a story unto themselves (pp. 65–70). A Berliner sees himself as far removed in humor, style, wit and wisdom, etc., from, say, a Bavarian as from a (German-speaking) person from Mars. And even within Berlin, the inhabitants of the various parts of the city—east and west in particular—often consider themselves entirely different breeds. This local identity phenomenon is not peculiar to Germany—what does a Boston urbanite think (s)he has in common with an Iowa farmer?—but it has to be mentioned here, and repeated elsewhere at regular intervals, since this book is about "the Germans," an entity which ethnologically, many Germans themselves refuse to recognize as even definable, much less describable. Nevertheless, I maintain that despite all the local differences, "the Germans" share so many common cultural characteristics that it is legitimate to talk about them as an ethnological phenomenon.

Given the significant differences between (1) the cities and rural areas and among the various regions; (2) ethnic, generational and gender diversity; and (3) class distinctions and variations in educational background, valid generalizations about German culture are difficult to make. But one entry point into this highly complex pattern is the central values and norms that have helped give the Germans a sense of commonality and tradition.

Greg Nees: *Germany: Unraveling An Enigma*

BLOOD OR CULTURE?

Germany is one of the few countries in the world where until the first day of this new century, nationality was primarily a matter of blood rather than place of birth—*ius sanguine* as opposed to *ius soli*. You were German if at least one of your parents was German, not because you were born in Germany. This rather narrow view of nationality has caused the Germans severe headaches in recent decades, because there are well over seven million "foreign" residents of Germany—almost 9 percent of the population—and several million of these were born here, as were many of their parents and even grandparents. So there are a lot of "foreign Germans" around—people who are every bit as German as any "real" German in terms of shared culture, but who have no automatic right to a German passport. At the same time, there are millions of ethnic (bloodline) Germans in eastern European countries who have never acquired an iota of German culture, have never even learned the language, but who can, and often do, claim to be bona fide Germans—millions have settled in Germany since the fall of communism and have German passports. These, then, are German foreigners. For more about German foreigners and foreign Germans, and about the new citizenship laws, see the chapter on the subject (p. 87 on). The point I want to make here is that having or not having a German passport says little about whether a person is or isn't culturally German.

It is characteristic of the Germans that the question, "what is German?" never dies out among them.

Friedrich Nietzsche: *Beyond Good and Evil*
(translated by Walter Kaufmann)

So—we're back to the "Who is a German?" question, and I'll solve it once and for all with my own definition for the purpose of this book:

A German is anyone nurtured and educated during the formative years in Germany or in a German environment, such as an expatriate enclave abroad, predominantly by people who themselves have a German cultural background.
I admit that my definition is not perfect, and we may be left with a few question marks, but it'll have to do.

MONOCHRONIC TIME, GERMAN-STYLE

What strikes a foreigner travelling in Germany is the importance attached to the idea of punctuality, whether or not the standard is realized. Punctuality, not the weather, is the standard topic of conversation for strangers in railway compartments. Long distance trains in Germany have a pamphlet laid out in each compartment called a Zugbegleiter *(literally, train accompanier) which lists all the stops with arrival and departure times and all the possible connections en route. It is almost a national sport in Germany, as the train pulls into a station, for hands to reach out for the* Zugbegleiter *so that the train's progress may be checked against the digital watch. When trains are late (and it happens), the loudspeaker announcements relay this fact in a tone which falls between the stoic and the tragic. The worst category of lateness which figures in these announcements is* unbestimmte Verspätung *(indeterminable lateness: we don't know how late it is going to be!) and this is pronounced as a funeral oration.*
Peter Lawrence: *Managers and Management in West Germany*

In the previous chapter, I talked about the relative importance of time in our cultural make-up, and said that time is a major organizing principle in German life. Which is not to say that other cultures—other northern Europeans and the Americans, for example—are not monochronic, time-conscious cultures. It's just that each culture goes about its orientation in its own way, and the German way differs from, say, the British or North American way. Time is precious, so all M-people are taught; it is too valuable to be wasted; it is *good* to be *on* and *in* time, it is *bad* to be late—or worse, not show up at all. The Germans take these edicts rather seriously, or at least more literally than most, and run their lives accordingly. Daily activities revolve around fairly inflexible schedules and routines. The logic of the schedules is not always apparent to anybody but themselves, but it is not for outsiders to reason why—to Germans, schedules and routines create order (see p. 42 on) and are *intrinsically good*. This is important for people who are less monochronic than the Germans to realize, because we're talking basic

The art of being German

values here, we're close to the core of Germanity! Germans have utmost respect for appointments, for prearranged engagements, for deadlines; delays, postponements and unplanned hitches are anathema, throw them off balance and can ruin their days. Punctuality is so close to godliness that in the old days, it wasn't enough to be simply be on time, you had to arrive five minutes early. Well, this may no longer hold true in general, but pre-punctuality (for want of a better word) is quite often observed by shops and supermarkets, where the personnel start cleaning up and emptying cash registers well before official closing time—and shut their doors pre-punctually in the faces of last-minute customers. So do bureaucrats working in offices (pp. 187-90). An indication of the sacredness of being on time: the recently partially-privatized railway system, Deutsche Bahn AG, put up large display boards in major stations giving the daily punctuality scores of its trains. This rapidly turned out to be a major embarrassment since the record was not impressive as far as the Germans were concerned, and led to loud complaints from people looking at the boards showing that some trains were up to five whole minutes late—on long-distance runs! The boards quickly disappeared. The German airline carrier, Lufthansa, recently admitted its punctuality record was unacceptable. In reality, the airline was towards the top of the world rankings in terms of punctuality, but this still wasn't good enough. As a contrast: I have it from several employees of the Pakistani national airline, PIA, that any arrival or departure within 24 hours of the scheduled time is considered punctual.

There are, as far as I can tell, only three people in German life who are habitually not punctual, and are not even expected to be: the doctor, the dentist and the hairdresser. All three keep their clients waiting for extraordinary lengths of time, but nobody seems to mind. The clients, on the other hand, are expected to turn up on the dot, and will automatically lose their place on the waiting list if they arrive a minute late for the scheduled appointment. Thus, there is absolutely no point in calling up in advance to find out how many hours late the doctor/dentist/hairdresser is running—you have to wait your turn on the premises. To be fair, I don't know any country where doctors, dentists, and hairdressers behave any differently—it's all a question of expectations.

ASSIGNED TIMES

To every thing there is a season, and a time to every purpose under the heaven.

Ecclesiastes 3.1

Punctuality is, of course, only one aspect of being time-conscious. Because time is so central to their lives, the Germans live with one eye on the clock and allocate time slots to the many activities that crowd their daily lives. This allocation is not just a matter of individual choice; the German world imposes a rhythm which is hard to buck, and which will make you unpopular or worse if you do. There are right times for certain tasks, and—logically—wrong times. This is particularly true of small communities, where an unwritten code regulates what the residents should do when, and vice versa. Accordingly, there's a time to go shopping and do the household chores: weekdays; a time to trim the garden hedge: Saturdays; and a time to go for walks in the woods: Sundays. There are regulated times when people can let their hair down, put on funny clothes and get roaring drunk without being arrested. This happens regularly once in early spring during the final days of *Karneval* or *Fasching* just before Ash Wednesday, and once again in the fall during the *Oktoberfest* (see pp. 224–26). During the summer months, the numerous festivals and wine fairs throughout the country also promote such revelry, albeit without the funny clothes. After football matches, the fans of the winning side can drive through town leaning on their horns to express their joy without risking a ticket. This is also the case if you are part of a wedding party driving to or from church (or wherever). There is just one time in the year when people can let off fireworks without special permission—New Year's Eve. And so on.

Even more rigidly regulated than what *should* be done at specified times, however, is what should *not*. The ignorant newcomer or visitor can incur serious local wrath—and end up being sued—by ignoring such conventions as the *Mittagsruhe*, or afternoon peace. The hours between 1 P.M. and 3 P.M. are designated as no-noise hours for those who wish to sleep or rest. In well-ordered suburbs—and most are—children are not supposed to play in the garden or in the street, not even quietly. Dogs must be kept inside and muzzled if necessary. Household appliances of the loud vacuum-cleaner sort should not be used. Music must be played low. All must be absolutely quiet on the suburban German front.

Bavaria Vows to Drink On

Bavarian beer gardens are famous, and they are open-air. According to federal law, they are required to send their guests away and shut down promptly at 10 P.M., to avoid breaching the peace of the neighborhood. The Bavarians, however, find that 10 P.M. is too early, and accordingly, have fought a battle all the way up to the highest court of the country (in Karlsruhe, which is not in Bavaria) for the right to stay open for another hour. No way, said the country's top judges. Just think what might happen if we were to make an exception—we'd risk total anarchy. The Bavarians, however, are not about to give up. Known for ignoring high court rulings—on such matters as hanging crucifixes in classrooms, which they shouldn't do but do do—they are waiting for the next hot summer night to show their independence. The beer gardens are probably counting on the cooperation of the police, who (they hope) as good, beer-drinking Bavarians themselves, will take a good hour to show up and shut them down.

This is also true of evenings and Sundays. As of 8:30 P.M., apartment dwellers must curb their desire to practice the piano or hammer nails into walls so as not to disturb the neighbors. Only muted sounds are allowed after 10 P.M.—a real party killer, but fail to turn down the music, and the police may turn up on your doorstep. Sunday is a day of such enforced peace—this is called for in the Basic Law or constitution—that the whole country practically closes down and communicates in whispers. Shops are tightly closed—exceptions are rare (see p. 203). All weekday activities such as housecleaning and doing the laundry should either not be performed at all, or in such a way that nobody could possibly notice. Mowing the lawn, for example, is a strict no-no, as is washing the car—both activities reserved for Saturdays.

You may think I'm exaggerating, but many an expatriate who has moved into a house outside town has learned the hard way how disapproving neighbors can be. The good news is that in inner cities, right and wrong times are not observed as strictly, if at all, and although neighbors are supposed to respect quiet times and Sunday remains relatively holy, metropolitan anonymity tempers the caveats. And even in the suburbs, some of the more restrictive, unwritten *mores* have been relaxed. Still, if you're sitting on the terrace or in the garden of an urban restaurant on a balmy, summer evening, chances are you'll be asked to move inside at either 10 or 11 P.M. to avoid disturbing the residents of the surrounding buildings. Don't even bother to point out that the area is non-residential—city ordinances are there to be obeyed.

I think it is easier for a polychronic person to be infected with the monochronic time bug than the other way round. After living in Germany for long enough, most polychrones tend to become pretty time-conscious—probably for reasons of survival. You just can't operate in a German environment if you don't have an accurate watch which you consult regularly. Nevertheless, it's hard not to smile sometimes: in Frankfurt airport, for example, where waiting passengers are informed to the second when the monorail train linking the two terminal buildings is expected: "The next train will arrive in 123 seconds." Or when the teacher trade union (GEW) calls a strike because they have a minute-limit to the time their members are allowed to work, and a particular school is asking their teaching staff to exceed the maximum by five whole minutes a week.

"Do come in"

MONOCHRONIC SPACE, GERMAN-STYLE

Being highly monochronic, Germans need a lot of personal space. Now, everybody needs a certain amount of space, so the difference between peoples lies in how much. In the case of the Germans, it's simply relatively more. Rich or poor, most Germans—first as individuals and later, as nuclear families—need to be able to retire within their own four walls, with a door they can firmly close. Whether the walls surround a large mansion or a cramped room in a student dormitory is irrelevant—the enclosed territory is personal and sacred. Entry by invitation only.

This need for space can be observed in almost all spheres of German life, and will keep recurring in this book (see, for example, the section on *Doing Business*, p. 105 on). There's an old adage that a man's home is his castle, and it is usually applied to the Brits, who are also highly monochronic, but in their peculiarly British way. In Germany, the castle is almost a fortress, and the moat surrounding it is deeper and wider than most non-Germans appreciate. A home is simply a very private place where only intimates (close friends) are welcome. Owned or rented, it is the pride and joy of the occupant(s), whose psychological attachment to it is very strong. This is one of the reasons why Germans are often loath to move, and usually only do so out of dire necessity—a change of job or circumstances, or an increase in the size of the family. If a person's home is invaded by a burglar or hit by a natural disaster—a relatively unlikely event in Germany—(s)he experiences the event as a personal violation. I've heard Germans discuss the reaction of Americans to the loss of their homes in floods, earthquakes, hurricanes and tornadoes with complete incomprehension. "How can they keep rebuilding houses in threatened areas?" they ask, after CNN has interviewed tearful but determined-to-rebuild victims. Homes in Germany are solid, built to last. The idea of a mobile home as a permanent address is not likely to catch on—and would almost certainly be illegal.

Outside the home, privacy is signaled by hedges and fences, be they ever so small and feeble in terms of physically keeping outsiders out. Enter through the gate and ring the front door bell, but don't expect to be greeted with open arms if you are arriving unannounced.

Unannounced Hospitality

More and more German companies are setting up abroad, many in the United States, hundreds in South Carolina alone. Most companies find that their German employees and their families have a hard time getting used to their new lives, because (surprise, surprise) the culture is so different and American ways so strange. A major problem has been caused by welcoming committees who turn up unannounced bearing gifts of cakes and other edibles on the doorstep of the unsuspecting German housewife. These well-meaning American ladies are completely unaware that they are invading German space. The housewife, at a loss and squirming with embarrassment—her hair is not combed, her kitchen is a mess, the carpet unvacuumed—lets the ladies in. They ooh and aah, and ask to be shown all the rooms, including the toilets. When her husband returns that evening, he finds his wife in floods of tears, ready to pack up and leave. After this pattern had been repeated countless times, one very large German company with a very large plant in a southern U.S. state decided that something had to be done. This wasn't the only cultural problem that had arisen, I should add. Experts were called in and in the case of the welcoming committee, a compromise was struck. The American ladies agreed that they would give the newcomers two weeks notice of their descent, and the Germans agreed to the invasion of strangers.

Germans don't take well to people dropping in and they don't drop in themselves. People can be neighbors for decades without ever having seen the insides of each other's homes. New arrivals in the street may be carefully observed through a chink in a curtained window, but there is no neighborhood welcoming committee to greet them.

This seemingly standoffish attitude has a lot to do with the development of the country. After the Germanic tribes had settled in the area during the early Middle Ages, Germany's population remained fairly stable. There were no vast waves of immigrants, so there was never a need for people from different cultural backgrounds to get to know and interact with each other as quickly as possible, just in order to survive. Historically, the sedentary Germans, many of whom had been in the same place for generations, formed their relationships over long periods of time and were not called upon to integrate strangers fast. The United States, of course, developed entirely differently: new people kept arriving and were, in general, welcome and welcomed. So, many Americans find this perceived German unfriendliness hard to fathom. It must be said that German society is becoming a lot more mobile today; nevertheless there are still many villagers and small-towners for whom a newcomer is anyone without ancestors in the community.

"The group from Frankfurt must have gotten in last night"

There is more to be said about the German home (see p. 59 on)—not everything can be explained by the monochronic need for private space. But this need for private space, like the importance of chronological time, is a vital key to the understanding of what makes Germans tick. The Brits have a favorite anecdote about the Germans, and it always causes them, the Brits, to howl with laughter. When the Brits and the Germans go on vacation—always south towards the sun, so they end up at the same crowded resorts—they usually spend half the night in bars and nightclubs. Bleary-eyed, the Brits wander down to the beach sometime the next morning, and fight for an inch of sand. The Germans, however, regularly set their alarm clocks for some ungodly early hour, rush down to the still-empty beach, and spread out their towels to mark their territory. Then they go back to bed. Most Germans I've told this story to fail to understand why the Brits find their behavior so funny. How else, they want to know, can you assure your place in the sun?

When you talk to Germans, there's a rule of thumb which says that you should never get closer than the finger tips of your outstretched arm. If you do—and P-people tend to—the German will start feeling uncomfortable and move backwards. If the P-person moves closer— which is likely—the German (or any monochrone— this does not apply exclusively to the Germans) will move further and further backwards until (s)he is up against an inconvenient object or wall, at which point (s)he may duck or move sideways. You can watch this little dance repeated endlessly at any mixed-culture cocktail party. There are photos in existence of Germany's former Chancellor Kohl and France's former President Mitterand, both seated, where Mitterand is leaning forward as he earnestly explains something, and Kohl is leaning so far back that it looks as if his chair is just about to topple over.

Germans are not normally physically demonstrative with people they don't know. The tactile bonhomie of strangers, the arm flung across a shoulder during an introduction, "Hey, Jack, meet my new pal from Germany, what did you say your name is? Helmut? Jack this is Helmut . . . ," is usually distasteful. Polite, and what appear to Americans formal, introductions are the order of the day, even in non-business settings. Only handshakes—firm, dry, short—are acceptable. Again, I should add that contact with other cultures is modifying German behavior, and young Germans are becoming far more casual. More on this topic in the *Business* (p. 105 on) and *Miscellaneous* (p. 209 on) sections.

Traditional German offices, in private companies as well as government buildings or German universities, are designed in such a way as to allow maximum privacy to the people working in them. Doors to offices are invariably kept shut. The more important the person, the more likely he—sorry, but it's seldom a she—is to have an office-shielded-by-an-office—that is, an office which is accessible only through another office which is occupied by a formidable lady (always a female) called the *Vorzimmerdame*, or anteroom lady, whose primary job it is to guard her boss's lair and prevent him from being disturbed.

I'll return to the subject of offices in the *Business* (p. 105 on) and *Practicalities* (p. 171 on) sections. Suffice it to say here that through globalization, joint ventures and all those mixed business marriages which are affecting traditional German ways, more and more offices are becoming open-plan. This can cause great discomfort to German employees, especially older ones, who have serious difficulties thinking if they are surrounded by people talking and moving around, and other noisy distractions such as telephones and the click of fingers on computer keyboards. I interviewed Germans working in open-plan offices not long ago, and some had come up with ingenious ways to shield themselves; they had erected walls of plants, for example, constructed bookshelves or brought in aquariums.

ULTIMATE COMPARTMENTALIZERS

Kant was determined, as no German had been before, to divide everything into distinct categories. He was notorious for driving his friends round the bend with his obsessive splitting of everything into smaller and smaller groups.

Stefan Zeidenitz/Ben Barkow:
The Xenophobe's Guide to the Germans

It makes sense—at least to me—that a highly monochronic culture, taught to do one thing after another (rather than simultaneously and higgledy-piggledy), respect schedules and value private space, is likely to end up compartmentalizing—sorting out its various activities into neat categories and then keeping the different "boxes" (areas of life) as separate from each other as possible, both in terms of time and space. The Germans are champion compartmentalizers. They do not mix work and family life, for example, and it is not customary to take work home, or home to the office for that matter—few secretaries know their boss's family in person. Friends are friends, but business acquaintances are just that, and are not invited home. It is relatively rare that colleagues socialize with each other, and if they do, the occasions are likely to be institutionalized—the annual Christmas party or the summer office outing which companies are required to allow on office time. That the Germans separate business from pleasure is in many ways understandable: Germans are at work to work, not to make friends. However, for foreigners working in the country, it makes it that much more difficult to befriend colleagues, the people with whom they have the most contact. Business lunches are fine as the time is reserved for work anyway, business dinners are more problematic—dinner time is traditionally family time, although modern business life is encroaching—and business breakfasts, an American "way" if there ever was one, are a real pain. Breakfast time in Germany is holy family time, and inviolate, however much each family member might prefer to have that extra hour of sleep—many school kids have to leave the house by 7 A.M. An unavoidable business breakfast is therefore quite often the second meal of the day.

Compartmentalization is pervasive. Germans like getting together for different activities, and club life plays a major role in people's lives (see *Social Life* p. 221). There are clubs for just about everything, and a lot of people belong to several. So they have a number of different club acquaintances (different from friends). But they

The Office Party

A friend of mine who heads an international financial news service in Frankfurt ran into a problem last Christmas. He has two teams working for him, one German, the other British. When the time to discuss the office Christmas party rolled around, unexpected difficulties arose. The Brits insisted that significant others be invited to the party, the Germans were equally adamant that they should not be. A vote was taken, and although the Brits won, out of deference to the host country, the final decision was to exclude friends, lovers and spouses. What was surprising about this cultural difference was not so much the way the two nationalities voted—that could have been expected—but the fact that the two teams were young, all under 30, and working in an industry in which the business culture is international, which normally means Anglo-Saxon. It turns out that the two teams have very different ways of working, and there is often friction—the German team finds the British team too loud, for example, and since they all work in an open-plan office, the noise is distracting. The teams do not socialize outside the workplace, although, as I found out after the party, they had a great time together on their one-night-of-the-year get-together.

rarely see their club buddies outside the club, or at times other than the regular club meetings. And their different buddies never meet each other. If I'm with Hans, Johannes and Peter, it must be Monday at the *Skat* (a German card game) club. . .

Compartmentalization at work is a topic in itself. One of its many manifestations lies in the responsibility a person is willing to assume for a task (s)he is supposed (or rather—that you suppose (s)he is supposed) to do. Let's say you, a customer, call up a company looking for information on the price of a particular washing machine. The person at the customer service desk (assuming that there is such a desk, see *Service with a Frown*, p. 177), is unable to answer your question because (s)he is responsible for general customer complaints, not information. He transfers you to the washing machine department, where you are again told you cannot be helped. It turns out that the person you are talking to is responsible for washing machine repairs, not sales. You finally get a washing machine salesperson, only to find out that he too is unable help you—he sells a different brand of washing machine. Fifteen minutes after you originally placed your call, you find out that the company doesn't even carry the model you were interested in, something the very first person could have told you. He didn't because it wasn't explicitly his job and he didn't want to risk stepping on the toes of a colleague. Then again, let's suppose you get as far as ordering a washing machine. You talk to the salesperson and arrange a delivery date. The machine does not come. This is particularly infuriating, because delivery dates are truly dates, not a specific time of the day, so you, poor customer, have had to take a day off work to spend the entire day at home waiting. You call up the company, and nobody knows anything about your order. It turns out that the person who originally took it is sick, on vacation, no longer in the same department or even at the same company. No matter. It is not unusual for the offending salesperson not to have passed on your order to anyone else. It was *his/her* order, after all.

NEED-TO-KNOW INFO

Put all of the above information about the Germans together, and one thing becomes very clear: the flow of information in Germany can only be slow. Germans are too ensconced in their physical and psychological private space for information to spread accidentally, or "leak," and so it takes a conscious act to pass it on. If the only available information around is information which has been disseminated by conscious act, then there probably won't be very much of it, and what little there is will have been carefully selected. There is perhaps an additional historical explanation for this. Germany's history has been marked by the frequent changing of leaders and even governing systems. When the chance existed that you could go to bed under the flag of ruler X and wake up under the flag of ruler Y (during the Thirty Years' War, for example), it became a matter of self-preservation to not speak out too loudly. Moreover, gossip can lead to a false rendering of the facts. The Germans are aware of this and, since wrong information is worse than no information, they act accordingly. Information, seen by the Germans as ultimate power and a means to compete rather than a way to synergize, is, in fact, guarded jealously, and imparted only when pertinent and necessary.

To find out about information flow in different cultures, some researchers played a game—a variation of one I knew as a child as "Chinese Whispers." They planted a piece of information in an office environment in different cultures, and waited to see what would happen. In most cases, the information eventually became "common knowledge." In some polychronic environments, the information spread almost instantly, and when people were asked how they knew, they looked surprised and said, "Well, doesn't everyone know?" Any guesses about what happened in Germany? Right—the information stayed right where it was planted and nobody else ever got to hear it. Which reinforces the conclusion that the Germans are not a nation of gossips, and that you can rely on them keep things confidential. Probably true, although I wouldn't bet my life on it . . .

German electronics giant Siemens . . . has a reputation for being weak at tapping its own knowledge. I once heard a management consultant who worked with Siemens remark: "If Siemens only knew what Siemens knows, it would be a rich company."
Thomas L. Friedman: *The Lexus and the Olive Tree*

The Germans, in other words, are extremely low context. They are not clued-in by their environment. The message here is: never assume that any(German)body knows anything that hasn't been made absolutely explicit—and I mean spelled out in capitals! It's a good idea to have important issues clarified several times, because if one tiny element is accidentally left out or taken for granted, horrendous misunderstandings can ensue. "But I didn't realize . . . you didn't tell me" is the standard excuse when the baby-sitter fails to show up because, although you had told her you were going out, and at exactly what time, and had discussed with her in detail the evening meal and the bedtime story—you forgot to actually ask her in as many words to baby sit. Granted, this is not the rule!

The flip side of this information constipation and literal-mindedness is that Germans, well aware that their fellows are unlikely to know what they haven't explicitly been told, also know that when a briefing is required, it has to be thorough. As a result, they will start at A and work meticulously through to Z, and appear, at least to those more polychronic people who had heard everything on the grapevine before they walked into the meeting, rather pedantic. Remember what I said about clichés at the beginning of this book? The Germans often appear to be stating the obvious, because to them, it is not always so obvious.

GERMAN DIRECTNESS

"You may on occasion be pulled up short by German bluntness and directness," says the *Xenophobe's Guide to the Germans*. I can certainly subscribe to that statement, perhaps in part because as a Brit, I was raised in a culture where bluntness—saying exactly what you think in the most direct way possible—is not considered good form. The Brits are the most indirect people I know, and our hedging, waffling, and generally beating around the bush can certainly confuse the message. "That costume you're wearing is quite nice," may not tell you what the speaker's real opinion is, but it isn't likely to hurt you either. If you really want to know if you look dapper in your suit, ask a German— but be ready for the truth. Most Germans have no patience with euphemisms, circumlocutions, or any kind of face-saving, polite indirectness. Things are right or wrong, good or bad, nice or horrid, and they owe it to you to tell you to your face. "Sparing other people's feelings is quite unnecessary since feelings are a private matter and have no business in public," quips the *Xenophobe's Guide*, and that strikes me as true, too. I've asked many Germans, including both my husband and daughter, how they can be so forthright at times, and they have not quite understood that I would occasionally prefer to be handled gently—they call it lied to—rather than be confronted with harsh reality. Coddling is what Germans would call the white lies my British soul craves for . . .

Germans are well-known for their directness, and most foreigners who are being culturally prepared for a stint in Germany are warned about it in advance. Since few other cultures can top the Germans when it comes to directness, nearly everybody has to be made aware of this bluntness. However, no amount of warning can soften the blow to the solar plexus when somebody comes up to you at the end of a presentation, a lecture, a recital you have given, or even a party you have hosted, and tells you, not unpleasantly or maliciously but simply for your edification, that (s)he found the evening a complete waste of time. This is perhaps extreme, but it happens. On the other hand, of course, when they tell you how great the evening was, you know they're telling the truth, and this is the valuable flip side of the direct approach.

To be fair, not all Germans are as undiplomatic as I have just made them out to be. Many of those who are used to dealing with other less direct cultures have learned to soften their blows. Some of my non-German friends who live and work in Germany maintain that their German colleagues are becoming increasingly convoluted—that is, indirect and polite—in their speech, and resorting to complex negatives, as in, "It would not be unwise to consider the undesirable consequences of your unfortunate decision." Blunt by any other formulation . . .

RESPECT FOR AUTHORITY

The Germans have great respect for education, knowledge and hierarchy, not necessarily in that order. Learned books delve into history and come up with interesting reasons for this phenomenon—one theory connects it to the fact that the Germanic nations missed out on revolutions and the overthrowing of tyrants. Be that as it may—educated people are assumed to know things by virtue of their education, particularly if that education was acquired in Germany; a doctorate from Italy, for example, is not always taken that seriously. A person who knows things best will, logically, rise to the top of a hierarchy. That is the reasoning, and the result is that academic or professional titles—used far more than in Anglo-Saxon countries, but considerably less than in Austria—are considered a magic guarantee of expertise, even when empirical evidence indicates strongly that the titled person is, in fact, a complete idiot. No matter. Knowledge confers authority, and authority is accepted fairly blindly. If the heating system continues not to work after Mr. Diploma-Engineer Schmidt has fiddled with it, the fault must lie with the owner, the weather, the time of year. A doctor (of anything) can pontificate on almost any subject no matter how unrelated to his field and his opinion is likely to be taken at face value: "But the Herr Doktor said . . . ." Medical doctors are particularly revered—but this is the case in most other cultures I know. I'll have more to say about the medical profession at a later stage (see p. 185–6).

Generations of children in German schools have been taught to place their trust in experts and that teacher knows best. I do agree that teachers are supposed to know best the world over, but what exactly they are supposed to know best and how they convey it is culturally determined. In Germany, there is generally more emphasis on the rote learning of facts, rules and formulas than on the learning of how to learn, and the understanding of the principles behind the facts, rules and formulas. German kids are not always encouraged to think independently; when they get to university, they often want predigested information, and are confused and even upset when told there is none available. It is my theory that young Germans have in the past been persuaded so thoroughly that so-called experts have all the answers that in later life, they are inclined to give their loyalty to paternalistic, trust-inspiring, authoritative leaders who promise to take care of them. Consider Chancellor Adenauer, who gave the Germans back a measure of their self-esteem after the war, and won election after election for 14 years; and later, Chancellor Kohl, who kept his office for 16 years. The more complicated, intellectual and therefore unpaternalistic postwar chancellors have so far been given short shrift. I admit that my opinions on this subject cause howls of indignation from some of my German acquaintances, especially the teachers among them. Nevertheless, my own several decades of university teaching (which includes teacher training) in Germany, as well as my participation on school boards, the school education of my own daughter, etc., have me convinced that German students diligently learn what they are told, but they are not challenged to question or dispute. Argument for argument's sake, playing devil's advocate, debating skills—none of these are given much priority in a system which tends to regard life in absolutes. White is white and black is black because a teacher or a text book says so, and arguing the opposite as an intellectual exercise is impertinent.

2 THE NEVER-ENDING FIGHT AGAINST CHAOS

Germans apply the random and often illogical practices and rules of bureaucracy in a more exacting way than most of mankind. Rules don't need to make sense, for they are respected as the necessary glue that holds society together.

Frederick Kempe: *Father/Land*

Re-imposing order on chaos

SPEEDY RECOVERY

The Germanic notion of time translates into a need for order. The most spontaneous events must be planned well in advance. Natural disasters, striking as they do without warning, are frowned upon. On the other hand, when the unexpected or the unplanned does occur, the Germans go into immediate action to re-impose order on chaos; they reorient and mobilize themselves with amazing thoroughness and speed. When German rivers burst their banks and cause extensive flooding at Christmas—this has happened a couple of times in recent years— the mop-up operation has been completed by the New Year. And what other nation could have recovered as quickly and successfully as the Germans did after World War II?

PANACEAN ORDER

People whose lives revolve around schedules and timetables are bound to be orderly. How could they not be? Life along the chronological time line is predictable. You know where you are and where you're going. You have, if possible, 10-year plans. But what comes first here, the chicken or the egg? Are the Germans orderly because they are so monochronic, or are they so monochronic because they need to impose a semblance of order on a world which constantly threatens to get out of hand—and indeed, which often does?

Extreme uncertainty creates intolerable anxiety . . . this feeling is, among other things, expressed through nervous stress and in a need for predictability: a need for written and unwritten rules.
Geert Hofstede: *Cultures and Organizations*

I have no answer, but I can venture some guesses. As I discussed in a previous section (p. 23 on) the Germans are a nation of worriers and they have perfected worrying to a fine art. Empirical experience over centuries has shown the world to be a fearsome place and worry is a natural—and permanent—reaction. So goes the apparent subconscious logic. The Germans worry about everything from ingrown toenails to the dying of their beloved woods—and that particular worry is deep and widespread. They worry about politics and the weather. Most of all, they worry about the economy and their health (more about these in later chapters). *Angst* is the word the Germans use for this free-floating heartburn, a feeling of unease that is not necessarily attached to anything in particular, but to the unpredictable in general. Whereas other cultures view the world and the unknown future with optimism (sometimes, it must be admitted, because their present existence is so awful that the future can only bring improvement) the Germans regard the future with suspicion, perhaps because their present is so good—and let's face it, they've never had it better—that the future can only be a letdown. Be that as it may: the injunction "Don't worry, be happy" would be considered by many Germans as naive advice.

Since imposing order is probably the single best way to get the upper hand on angst (although I'm not sure that Freud would have agreed), the Germans try very hard to control whatever is controllable—and often what is not controllable. They circumscribe their lives and their environment with as many rules and regulations, ordinances and laws as possible in an attempt to ward off chaos. The way I see it, in many cases these prescriptions themselves give rise to even more worry than would otherwise have been experienced; for example, the more uptight someone is about following instructions, meeting a deadline or being on time, the more likely it is that something will go wrong—and worry about this eventuality will increase the stress levels, increasing the likelihood . . . and so on. The circle can be vicious indeed.

A REGULATED WORLD

Obtaining approval to do something—chop down a large tree, for example—or getting official recognition for an act such as moving to a new residence or buying a car is—well, a royal pain. Since permissions and approvals (as they are called, albeit in German) can usually only be obtained on Monday, Wednesday and Friday mornings, and now sometimes on Thursday afternoons, a lot of acts take a long time to get done if they ever get done at

VERBOTEN

all—and if they don't, German logic is that they weren't worth doing in the first place. Given the Federal Republic's meteoric rise to economic success, it boggles the mind to imagine what the country might have accomplished in its relatively short life if it hadn't been constantly hampered by bureaucratic red tape and rubber stamps. On the other hand, if it hadn't had the Rules and Regulations to organize itself around, it might have accomplished nothing at all. Ah well. . . .

The Germans fear society without order and organization . . . This is the reason for an extraordinary slavishness to deep-seated principles of hierarchy, and to rules and regulations in general.
David Marsh: *The Germans*

Here it must be said that German officialdom is currently undergoing something of a revolution. There are attempts being made in a number of cities to facilitate dealing with the bureaucracy by putting it under one roof, so that any given act—getting a residence permit or a work permit—which used to take five separate trips to five different offices will now be accomplishable in one. There is even talk of eliminating that one trip, and having some acts performable via the Internet. I am skeptical, because the Internet can't stamp the necessary papers with real ink. German officialdom refused to recognize my divorce decree from the Los Angeles Superior Court because the document, admittedly suspect because it was pink and flimsy, had no stamp on it. But who knows? Miracles happen.

(PRACTICALLY) NO EXCEPTIONS

The German need and desire to conquer chaos by removing as much uncertainty as possible from an inherently uncertain world leads not just to an incredible abundance of bureaucratic red tape, but to a blanket, across-the-board application of the bureaucracy which rarely permits exceptions. It's no good pleading special circumstances, throwing yourself on the mercy of the person in charge, offering bribes and/or threatening suicide: it is rare that a rule will be bent or a law circumvented—forget about broken—to accommodate an individual. Accordingly, the Germans often appear heartless and cold (remember those stereotypes?). However, with anarchy constantly lurking, and tomorrow, that fearsome unknown, rapidly approaching, who can blame them? The fact is that

Inflexible Rules

My daughter is British, although born and raised in Germany, and she started out in life with my surname. A few years ago, she decided she wanted to bear her father's name, so we—she was still under 18—went to the British Consulate in Frankfurt and changed her name. The whole procedure took about 10 minutes. Then I figured that I'd better let the German authorities know what her new name was, so I trotted off to the appropriate office. The officials there were not impressed. Once they had established that her father was German, and that he and I were legally married—which we hadn't been when she was born—they told me that our daughter had become German the day we got married and therefore, under German law, could not change her name. Period. In that case, forget about her being German, I said, somewhat incensed, she's been British all these years, and can do without being German if that's only going to create difficulties. Anyway, you don't like dual citizenship, I added nastily. No way she can renounce being German, they replied. Once German, always German. This is not quite true, as I later established, but almost: she'd have to leave the country for a century or so before they'd let her go. And so the story would have ended, with my daughter having one name in Germany and another in the rest of the world, if I hadn't raised Cain and made such a pest of myself that the officials finally relented.

most Germans consider that rules exist in the abstract and that bending them is both dishonest and dangerous. They do bend them, of course, but whereas this makes some other cultures feel good, it simply makes the Germans nervous.

The categorical imperative which no German escapes is "**Ordnung muss sein,**" *Order Must Be.*

Zeidenitz/Barkow:
The Xenophobe's Guide to the Germans

I was talking to a German official recently—a man with a legal background, and considerable experience in non-Germanic countries. He agreed that German laws and regulations, etc., are pretty inflexible—but he claims that the Germans do have a way to circumvent this inconvenience, namely, by changing the case itself rather than the rules. Other cultures move the mountain, the Germans disguise Mohammed as someone or something else. Where there's a will, there's a way, said my friend, but then again, the Germans don't always have the will.

There is an old joke to the effect that whereas in most countries of the world, everything which is not expressly forbidden is allowed, in Germany, everything which is not expressly allowed is forbidden. For visitors to Germany, there often seems to be some truth to that. However, there is one notable exception: smoking is still allowed, albeit not expressly, in a great many places—and even where it is expressly forbidden, it is frequently tolerated.

FUTURE PERFECT

From all I've said in the sections above, it is clear that "the" Germans are not likely to embrace the future with as much fervor as, say, "the" Americans, who are the most future-oriented people I know. And yet, I am loath to create the impression that the Germans are future-resistors by culture—certainly not by nature! They have a lot more respect for history than do many other cultures; they believe that the lessons of the past should be a guide to their future. To put a different spin on matters: Their traditional way of looking at the world is simply cautious and anticipatory as opposed to adventurous and foolhardy. That said, I must quickly add that new generations of Germans are shedding a lot of their cultural conservatism and overthrowing many of the constraints that their parents clung to. In this respect at least, I do believe that turbo-convergence has taken over. For in our global world, curtailing maneuverability and flexibility— the inevitable result of trying to control the future—is a serious hurdle to success. So—although young Germans continue to think and plan ahead, they are learning fast to adapt to unforeseen circumstances and not be thrown into a tailspin of panic. As we will discover later in this book (see Business section, p. 105 on), business Germany has already become very nimble very fast, and with considerable, sometimes spectacular, success.

So far, the German system has been based on absolute security, so that many young apprentices starting their careers could foresee with remarkable accuracy what they would be doing 40 years later. Until recently, they could even have had a pretty good idea what their pension would be at age 65. Few expected to change careers after finishing their education—some did not expect to switch companies during the course of their working lives. The idea that a person could start out as one thing—a banker, for example—and in the course of his/her life become in turn a lawyer, a garage mechanic, a salesperson, a computer consultant, was almost inconceivable. No longer. The notions that life consists of phases and that the successful in the future are likely to be those who are ready to take risks and jump at opportunities are becoming more widespread. At least among the young. It's the middle-aged who are the least able to adapt and who feel the most threatened. They are too old to build up security for their old-age outside the state system, but young enough to be the victims of a state which can no longer pay them their expected pensions. Angst is prevalent—and not without some good cause.

Funnily enough, the Germans ought to be well suited to adopting a portfolio life containing different phases and occupations since they have a natural ability to compartmentalize. So although they may find it difficult to abandon control of the great unknown, the challenge to add more compartments to their futures shouldn't in the end prove too difficult. The British sociologist Lord Ralf Dahrendorf recently commented in an interview for the business magazine, *Wirtschaftswoche*, that German women will have an easier time becoming portfolio people than will German men because women have traditionally been forced by circumstance to combine several roles.

Culture Quiz

Guess to which cultures the following self-descriptions apply:

1. Culture X is highly communicative: communication is the elixir of life, it imparts a feeling of well-being, it involves the mouth, the diaphragm and the index finger. X people say whatever comes into their heads, even if there's nobody around willing to listen to them. Mediterranean types, they communicate very loudly, and on the most intimate of topics . . . They are extremely social, and welcome contact with strangers; they enjoy physical contact and kissing, but only as long as this latter doesn't interfere with their conversation flow . . . They don't take appointments seriously, they consider not being punctual a virtue and part of their Mediterranean heritage. Meetings don't have precise beginnings. If an invited guest should happen to arrive at the door at the agreed-upon time, the host will invariably still be in bed, in the shower, or out shopping.

2. Culture Y is orderly, hardworking, accountable, direct. The zeal with which Y people combat chaos takes on almost mythical dimensions. Known as innovative designers of remarkable machines, they are also the unsung inventors of a world-renowned filing system, and they conscientiously file away every single item in their lives, in strict alphabetical and numerical order, so that everything can be found again for as long as mankind continues to exist. They sort out the washing they hang out to dry according to color and category . . . And of course, since the best way to keep order is to be in control of time, punctuality must be strictly observed. Indeed, this culture is so exact with regard to time and so concerned that nothing should ever take them unawares that a local 16th-century mathematician worked out that the world would come to an end on October 19th, 1533, at 8 A. M.

Well, some of you may have ventured the educated guess that Culture X is polychronic, southern European—maybe Spain or Italy? And Culture Y is monochronic and more northern—maybe Germany or Switzerland? Wrong! Culture X is German—the above passage is a description of the Rheinländer, the people who live along the Rhine river and inhabit the area which boasts the city of Cologne and the former capital of the Federal Republic, Bonn. The *Rheinländer* have a reputation within Germany for being easy-going, laid-back and witty. And Culture Y is German too! The people described are Swabians, natives of the more southern area around Stuttgart and all the way down to Lake Constance. Both passages were condensed from two books written by authorities on the respective regions: *Die Rheinländer Pauschal* and *Die Schwaben Pauschal*. It all goes to show the relativity of culture. Or the way we see ourselves versus how others see us.

3 CONTRADICTIONS

Foreigners stand amazed and fascinated before the riddles posed for them by the contradictory nature at the bottom of the German soul.
Friedrich Nietzsche: *Beyond Good and Evil*
(translated by Walter Kaufmann)

SENTIMENTAL STREAKS

What makes the Germans thoroughly human is that they are a mass of contradictions. Ask them to describe themselves, and 70 percent of them will tell you that they consider diligence and efficiency as their greatest virtues (Alan Watson: *The Germans*); at the same time, they actually work less hours per year than any other industrialized nation (see p. 138). They claim to love order—but simultaneously see themselves as unworldly dreamers, spiritual descendants of the 18th and 19th century Romantics. It is not uncommon to catch a German crying into his beer over *Gott und die Welt* (God and the world) and holding forth on the meaning of Life, Love, The Mysteries of the Soul and major German poets, all dead. And while the Germans are about as neat and tidy as people can possibly be, matched only by the Swiss and the Singaporeans, they are the inventors of the word, and presumably of the concept, *Gemütlichkeit*.

GEMÜTLICHKEIT

This hard-to-translate quality is an essential part of the German character and it's probably what prevents worrywartism from driving the German round the bend. Gemütlichkeit is a feeling or atmosphere of coziness and harmony which most Germans hanker after and which they have to cultivate carefully since it is basically not compatible with their meticulous neatness. When order has prevailed at the end of the day, when the dishes have been stacked away, when stress and tension have been blocked out, when the problems of the world have been relegated to some distant corner of the consciousness, the Germans feel a need to retreat into the womb of their own four walls or of their local pub, and over a beer or two, feel at one with their surroundings.

To this end, they try very hard to makes these surroundings *gemütlich*. Gemütlich rooms generally contain a lot of rustic wood, rugs and wallpaper of different colors and patterns, knickknacks, soft armchairs and crowded furniture. But since German coziness tends to be rather tidy and geometrical, with the cushions lined up in neat rows along the couch and even the plants standing to attention, visitors from sloppier cultures don't always appreciate how snug and relaxed a German home is. One person's Gemütlichkeit . . .

ATTITUDE TO KIDDIES . . .

W. C. Fields is supposed to have commented that a person who hates children can't be all bad. The Germans probably rated high in his estimation, because in a cultural comparison, they are not obvious children-lovers, and babies—by their very nature disruptive of peace and order—leave them . . . well, relatively cold. Proud parents goo and coo over their rambunctious offspring in silent company, and should baby start howling, especially during the famous quiet hours (see pp. 28–29) or in a public place such as a supermarket or restaurant, the reaction is not likely to be encouragingly sympathetic. Babies and children are expected to be seen if necessary, but preferably not heard. When they go on vacation (older) Germans are often perplexed by the seemingly lax attitude Mediterranean parents have towards their children, who are allowed to run around seemingly uncontrolled and make as much noise as they want until all hours of the night. My mother-in-law, a loving grandma and generally very fond of children, gets very upset when children stay up late or "have no manners." Her annoyance is directed not at the children, but at their parents: Don't they know that children need sleep? she worries, and has been known to lecture complete strangers on the necessity of strict education.

To be fair—and I always try to be!—younger Germans have an altogether more relaxed and friendly attitude to kids in general. The late 1960s saw a revolution in child-rearing theories and practice, and the '68ers went the whole hog. They became anti-authoritarian with a vengeance and a generation of German children was raised in a pretty anarchic environment—no rules, no punishments, no controls.

Older Germans watched in horror. But radical anti-authoritarianism produced a generation of what I can only describe as mildly disturbed, confused adults and when they in turn started having kids—not very many, I might add— they didn't know what approach to adopt. Now, three decades later, the pendulum is coming to rest somewhere in the middle, and although a lot of the old controls and child-rearing principles are back, children are viewed more tolerantly, even when they behave—well, like children. (For a few more words on this topic, see *Gender Roles*, p. 71 on.)

. . . AND TO ANIMALS

The German dog lobby is like the Miami Cuban lobby—nobody can touch it. The dog is so close to the German soul that not even an estimated 20 tons of dog excrement a day, much of it on the street, produces an official response.

Peter Schneider, German author, quoted by
Roger Cohen in the *New York Times*, June 20, 2000.

The German attitude to animals, however, is quite different. Animal lovers to the core, there is almost nothing a pet is not allowed to do, and the very same people who will not budge an inch to make way for a harried mother pushing a baby carriage along the street can go into raptures—and cause a serious traffic jam—over a furry, four-legged beast. Germany is animal paradise. There must be more parental-aged men and women who own a dog than those who have children. The reasons for this are endless: costs, time, the decline of the nuclear family, the demands of a career (see p. 129 on), but suffice it to say here that society's written and unwritten rules which militate against children and in favor of pets have helped to increase the gap in recent years. There are even regulations concerning how much time and attention a dog-owner must devote to his pet every day. Children, on the other hand, have to rely on their parents' goodwill for daily attention. Animals—well, dogs—are welcome in most pubs, bars and restaurants, whereas children are not. And here comes one of the greatest contradictions I personally have ever encountered among the Germans: obsessively clean and tidy as they are reputed to be, they have not until recently required animal owners to clean up after their pets. Unbelievable but true. Some cities, such as Hamburg and Berlin, are now attempting to tackle the problem and provide vending machines from which an owner can purchase a rubber glove to remove his pets' doings and comply with new regulations. But throughout much of the country—certainly in my own Frankfurt—droppings remain the curse of German streets, and visitors are well advised to keep their eyes to the ground at all times (see also *Walking* p. 197).

HALF-EMPTY GLASSES

The angst mentioned so frequently in previous chapters is closely related to a pessimistic mind-set that can irritate as well as baffle the unprepared foreigner. In an interview that American author Frederick Kempe had with former Federal President Roman Herzog, the latter said, "*Newsweek* speaks of the 'German disease'. That is certainly exaggerated. But this much is correct: whoever reads our media has the impression that pessimism is our general attitude of life . . . ." Well, it's not just the fault of the media. The German tendency to downplay the positive and moan and groan instead (they themselves call it *jammern*) is pretty widespread. Is this a contradictory trait? Compared to most of the rest of the world, Germans have it exceptionally good, and yet, to hear many of them bellyache, you'd never know it. Germans find it difficult to rest on their laurels because they know that perfection has not been fully achieved. And although they realize that they could have it a lot worse, they also feel in their heart of hearts that they could have it better. Take their economic situation. Not all Germans are rolling in money, but their standard of living is indisputably high. And, while the economy goes through its ups and downs, worry about it has little to do with reality. The West German economy did brilliantly for decades prior to unification and the world recession of the early 1990s, but still the Germans worried. They haven't forgotten the catastrophic monetary upheavals that got them into dire trouble early in the 20th century, so the mere mention of inflation throws them into panic. However, so does the mention of deflation. Whenever the economy does slow down, they feel their fears are vindicated. The facts that Germany remains, and in all likelihood will continue to remain, one of the strongest economies in the world, that average per capita wealth is higher in Germany than most any place else, and that Germany still has a social security net second to none, makes no difference. The Germans are worried that economic doomsday is just around the corner, in about 20–50 years.

As with wealth, so with health. On that subject, the Germans can become quite frantic—really, quite ill. They worry about all the health problems common to Western (wo)man, but above all, they fear a disease completely unknown as such in the rest of the world and called *Kreislaufstörung*. This roughly translates as circulatory problems, and covers everything from mild headaches and dizziness-caused-by-a-change-in-the-weather to major heart malfunction. Since the disease is so all-encompassing, most Germans suffer from some form of it quite regularly, and it is often difficult to determine just how serious it is in any given individual. It keeps people off work for long periods of time, thereby impairing Germany's competitive viability as an industrial location and giving the Germans yet another reason to worry.

Not long ago, I visited an office of the German government in New York on an unexpectedly hot day—the temperatures had soared overnight—and none of the German staff were around. A lonely American I tracked down told me they had all called in sick for circulatory reasons. (Note: all nations seem to have a national ailment—the Americans have heart disease, the French have liver complaints, the Brits have viruses . . . Kreislaufstörung is simply the German variety.)

NEED FOR LOVE

The Germans, outwardly often glum and cautious, are inwardly desperate for affection and popularity. They want to be cherished just as the rest of us do.

Richard D. Lewis:
Cross-Cultural Letter to International Managers

Also closely akin to worrying—maybe an aspect of it—is the German anxiousness to be loved by the outside world. They'll settle for being liked, but anything less than that is intolerable. True, the Germans did not prove themselves to be especially lovable in the 20th century, but after over 50 years of good behavior, most non-Germans are willing to let bygones be bygones and judge contemporary Germans on their present merits and defects. (I'll make one exception to that last statement: American Jews are not always willing to recognize that the sins of the parents are not passed down to the children and grandchildren, and occasionally show animosity. See *Legacy of the War*, p. 98 on) The Germans are acutely sensitive to any perceived or imagined negative vibes emanating from beyond their borders and go out of their way to avoid criticism. Since Germany has become the most populous and economically most powerful country in the European Union, this is an incredibly difficult task, because as someone once remarked, you can't please all of the people all of the time.

The Germans long to be understood and liked by others, yet secretly take pride that this can never be.
Stefan Zeidenitz/Ben Barkow: *The Xenophobe's Guide to the Germans*

This longing to be loved, or at least liked and accepted in the family of nations, may be changing. There has been much talk of late of a new spirit of assertiveness issuing from Berlin—more willingness to take a political lead and if necessary, risk the wrath of allies. Germany has traditionally been extraordinarily forthcoming with so-called humanitarian aid, second only to Sweden in its bounty. Germany also used to have one of the most relaxed qualification processes for accepting asylum seekers. If it disagreed in a matter of international policy, it tended to acquiesce or abstain rather than go against the grain. One lasting effect of occupation was that the country saw its role as reactive rather than proactive. That attitude, which started changing in the early 1990s, went through a transformation during the Kosovo war, when it was Germany, militarily engaged for the first time since 1945, who was given most credit for negotiating the peace agreement. Beyond that the government has not been put to any serious test, but I would not be surprised if the Germans had developed sufficient self-confidence to risk being less liked and support what they believe to be right.

PASSION FOR POSSESSIONS

The German need to be loved is somewhat at odds with their general unwillingness to lend their belongings to anyone, including to their best friends. The Germans are avid owners. Whatever belongs to them is an extension of themselves—and is treated accordingly. Most Germans take care of their possessions, mentally accounted for down to the last button, with great feeling. And just as most other people would think twice about lending out any of their limbs, other than a helping hand, the Germans are not too happy at parting with anything they own, not even temporarily. Property, from real estate to a paperback book, demands the utmost respect.

This deep-seated sense of ownership has a number of ramifications for visiting non-Germans with a different attitude towards their own and other people's belongings. Coming from a different culture, you may take lending and borrowing for granted, and not give much thought to either. "Do take my car/laptop/camera/sweater, I don't need it tomorrow," you say unsolicited. Your German acquaintance hesitates—(s)he doesn't know what to make of your offer. If he accepts, he is burdened with responsibility for something which is not his. Moreover, he may be expected to reciprocate sometime. Puzzled over your unexpected and probably inexplicable gesture, he declines regretfully. If you ask to borrow or use something of his, he'll be even more embarrassed. So don't ask if you can use his mobile phone, work on his computer, borrow his bicycle or, heaven forbid, his car. Without meaning to, you may put him on the spot.

GAS-GUZZLERS AND GARBAGE-SEPARATORS

Strict hours

Does it make sense, I ask myself, that people who consider it their unalienable right to own a car and drive it as fast as they want are the same people who think greener than anybody else in the world? The Germans have a torn soul. As the world's champion tourists and globe-trotters, they drive and fly to their heart's content despite the damage they know both activities wreak on the environment—but as conscientious burghers, they assiduously save energy, cut down on the amount of water they flush their toilets with, and separate their garbage with a scrupulousness bordering on the fanatic. Although I have never actually been in a German kitchen that contained six or seven garbage pails for the different kinds of waste, I am assured that such kitchens exist. What more visibly exists is the assortment of colorful plastic garbage containers located outside each house and apartment building and otherwise permanently dotting and blotting the landscape— they are not dragged to the edge of the curb on garbage collection days. They also decorate such public spaces as airports and train stations, albeit in smaller, designer-shaped versions. Then there are separate containers for batteries, pharmaceutical products, electrical items, and so on. Just in case there might be confusion as to what garbage goes where, municipal authorities distribute free booklets to all residences, explaining in great detail all of the ordinances concerning trash, and explaining, for example, whether plastic yogurt containers should be washed out before being thrown into the yellow bin—they should be, but along with other dishes so as not to waste water. Some garbage is collected directly outside the place you live; other garbage has to be taken to a collection point. Throwing-away-bottle hours are from 7 A.M. to 7 P.M. only, so as not to disturb the local residents.

All of this would be all well and good, if it weren't for the disturbing rumor that when the carefully sorted garbage reaches its final dumping destination, it is lumped together again because the facilities are not up to the disposal job.

GERMANS ABROAD

The German soul is above all manifold, of diverse origins . . . A German who would make bold to say, "two souls, alas, are dwelling in my breast" (Goethe's Faust, line 1112) would violate the truth rather grossly, or, more precisely, would fall short of the truth by a good many souls . . . the Germans are more incomprehensible, incalculable, surprising, even frightening than other people are to themselves: they elude definition and would be on that account alone the despair of the French.

Friedrich Nietzsche: *Beyond Good and Evil*
(translated by Walter Kaufmann)

It's not just the Germans who let their hair down when they go abroad, especially on vacation, and act differently from the way they act at home. People from other cultures certainly do too. There are the famously "ugly" Americans and "ugly" Brits—one southern Italian town once banned British women on the grounds that they were corrupting the morals of their young men. But the way some Germans throw off their basic inhibitions and go native is remarkable and to me, contradictory. Given the German need for private space, it is quite amazing to see them skin-to-skin on a Spanish or Italian beach—whereas they construct ingenious ways to preserve privacy on their own home beaches. On the north German coast, for example, they ensconce themselves in wicker baskets, ostensibly because of the wind, and have no communication at all with their fellows. Or they build huge sandcastles surrounded by moats and disappear inside them. It is true that when abroad, they get up early in the morning to stake out their piece of beach with their towels (see p. 34), but this territorial claim aside, they often seem like different people. They become informal, almost garrulous. They jostle and push in markets and bazaars as if to the manner accustomed (come to think of it, they push in German shops too. Strike that last remark). They even accept delays at airports with the most amazing stoicism.

HOME SWEET HOME 4

The scale of everything is smaller in Germany than in the United States . . . Americans find German houses, apartments, and even appliances inconveniently small . . . Homes are protected from outsiders by a variety of barriers: fences, walls, hedges, solid doors, blinds, shutters and screening to prevent visual or auditory intrusion. Front yards are beautifully maintained but rarely used, and residential streets often appear deserted. Outside activities—sitting in the sun or visiting with family—are restricted to the back yard, away from the street and eyes of others . . . Life in the home with one's family is treasured.

Edward T. Hall and Mildred Reed Hall:
Understanding Cultural Differences

HOUSE AND GARDEN

Since Germany is one of the most densely settled countries in Europe, people have to live relatively close together, mainly in apartment buildings or in houses divided up for several families. One-family houses standing in splendid isolation are a particular luxury. To accommodate the many Germans who still want to live in a private house despite the space problem, a lot of modern residential developments consist of two-story-plus-attic houses joined together and known as *Reihenhäuser*—row houses. Each Reihenhaus has its own yard—sometimes one in front (for show) and one in the back (for family use). The most coveted houses in the row are at the two ends, because the yards can extend around the side, and there is only one attached neighbor to share a wall and fence with.

Germans like greenery and fill their homes with plants. Many urban apartment dwellers hanker after their own private yard or garden, and some are lucky enough to get one, albeit not on their own doorstep. A lot of communities own areas of land which they divide into garden plots called *Schrebergärten* and rent to local residents. The renter erects a wooden hut on his allocated piece of turf—sometimes the hut is little more than a shed for gardening tools, sometimes it is an elaborate mini-house—and has to promise to keep his plot in tiptop order. On summer evenings and weekends, these areas are a flurry of gardening activity. If the foreign visitor doesn't know what Schrebergärten are, he could get the impression that some Germans live on a very small scale (as a guest of mine exclaimed as we drove into town from Frankfurt airport). The Schrebergärten may be a doomed institution, though, as land becomes more expensive and scarce and communities rezone to make way for more lucrative projects.

CLOSED DOORS . . .

As has already become very clear from the first chapters of this section, whatever their financial means and whatever type of dwelling they occupy, most Germans live behind tightly shut doors. Not only are the outside doors to their homes closed—locked and bolted in urban areas, as in urban areas throughout the world—but within their homes, most of the doors to the individual rooms are kept closed. Since people do come and go, this of course leads to the constant opening and closing of doors, which is a characteristic sound of German households. For the visitor, the closed-door syndrome can lead to confusion and the occasional nasty shock. Since you never quite know who's lurking behind the doors, people sometimes pop out unexpectedly and surprise you. Americans have been known to suffer agonies because they thought the room containing the toilet—a small room often separate from the bathroom—was permanently occupied behind the closed door, when in fact it was empty all the time. It's always worth knocking to find out.

. . . AND OPEN WINDOWS

Doors are kept closed, but windows are constantly opened and shut, because most Germans are fanatic about airing their rooms. "It's stuffy in here," says the housewife (rarely houseman) wrinkling up her nose. So she throws open the windows. A few minutes later, someone—often the same person—will complain, "*Es zieht*," meaning, there's a draft coming from somewhere, and the windows are immediately closed. It requires a lot of skill to navigate between stuffy

Door-training starts early

smells and dreaded drafts. Drafts, by the way, are something a great many Germans are extremely sensitive to, and the cause of many ills, from stiff necks to bad colds, pneumonia and worse—the dreaded Kreislaufstörung (see p. 54).

ENERGY SAVERS

Ask the Germans why they keep doors closed and air rooms individually, and they'll tell you it's to save heat. The Germans are indeed great energy savers. Lights are only on when needed, so you should remember to turn off the lights whenever you're the last to leave a room. Central heating systems are often regulated to turn themselves to low at night. Water is used sparingly and there are special water-saving devices on many toilets. In some older and more modest households where the heating system is not central, each room has a stove or space heater and water is warmed by a small gas or electric appliance only when the faucet is turned on. Not infrequently, a small water tank provides the hot water, and when it runs out—after a few minutes—you have to wait for a new tank of water to be heated.

On the subject of heating: There is often none available during the summer months. Heating systems are simply put to bed, which in rented places means turned off at source. So if there's a cold spell in May, and your landlord is the unaccommodating type, you're in for a bracing time. Heat is saved during the cold winter months, too: I recently had a set-to with the apartment owners in the condominium building where I live because they wanted to have the central heat turned off automatically every night at midnight. Since I don't keep German hours, this did not suit me at all. And from heating to cooling: air conditioning is practically never found in private homes. When it gets really hot, shades are drawn and the butter runs freely. This is one of the rare times when doors and windows may be kept open simultaneously, to create a breeze. People who live and work in old buildings with thick walls have a cooler time than those in flimsier, postwar buildings.

In most apartment buildings, even in the luxury category, the lighting in the stairwell is controlled by a time switch. After a minute or two, the lights go out, and if you happen to be between flights—too bad. On each floor, the light switch glows to show you where to press. Invariably, the doorbell to someone's apartment is right next to the light switch, so aim your finger carefully.

BEDROOMS

The one room in a German house about which Americans in particular should be forewarned is the bedroom. Quite often, bedrooms contain no built-in heating element, not even in homes that are centrally heated. This is because a lot of hardy Germans, including the young, consider it healthy to sleep in an unheated room with the window open, even during the coldest months. They may be right, but it's the kind of Spartan experience which I personally can forgo. Once in bed, they traditionally cover themselves with a thick feather- or down-filled comforter stuffed inside a large, bag-like sheet. This huge, puffy covering either smothers you or, when you throw it off in exasperation, leaves you freezing. It takes a lot of getting used to, as do the similarly-filled pillows into which your head sinks endlessly. Fortunately for featherbed fighters such as myself, these costly eiderdowns are being replaced by the duvet, an altogether more comfortable comforter.

PART THREE

Germans and Other Germans

EAST AND WEST AND WALLS IN THE HEAD

After 40 years of life apart, how long will it be until former "east Germans" and "west Germans" become simply Germans?

The Economist

CULTURE SHOCK

In 1996, a lengthy, footnoted and annotated book entitled *Kulturschock Deutschland* (*Culture Shock Germany*) first appeared on the German market. The author, Wolf Wagner, starts out by talking about the culture shock he experienced when he went to the American Midwest for the first time as a 16-year-old and experienced classical culture shock symptoms: first euphoria, then a feeling of uprootedness, then a surge of strong attachment to the familiar home culture and a simultaneous rejection of the foreign culture, then depression caused by feeling misunderstood, and only eventually, acceptance and tolerance of the new environment. His book, however, is not about the shock that foreigners experience when they visit Germany—it is about the shock experienced by Germans themselves within their own expanded borders. And the point he makes throughout the book is that Germans of the former communist German Democratic Republic (*Ossis*) and Germans of the pre-unification Federal Republic (*Wessis*) are still, a decade after unification, so culturally different as to make communication between them not simply difficult, but often acrimonious and resentful.

FIRST THE WALL CAME TUMBLING DOWN

Nobody who was living in either of the Germanys at the end of the 1980s will ever forget the "Great Country Disappearing Act," as Jim Neuger and I dubbed it in a book we wrote called *Ten Went West*.

Over a period of months, the "Wall"—a real wall only around Berlin;
otherwise, a 10-foot high steel and barbed-wire fence backed up by
mine fields and parallel fences, snaking 900 miles through the countryside from the Baltic Sea to Czechoslovakia—crumbled before our
eyes, as an entire nation, or so it seemed, assembled peacefully on
Monday nights to protest a regime which was no longer tenable. "We
are one people," chanted the citizens of the German Democratic Republic (East Germany), and meant one people with the Germans in
the Federal Republic (West Germany). In both Germanys, the spirit
of brotherhood and solidarity was all-pervasive. The events leading
up to the opening of border crossing points from East Germany to
West Berlin and West Germany on the famous night of November 9,
1989, have been recounted innumerable times. Suffice it to say that
the metaphorical falling of the wall signaled the end of East German
communist rule, and for a short moment in history, East Germany
was an independent non-communist nation-state. The reasons for
unification with West Germany are complex, but can be summed up
briefly: East Germany was a bankrupt wreck of a country; West Germany was the prosperous economic leader of Europe. East Germans,
deprived for decades of the material comforts of life, wanted what the
West had, and were not about to wait. They poured into West Germany, and would have stayed there permanently if their own country
been left to its own devices and been forced to restructure without
massive help. And stay in West Germany they could have, since the
Federal Republic was bound by its constitution to recognize them as
its own citizens. When it became clear that it would not take long for
most of the East Germans to settle in the West, adding 16 million
new residents to the already-crowded Federal Republic and leaving
the Democratic Republic virtually empty, the decision to merge the
two countries into one was in part a measure to keep the Ossis where
they were. If the wealthy West took responsibility for the impover-
ished East, the Ossis would have an incentive to stay put.

Unification was accomplished in record time. Barely 11 months
after the Wall had come down, the Democratic Republic was absorbed lock, stock and barrel into the Federal Republic. That was on
October 3, 1990. Already in July of that year, social and monetary
union had taken place—and literally overnight, the West's way of life
became willy-nilly that of the East. The ramifications were mind-
boggling. There simply hadn't been time to think through what
could, would and might happen when the entire legal and social system of one country (western democratic) was imposed on another

(communist totalitarian), and when one culture—and all that implies: way of thinking, acting, the whole value system—was supposed to replace the other. The immediate consequences went from the sublime: the East gained the precious D-Mark—to the ridiculous: the plastic, exhaust-spewing East German cars, *Trabants* or *Trabis* as they were known, quickly became collectors' items in the West. But "minor" irritations soon came to the fore: shops in the East were obliged to stick to western closing hours, which at the time were even more restrictive than they are now (see the section on Shopping, p. 203 on). Hairdressers, a focal point of the East German social infrastructure, were also obliged to close in the evening and thousands went out of business. West German wares replaced East German ones on supermarket shelves, usually at the insistence of large western suppliers who saw the chance to carve up the market for themselves. Wessis poured in to "teach" the Ossis the basics of capitalism, and were soon the clear bosses, running the administration, the judicial system, education and industry. And so on.

Time went by. A super-institution, a national privatization agency called the *Treuhand*, was set up (by the Wessis) to break up and privatize the huge, totally inefficient, cumbersome state monster that had been East German industry, and in the process, close, sell off and rationalize in such a way—and tragically, it was certainly the only way— as to make huge numbers of workers redundant. In an ex-country where unemployment had been virtually non-existent, the jobless rate soared up to 90 percent in some unfortunate areas—indeed, the overall average often reached around 30 percent in those early years. And throughout this almost unimaginable period of radical change, the west, which became known as the old *Länder* or states, kept telling the east, the new Länder, what to do and how to do it. The Wessis always seemed to know everything better, and since it was their money which was being poured into the new Länder, many felt they had the right to dictate terms.

OSSIS AND WESSIS

The above mini-account of unification is hopelessly inadequate to convey what actually happened at the beginning of the 1990s. Hardly had the whole of united Germany recovered from the heady celebrations which marked the historic events when cold sobriety set in. The sheer enormousness of the undertaking in both economic and human terms left everybody reeling. The Wessis began to comprehend what unification was going to cost them on a very personal level, and despite government promises to the contrary, a hefty solidarity tax—7.5 percent of income tax—was introduced fairly fast. It has since been reduced to 5.5 percent, but is obviously around to stay for quite a while. At the same time, the Ossis began to comprehend that things were going to get much worse before they got better. Nasty epithets started to fly freely across the non-existent border. Then came the *Stasi* (East German secret police) revelations, and the realization that the Stasi had infiltrated the country to a horrendous extent, enlisting "help" from ordinary citizens who had supplied them with sometimes damaging, sometimes innocuous information in return for favors. These favors were often no more than a better education for their children, permission to see family in West Germany or the right to travel outside the communist bloc. So, as it later became evident through extensive investigations, a large percentage of the East German population had "worked" for the Stasi as "informal collaborators" (IM). This to the Wessis was an unforgivable sin, no matter what the circumstances, and caused the hoards of ex-IMs to become social outcasts, with many losing their jobs. Many, no doubt, deserved to. But part of the human problem lay in the Wessi attitude of superior rectitude, and the growing feeling on the part of the Ossis that unification, once viewed as a friendly merger, was more of a hostile takeover.

Resentment grew daily. The Wessis started dismissing the Ossis as lazy, stubborn, greedy and corrupt and the Ossis saw the Wessis as arrogant, know-all, greedy and corrupt. The divide, which quickly became known as the "wall in the head," grew even deeper. It still exists today, although it is no longer quite as widespread. The most bitter Ossis are those who lost their livelihood and way of life at a time in their lives—I'd say over 35—when they were set in their ways and unable to make the quantum leap required to shape up in a foreign western world. The younger Ossis, children and youth at the time of unification, have had a much easier time. But the fact that the PDS, the socialist successor party to the communist state party SED, continues to enjoy considerable support throughout the new Länder says a lot about the nostalgia that many Ossis feel about the old days, which may not have been all that good, but were certainly nowhere near as bad as the Wessis make them out to be.

"Wall? What wall?"

THE CULTURE FACTOR

> *Detailing the differences between East and West Germans is difficult because not only did the forty-plus years of communist rule leave its mark, but also regional differences had existed in the east prior to the takeover ... West and East Germans are getting to know one another better, and many of their negative stereotypes are being revised or set aside entirely.*
>
> Greg Nees: *Germany: Unraveling An Enigma*

One (of many) factors which was ignored or brushed aside at the time of unification was the cultural one. And of course, I mean the software-of-the-mind kind of culture. Ossis and Wessis were, and still are to some degree, differently programmed, and 40 years of socio-cultural programming leaves an indelible mark. Many of the cultural characteristics I have attributed across the board to the Germans—their monochronic way of viewing time and space, their attitude toward risk-taking and ambiguity, their way of compartmentalizing, etc., etc.—can also be attributed to the Ossis, but not in quite the same way. It's as if they had been programmed with a different version of the same software. For example: The communist state did not eliminate a chronological orientation towards time, and punctuality was important, but since time and money were somewhat unrelated in the minds of the Ossis, who had not been rewarded for performance so much as for simply turning up and being around, and who had never had to fear unemployment, time had a different quality to it. Likewise space: the Ossis lived within their own four (often crumbling) walls, but since the social infrastructure was far more collective than in the West—from collective baby-care centers through collective kindergartens, state schools, political clubs, to the ubiquitous state enterprises which were as much social meeting places as serious workplaces—personal space and human contact were viewed differently. Information flow was completely non-existent on one level—the state was, after all, totalitarian—but informally and often secretly, information flowed fast and freely, a common feature of totalitarian states. The Ossis were not programmed to think much for themselves; they were not taught the supreme value of hard work; they knew nothing about getting ahead on their own merit; they were not encouraged to be efficient, methodical or even dependable. They did, however, come to see the state as completely responsible for their material and physical well-being.

Are the Wessis so different? The good old yes-no word: *jein*. The Federal Republic, with its remarkable, and regrettably no longer financially feasible, comprehensive social system and its "the state knows best" attitude (see p. 165 on), does not, in the eyes of the far more individualistic Americans, for example, encourage its citizens to take care of themselves. Rather, it takes it upon itself to finance through mandatory taxes almost all educational facilities including universities, and all cultural institutions including opera and museums. Citizens need to be educated! The state obliges them to contribute to the state pension fund, have medical insurance, and even support state broadcasting through a mandatory tax on TV/radio owners, etc. In return, the state guarantees far more security to its citizens than Americans are used to. But not, of course, the degree of security the Ossis were used to. So notions such as collectivism and individualism are relative. So too is the attitude toward risk-taking, tolerance of ambiguity, and so on. What the Wessis find irritating in the Ossis—an unwillingness to stand on their own feet and the sometimes querulous expectation that the good things in life are "owed" to them—the Americans could find irritating in the Wessis.

OSSIS (AND WESSIS) AND FOREIGNERS

Ossis are, on the whole, friendly people towards strangers, perhaps more immediately friendly than the Wessis seem to be. The Ossis may be faster than Wessis to invite you to their homes—that is, if they are not ashamed that you may be shocked by their meager standard of living. They are curious about you, and will ask more personal questions than the Wessis will. In other words, they appear less formal and more open. All of this can be explained—if one wants to be clinical!— by their history and social programming. At the same time, and this often appears as a contradiction, some of them are suspicious of foreigners, especially foreigners who look foreign, i.e. different from them. The Ossis were hardly exposed to foreign-looking foreigners in East Germany—there simply weren't more than a handful of them from such kosher communist countries as North Vietnam. The foreigners they met—if they ever met any, and most didn't—were other white Europeans from neighboring communist countries such as the Soviet Union, Poland, Hungary, etc. When the Ossis first started traveling in West Germany, even before unification, they were astounded by the number of foreign-looking foreigners they ran into: Turks, southern Europeans, Africans, Asians, black Americans . . . These people at first seemed exotic. But after things started going sour, and more and more Ossis became unemployed and disillusioned, their anger turned on those whom they saw as preventing them from getting jobs. A wave of xenophobia hit the new Länder in the early 1990s. It was by no means confined to the new Länder I should add, and young, white males—the perpetrators in practically all cases—took to the streets, fire-bombing homes of Turks and refugee shelters and causing injury and deaths. The incidents were undeniably ugly. In one town in the new Länder, bystanders applauded as refugees were driven out of their torched quarters. This shocked the world, and particularly the Germans, who quickly got together in the hundreds of thousands to demonstrate support for the foreigners among them.

Serious xenophobic incidents decreased over the past decade but are now again on the rise. Hooliganism is a serious problem. Then again, where is it not? The new Länder are unfortunately becoming dangerous places for foreign-looking tourists, especially in areas of high unemployment—the jobless rate continues to hover around the 15 percent level in the new Länder, rising sharply to over 30 percent in hard-hit areas. Foreign workers claim to feel uneasy, and refugee settlements are all too often vandalized. This latter is illogical, because the refugees are not allowed to work, and are certainly not taking jobs from anyone. But logic is not something hooligans are known to possess in any significant quantity.

GENDER ROLES

Partnership and children are the lifestyle priorities for most (German) women, followed by employment . . .
German Federal Government Report for the 4th World
Women's Conference, Beijing, 1995

FAMILIES

Home and family—this constellation, always important in German history, played a rather major role in Germany in the early Hitler years, when it became grotesquely idealized. Family roles, already firmly anchored in societal consciousness, were to be taken deadly seriously, with the men going off to provide (and eventually fight for the fatherland), the women relegated to house and hearth, bearing and raising children, and the cleanly-scrubbed children looking angelic and singing in choirs. This was not quite the way the family developed as the war dragged on, and Hitler discovered that he needed the women he had "freed" from non-family activities, such as studies and professions, to help run the country he had depleted of men. During and after the war, women proved themselves capable of manly deeds, from physically clearing the mountains of rubble from the streets to running farms, offices and businesses—all without neglecting their household duties, of course. Curiously enough—understatement: I find this completely incomprehensible—when the men returned, the women in the western part of Germany meekly withdrew to their kitchens. It took until 1977 for a West German woman to have the legal right to be employed outside the family against her husband's will, and for §1356 of the Civil Code, defining housework as the woman's duty, to be abolished. In East Germany, the fate of women was somewhat different: they were not simply permitted to work outside the home, but required to do so. They also took care of the family. The male-female "equality paradise" which the East German propaganda machine was so proud of does not bear careful scrutiny—women had no choice but to shoulder double and triple burdens.

Today, in united Germany, the nuclear family consisting of Mom, Dad and 1.71 children is still considered the mainstay of German society. Indeed, one feature of German life that often strikes Americans is the visibility of entire families, Mom, Dad and teenage kids, on the streets, in cafés and restaurants. Families are likely to go on va-

"Dad's home!"

cation together long after the "children" are grown up enough to take off on their own or with friends. Children often live at home seemingly forever—that is, until they are well into their 20s and beyond. More about this in later sections. But at the same time, more and more people have different lifestyles, and live as singles, one-parent families, or as cohabiting couples with or without children. Even the nuclear family is not always what it was, with Dad sometimes taking a more active role in the raising of the children, and Mom often working part-time. Which brings me to the next section of this chapter, namely . . .

WOMEN

The subordination of women had ancient roots in Germany and was sanctified by custom, religion and law . . . (In the 19th century) what was unique to Germany was that the subordination of women was more stubborn and more protracted than in the advanced Western countries.
Gordon Craig: *The Germans*

The 4th World Women's Conference in China in 1995 was a reminder: nowhere, it seems, are women getting a really fair deal and even in countries of the so-called western civilized world, they are still struggling for true parity. So the positive news is that compared to women in many, indeed in most other nations, women in Germany have it good. They certainly do on paper, since equal rights are enshrined in the Basic Law (constitution), and on federal and state legislative shelves there are stacks of laws, articles and paragraphs designed to protect and promote members of the female sex. True enough, women in Germany—and in a country of 82 million, they are in a 3 million majority—are neither persecuted nor downtrodden. They are to a great extent free to determine their lives; they are an important part of the workforce; they are the backbone of the family. They are also over-worked, underpaid and generally discriminated against—and nevertheless, curiously uncomplaining.

Reality is complicated, as can be surmised from a recent amendment to the Basic Law. At the end of 1994, the original article affirming the equality of men and women received an addendum: "The State supports the actual bringing about of equality between women and men and is working towards the removal of existing disadvantages." No need to say which sex is disadvantaged. Many women have jobs—55 percent of the female population between 15 and 64 are employed outside the house, and the percentage would be higher if there were more jobs to go around—but in industry, they receive only between 64 percent and 74 percent of what men earn. Moreover, women rarely make it up the career ladder to the highest positions (see also the section on Women in German Business, p. 129 on).

It used to be that German women lived according to the "three Ks:" *Kinder, Küche, Kirche*—children, kitchen, church. This is certainly no longer the rule, but the first two "Ks" continue to exert undue—says I—influence. Germany means well with its women, but the gut feeling (on the part of both sexes) that whatever her legal rights, a woman's top priority *should* be her family, still prevails. It is this deep-rooted, gender-role prejudice that keeps women from more energetically striving for the equality they are legally entitled to. Although there are activists who demand that society treat women more fairly, women in Germany are remarkably accepting of their fate and indeed, tacitly support practices and policies which keep them firmly in their place—at home. For example: most German schools have no fixed hours, no midday meals and no classes in the afternoon. Children can be sent home for whatever reason, hot weather, for example, and at any time if classes are cancelled because the teacher is sick, on a school outing, at a meeting or otherwise indisposed—a ridiculously frequent occurrence. And yet, few mothers are willing to go to the barricades to change this situation. There is a law enabling a parent to take a three-year, child-rearing leave from work with a guaranteed job to return to. Most couples—well over 90 percent—take advantage of this possibility, although not necessarily for the full three years. Until recently, under 1 percent of Dads have taken this leave and only now, in the year 2000, have 1.5 percent of the applications come from men. The law is certainly noble in concept, but unfortunate—I would say dire—in its consequence: women of child-bearing age are considered a liability in career-track jobs and are too often not hired, despite all the legal protection they are supposed to enjoy. I have interviewed major German companies which, off the record of course, quite freely and even regretfully admit that they will resort to the basest of tricks to keep out "liability" women. In the early years of unification, some women in the eastern part of Germany went as far as to get themselves sterilized to "prove" to prospective employers that they would not become a burden. But on the whole, women dismiss the Catch-22 aspect of the law with a shrug.

This was at first incomprehensible to me. But here comes the all-important question: do German women really want to be equal in those domains traditionally considered male, i.e. the money-making world? The answer seems to be "not really." Women with children tend to opt for the so-called Three-Phase-Model: They drop out of the workforce when they have their first child, spend the next ten years or so bringing up their offspring, and then return to the job market on a part-time basis. This model does not work quite so well at times of high unemployment, when older women have a difficult time finding a job even after a period of re-training and often remain jobless after the children have left the nest. What has changed in recent times is that an increasing number of younger women decide not to leave the workforce completely while their children are very small, but prefer to combine child-raising with a part-time, outside job. A recent public opinion survey (*Allensbach*) shows that 50 percent of all German women, with or without children, consider that being a mother with a part-time job is an ideal solution. In the old German states, 33 percent of women say that they can well imagine being a full-time mother and housewife; in the new Länder, only 13 percent find this traditional role acceptable.

Reality is indeed complicated. I used to think that German women were badly off, but after years of futile activism while my own daughter was growing up and I was a working mother, I came to the conclusion that the majority—at least the 50 percent quoted in the paragraph above—are getting pretty much what they want. Which can't be knocked.

CHILDREN

Germany has a future-generation problem. Although German adults are still producing offspring, the birth rate is alarmingly low: according to 1999 figures, there are only 10.5 births per 1,000 inhabitants. In the new Länder, the birth rate temporarily dropped through the floor after unification. Germany, as I have already mentioned (see p. 51) is not a child-loving land, and I don't see any indication that it will become one. Because this bodes ill for the perpetuation of the German species, and because even the most diehard childophobes realize that their pensions will be seriously endangered if the supply of the able-bodied young dries up, there is perennial talk about ways to encourage childbearing. In the 1980s, the government introduced a number of reproduction-friendly measures, including comprehensive protection for pregnant women, various forms of compensation for the progenitors and generous leave provisions for an infant-rearing parent. Which is all well and good, but once Mom and/or Dad decide to get back to the workplace, they're on their own. I speak from hard experience. There are practically no affordable daycare centers, kindergarten places are still at a premium, and as I have already said, after children start going to school at around the age of six, there are no fixed and dependable school hours, no school lunches and no school in the afternoon. What's more, substitute teachers are very rare, so if a teacher drops out for some reason, the kids are simply sent home.

During school vacations, families generally stay together and vacation together—with the result that there are very few organized possibilities for children to go away without their parents and with their peers. Day camps, summer camps and the like are practically non-existent; occasionally a community or church organization will arrange short, subsidized trips for local kids, but "sending children away" is not really a German thing to do, and there is a certain stigma attached to it. Consequently, the private sector sees little need to offer supervised recreation programs for young people. Study tours, on the other hand, are increasingly the rage, and older children can take language courses in various European countries, where they are usually accommodated in a family.

MEN

Germany is a very man-friendly country. And no wonder. Since they meet with so little opposition from their women, men benignly do what they have been doing for centuries: rule the country and the roost. Which is not to say that enlightened men and even househusbands don't exist—they are simply a rare breed.

3 RELIGIONS IN A SECULAR STATE

Considering the number of times that German intellectuals have declared that God is dead, newspapers devote a surprising amount of space to news about religion.

Gordon Craig: *The Germans*

UNIQUE RELATIONSHIPS

State and church, throne and altar, president and priest (or mullah or rabbi)—the political entity representing or ruling the people of a particular country of the world and the so-called organized or established religion or religions within its midst always have a unique relationship. In many cases, this has evolved and matured over the centuries. From pure symbiosis to total mutual independence, the range of possible ways that the secular and the religious can co-exist is exceedingly wide, and the number of variations on a theme seemingly endless. So it is hardly surprising that the relationship between the secular and the religious in the Federal Republic is uniquely German and not comparable to that of any other country. This has to be kept in mind, because the German model often causes confusion, and its subtleties are not always understood. Nevertheless, for all its apparent anomalies and contradictions as seen from a foreign perspective, it functions remarkably well.

COEXISTENCE

In a recent article in the *New York Review of Books*, journalist Josef Joffe talks about "the peculiar cohabitation of 'throne and altar' in Germany. Germany is one of the few countries in the West where church and state live in an intimacy that is proscribed by American standards. Congress 'shall make no law respecting an establishment of religion,' the First Amendment says. But in Germany, there are 'established religions'—three, to be precise: 'the Lutherans, the Roman Catholics, and the (Orthodox/Conservative) Jews.'"

What does Joffe mean by "established" religions? He's referring to the legal status given to them by the state as "corporate bodies under public law." This entitles them to certain privileges I'll return to later. In fact, the relationship between church and state is based on the principle established in the Basic Law, Germany's constitution, of a strict and legal separation: "There shall be no state church." The state is required by the constitution to take a neutral stance on ideology. This, however, does not mean that the state is indifferent to religion or that it rejects any value orientation. On the contrary, its neutrality is realized in a positive way in a diverse network of relations regulated by concordats and a variety of agreements, together known as "state church law," with cooperation taking place in various fields of common interest—particularly, as we shall see, in the field of social services. Thus, the German view of a partnership between church and state differs considerably from the U.S. or French view, with their greater emphasis on independence and separation, or the British, Swedish, Russian or Greek view, where the state church is privileged. Germany's Basic Law recognizes the duty of the state not simply to tolerate free forces in society, but to actively support their development. The Basic Law does not specify, however, that the state must support all religions equally, and indeed, only certain religions receive this backing.

CORPORATE BODIES UNDER PUBLIC LAW

Freedom of faith and conscience as well as freedom of creed, religious or ideological, are inviolable. The undisturbed practice of religion shall be guaranteed.

Article 4 of the Basic Law

The support offered by the state on these "specific" religions comes in the legal sense mentioned by Joffe above: the privileged status of a corporate body under public law. This major difference in Germany's established law requires the understanding by others, because these legal entities have what might be considered in economic terms an "unfair competitive edge" over other religions, since they alone can collect mandatory dues from their followers—and it takes an act of state for a person to leave the church and cease to become a follower. The levy, or "church tax" as it is commonly known, even when it applies to non-Christian religious communities without "churches," is a percentage—around 9 percent—of a person's income tax, and is collected by the state, normally by tax authorities, and passed on to the religious community the person belongs to. The state, it should be added, charges a hefty fee for this administrative service, but the benefit to the churches of this means of collection far exceeds the cost. There is no way for a taxpayer to avoid the church tax without officially leaving the church. If the churches had to support their own tax collection offices, it would cost them around 20 percent of their tax revenues. And not only do the churches have none of the bother of finding ways to support themselves—in other words, they don't have to get heavily into the fund-raising business—but the money they get is directly tied to national income.

The right to impose church taxes, however, is not the only privilege granted to what might be called the established religions. They can offer religious education in state schools—and almost all German schools are public, state-financed institutions—which is almost certainly an effective way to spread the "good word" and keep the faithful in the fold. In sum, they are freed from a number of taxes; they have a say in public broadcasting; they are allowed to minister to the needs of people in hospitals, prisons and the military. And essentially all the state requires in return for all these privileges is that the churches recognize the state's right to exist.

THE INTERPLAY BETWEEN CHURCH AND STATE

The state does, however, reap considerable other benefits, benefits which go beyond the purely religious or spiritual work of the established churches. Their activities in the area of social and welfare work are indispensable and relieve the state of many responsibilities it would otherwise have. Thus, the sick, the needy, the old and infirm, the handicapped and all those who, for whatever reason, require short or long-term care or assistance can turn to the churches, whose welfare associations (*Deutscher Caritas Verband* in the case of the Catholic Church, *Diakonisches Werk* in the case of the Lutheran, and the Central Welfare Organization of the Jews in Germany) provide kindergartens, hospitals, old people's homes, nursing homes, rehabilitation centers, domestic care, counseling centers for foreigners and refugees, family planning centers and so on. All these organizations are intricately tied to the state, legally, financially, and even in terms of human resources, since conscientious objectors, who may choose to replace obligatory military service with "civil" service, provide a significant part of their workforce.

A complete discussion of all church contributions to society would require much more space than is available here. Suffice it to say that the established churches are also extremely active in development work in Third World countries, and provide assistance wherever emergency support is needed in catastrophe areas. Here too, the relief organizations work closely together with the state to share at least a fraction of Germany's wealth with poorer, less fortunate nations.

Since the churches provide the state with their multifold services, the state provides the church organizations with funding for their good works. State subsidies form an impressive line in annual church budgets, as can be seen from the following example: In 1993, of the DM16.3 billion (around $10 billion) that the Lutheran Church (EKD) had at its disposal, DM8.4 billion came from church taxes, another DM3.1 billion from public subsidies, DM2.3 billion from income from its own assets, and the remaining DM2.5 billion from donations and fees.

A CHRISTIAN COUNTRY?

We are a country in which Christian tradition and the Christian Churches play an important role, but we are not a Christian county. The Christian Churches cannot claim monopoly right . . . Nevertheless, in this land in which we live, with all its different cultural traditions, the Christian tradition has a special meaning and special importance.

Wolfgang Huber, Bishop of Berlin-Brandenburg

Based on numbers alone, the Federal Republic is definitely a Christian country. By the latest count, and despite a considerable decline in church membership in recent years, there are 27.6 million Lutheran Protestants and another 27.5 million Roman Catholics: these together add up to around 67.5 percent of the population. Add another 1.5 million Christians of other denominations—over a million belong to one of the Orthodox churches, and most of the rest are either Baptists (87,000) or Methodists (68,000)—and almost 57 million of the 82 million people in Germany—69 percent—are declared, i.e. church-tax-paying, if not active, Christians. It should be noted that while 96 percent of the Federal Republic's (West Germany's) residents belonged to one of the two main Christian churches in 1950, times and the composition of the population have changed. The solidarity tax mentioned in the section on east and west Germans (p. 66) caused many church-tax-payers to formally leave their church to balance out their paycheck deductions. Unification added over 16 million primarily non-religious residents to the united country. In addition, well over 7 million of the present population are not German nationals, and 2.6 million of these are Moslems.

A STORMY HISTORY

Christianity has had a stormy history in that part of central Europe which is now the Federal Republic. Dissatisfaction with the Church of Rome in the late 15th century led to the Reformation, the great revolution led by Martin Luther which effectively ended unity of the German church. Thereafter, Protestants—not just the Lutherans, but others such as the Calvinists and Pietists—remained in the ascendancy; by the middle of the 16th century, they accounted for four-fifths of the population of Germany. But the Roman Church did not fade from the scene as expected: it, too, underwent reform and made a dramatic recovery. The clarification and redefinition of Catholic doctrine took some wind out of the Protestant sails, and led to the Counter-Reformation. The Catholics remained a minority religion, but by the end of the 19th century, they were better able than the Protestants to meet the challenges of modern science, industrialization and urbanization.

The came the 20th century, in many ways an unholy one for Germany. "Both the Catholic and Protestant Churches share something of a bad conscience over the Third Reich," writes Alan Watson, a British journalist. Indeed, leaders of these churches failed or refused to recognize the dangers, and passively or actively supported Hitler. (In 1933 the Catholic Church signed a concordat with Hitler, and the Lutheran Church allowed itself to be incorporated within the National Socialist State as a National Church.) It did not take the churches long, however, to discover that the new dictator was not about to tolerate the promised religious independence, and would have any critic or dissident arrested, whatever his ecclesiastical rank. However at first, despite occasional notable—and successful—resistance to Hitler's attempts to subdue the churches completely, there was little outcry at the evils that were taking place: censorship and the increasing interference of the state in the lives of the population, the visible dispossession and humiliation of the Jews, the arrest and incarceration of political opponents and other undesirables. As the horrors of National Socialism became worse, many brave individuals did take to the pulpit to denounce them, and many forfeited their freedom or their lives in acts of selfless heroism. Names such as Cardinal

Count Galen, Martin Niemoller and Dietrich Bonhoffer live on, but when the nightmare finally ended, many Christians felt they could and should have opposed it more forcefully.

THE SPECIAL RELATIONSHIP, CONTINUED

What I find more remarkable (than the decrease in church attendance) is that the Catholic and Protestant churches still play so lively and vital a role in the life of Germany.

John Ardagh: *Germany and the Germans*

After the war, the close relationship between the state and the Churches in the Western part of Germany was reconfirmed rather than redefined. In fact, Protestants and Catholics joined in the formation of the Christian Democratic Union (CDU), the political party which came into power under Konrad Adenauer when the Federal Republic was created in 1949 and which was in power for all but 13 years until 1998. Similarly, the Christian Social Union (CSU), sister party to the CDU in Catholic Bavaria, is even more outspokenly Church-oriented, in some ways similar to the Conservative Christian coalition in the United States. In the East German Democratic Republic, religion was discouraged, but the Protestant Church managed to survive within the all-powerful communist state and provided a limited forum for dissent. Certainly, the Church as a symbol of freedom and organizer of resistance played an important role in the peaceful revolution which led to the downfall of the regime and to unification in 1990. In 1991, after decades of separation, the regional Protestant churches in East and West Germany were legally and structurally reunited and are known today as the EKD, *Evangelische Kirche in Deutschland.*

THE LUKEWARM AND THE FERVENT

The established churches today are concerned that their followers may be losing interest in religion, that they are becoming "remote." As I have already mentioned, after unification, and with the introduction of the mandatory "solidarity tax" to help pay for the costs of improving life in the new states or Länder, many people left the church to reduce their hefty taxes (see p. 66 and p. 79). In 1992, the peak of secession, almost 200,000 people left the Catholic Church—annual secession now hovers around 155,000. But church attendance, that is the number of persons actually attending services at these same churches, has not declined at the same rate. Church leaders recognize that the great majority of their members are not regulars, but rather people who remember their religion only on particular occasions like christenings, weddings and funerals, and at particular times of the year like Easter, Christmas, etc. Both churches are seeking ways to reverse the downward trend. And yet, there are occasional demonstrations of religious fervor which cause a stir throughout the country. When the Federal Constitutional Court ruled in 1995 that a mandatory religious cross in each state school classroom was illegal, politicians and the people of the Free State of Bavaria took to the streets in protest. The so-called "Crucifix Decision" proves that for a part of the country at least, God was far from dead.

THE JEWS IN GERMANY

Some 100,000 members of approximately 80 Jewish communities are currently living in Germany and the number is rising by the month. In terms of relative growth, Judaism is the most dynamic of any of the religions in Germany. As one of the three established religions, it shares all of the privileges granted to the "established" Christian churches: it benefits from the church tax, receives state subsidies, has representatives sit on broadcasting councils, provides social and welfare programs, runs kindergartens and schools. In a population of 82 million, it is a group whose exceptional past has led to an unexpected present.

The Jews in Germany have had a long and often turbulent history which dates back more than 16 centuries. In A.D. 321, the rights of the Jews in Cologne were defined (and restricted) by the Roman Emperor Constantine in a document still preserved in the Vatican. The emperor Charlemagne, not known for his tolerance of non-Christians, accepted Jews in his empire. But over the centuries, the Jews have never had an easy time in Europe in general and in the German territories in particular, and all too often became the scapegoats for the ills that befell the rulers and the populations.

Nevertheless, and this in itself testifies to human perseverance, the Jews managed to survive, and were actually doing quite well by the late 19th century, when Bismarck unified the German nation. In 1872, they were formally granted equal rights, although they remained far from equal in practice and pressure on them to convert persisted into the 20th century. Throughout this period, they did integrate and assimilate to an astounding degree, considering the earlier hostilities and restrictions. Jews fought—and 12,000 died—for their country in World War I. They considered themselves to be Germans first and foremost, and as surprising as it might seem in retrospect, they were completely unprepared for the unprecedented genocide, the holocaust unleashed upon them by Hitler and his thugs.

Prior to World War II, there were 530,000 Jews in Germany. At the end of the War, around 15,000 remained. Not all of the 485,000 had been killed—some, of course, had escaped. But at what price. This is not the place to talk about the horrors of the Holocaust, and I shall not attempt to do so. In an irony of history, the Jewish population in Germany rose to well over 200,000 right after the Holocaust—these were the so-called Displaced Persons (DPs) from other countries, almost all on their way elsewhere.

Within five years, most had moved on. The members of this "new" West German Jewish community—for now it was made up primarily of Eastern European Jews, most of them from Poland—spent their time filling out visa applications while they "sat on packed suitcases" and waited for their turn to emigrate further west, or to Israel. In 1950, some 30,000 were left. Left, not because they wanted to stay, but because many were too ill, too broken to get the visas they so much wanted from the United States, Canada, Australia. And when one family member was turned down, how could the rest, more able-bodied, leave them behind?

The years passed. Some of the survivors died, while others founded families and had children. Despite significant emigration restrictions enforced by the Soviet leadership, more Jews joined those already in Germany in periodic waves from countries of Eastern Europe, including the Soviet Union, as well as some from places such as Iran and even Israel. With all the fluctuations caused by death, emigration and immigration, the Jewish community in Germany continued over the years to number around 30,000 and to consist mainly of people with an Eastern European background who practiced an Orthodox version of their religion—as opposed to the more liberal versions practiced by the majority of the pre-war "German" Jews. And surprisingly to many observers, this new community (subdivided into communities throughout the country, with the largest ones in Berlin, Frankfurt and Munich), prospered and took root, so that by the 1980s, this realization led to a different mind-set on the part of Jews towards their environment. Instead of maintaining the illusion that they were only temporarily in Germany—the "packed suitcase" syndrome mentioned above—they began to feel more as franchised members of the population. Most of them were by now German citizens, and had become literally the "new" German Jews, although many continued and indeed continue, to think of themselves as Jews in Germany, rather than as German Jews.

In 1989, the official number of Jews in Germany was 28,400. Then came Gorbachev and *Peristroika*. Almost overnight, it became easier for Jews, not necessarily persecuted, but certainly living in a hostile climate, to leave the Soviet Union. For a number of reasons, some chose to head for Germany rather than Israel. The then head of the Central Council of Jews in Germany, Heinz Galinski, entered into discussions with the German government aimed at creating special provisions for these Soviet Jews to take up residence in Germany. What Galinski wanted, and ended up getting, was an open immigration quota. Since Germany is a country which, despite overwhelming evidence to the contrary, insists that it is not an immigration country, Galinski's success was impressive: there is no similar open quota provision for any other group. Israel, it should be noted, continues to oppose this immigration, and in another irony of history, would like Germany to close its doors to the Russian Jews, whose duty it is, according to the Israelis, to move to Israel. The German government, however, continues to keep its doors open.

Since the collapse of the Soviet Union, over 80,000 so-called Russian Jews have established themselves in Germany, and they are arriving at a rate of about 10,000 a year. Actually, the official number of these immigrants is far higher, since the Germans allow not only Jews but also their non-Jewish families to enter the country, while the Jewish community accepts and counts only those Jews who are Jewish according to Orthodox religious law—that is, those who can "prove" they were born to a Jewish mother.

This dynamic growth of the Jewish community in Germany is leading to dramatic change. The Russian Jews are younger, better educated and more secular than the traditional (read: post-1950, pre-1989) establishment, which now numbers under 20,000 according to my own mathematics. The Russians are still in the process of fitting in, learning German, finding jobs and becoming integrated, but into which society? The Orthodox Jewish community, or mainstream Germany? Time alone will tell.

Another development in Jewish life in Germany today is the growing diversity in religious life itself. The postwar community calls itself an *Einheitsgemeinde*, a unified community, which has always favored the Eastern European Orthodoxy mentioned above. Liberal and Reform Judaism did not re-establish themselves after the war. Now, initiated by young intellectuals and encouraged by progressive movements outside the country, Liberal Judaism—in American terms, Conservative Judaism—is taking root. This is not happening without fierce opposition from the establishment—but that in itself is healthy (again, says I) since internal squabbles are part of the tradition. Moreover, the fact that the Jews in Germany can afford to squabble is a sure indication that they are not facing external problems such as serious anti-Semitism. (For further reading on related topics, see *Jews from the Ex-Soviet Union* pp. 91–92 and *The Legacy of the War*, pp. 98–102)

ISLAM IN GERMANY

Islam is the third-largest religious community in Germany. Its 2.6 million followers, not all of whom are particularly religious, make up just over three percent of the population. In Cologne alone, there are about 70,000 Moslems. Dotted throughout Germany, there are around 2,500 mosques and other Moslem places of worship in local communities. The vast majority of these places of worship are in private homes and cramped backrooms, inaccessible to all but the initiated. Nevertheless, Islam is visible, and becoming more so.

Islam in Germany dates back to the 18th century, when in 1732, the Prussian King Friedrich Wilhelm I decreed that "his Mohammedans"—twenty soldiers given to him as a gift—be allowed to form a community and practice their religion in a place set up as a mosque in Potsdam. From then on, there have always been Moslems in Germany. But it was not until more than two centuries later that the "community" became a sizeable one. During the 1960s, West Germany needed a larger workforce than it could itself provide, and invited "guest workers" from a number of countries in the general non-communist vicinity to contribute to German prosperity. Most of the foreign workers who took up the offer came from Turkey. The general idea at the time was that the "guests" would stay for a few years and return home. This did not happen. Germany proved to be too attractive to leave, so the guests settled down and sent for their families. Not even the offer of cash incentives to return to their homeland was sufficient to reverse the trend. De facto, by the mid-1970s when an influx of foreign workers was no longer needed, Germany had a large permanent foreign element in its midst, and Islam had become part of the West German scenery.

Thus, the vast majority of Moslems living in Germany today are Turkish Sunnites—the Turkish population of Germany now numbers over 2 million. And Turkish many will remain, although the new citizenship laws (see p. 87) will allow those born and raised in Germany to opt for German nationality, and confer German citizenship automatically on future offspring.

While religious freedom is guaranteed by the Basic Law and Moslems are as free as anyone else to practice their beliefs, Islam in Germany is not on a par with Christianity and Judaism, if only because it is not a corporate body under public law. Nevertheless, Islam is thriving and Moslems are generally well accepted. The problems they may encounter would appear to have more to do with resistance to immigration, especially during times of high unemployment, than with religious intolerance. There has been little protest in Germany—as for example there has been in France—over traditional dress codes. In fact, in some public schools where there is a high concentration of Moslems, Islamic religious teaching is on the curriculum, even though this is a privilege usually reserved for the established religions.

Finally, I should add: While the majority of Moslems in Germany are Turkish, around 17 percent are nationals of other countries. The entire spectrum of Islam is represented.

IN CONCLUSION

In Germany, the state and its established religions are involved in a well-functioning, synergic relationship. The strict legal and organizational separation between state and church stipulated by the Basic Law is not always apparent; the lines between political parties and the church often appear fuzzy, despite the fact that they are regulated by "state church law." Curiously enough, however, these intricacies do not seem to lead to undue interference by either side in the matters of the other. Generally, consensus reigns. Occasionally, the more conservative Catholics will lobby against what they consider to be moral infringements—legal abortion, the Crucifix Decision, the giving of legal status to same-sex couples (see p. 159)—but for the most part, religion in everyday life is involved with the same underlying values which are more or less the same throughout the western world, and which are neither strictly denominational nor particularly controversial. Funnily enough to many Germans, it is in the United States, where separation of church and state has in itself become something of a religion, that in public speeches at secular events politicians like to appeal to God to bless America and the Americans. In Germany, invoking God to bless the Germans would very likely be considered inappropriate.

GERMAN FOREIGNERS, FOREIGN GERMANS 4

The atmosphere in this country is going to change as the notion that we are all German citizens, independent of our roots, takes hold. It will take a long time [to change attitudes], but it will happen.

Safter Cinar, a Turk in Berlin,
quoted in Frederick Kempe: *Father/Land*

GERMAN FOREIGNERS

It was Mark Twain who said "There are small lies, big lies and statistics" (or words to that effect). When it comes to talking about foreigners in Germany, it's wise to keep this in mind, for the statistics can easily give rise to serious misinterpretation. That said, here goes:

At the time of writing, the start of the 21st century, there are 7.3 million foreigners in Germany, around 8.9 percent of the population of 82 million. This may sound like a lot of foreigners, but since several million of them were born in Germany, as were many of their parents and even grandparents—25 percent of all foreigners have been in the country for over 20 years—the statistics say very little, because in the United States, for example, these several million would, of course, automatically be U.S. citizens by virtue of their place of birth. So we can't meaningfully compare German and U.S. statistics on foreigners. The reason for all these foreign Germans—and after one or two generations of living in Germany, they are as German as any German, but they retain foreign status, their foreign citizenship and passport—is to be found in the "old" naturalization laws, which have only just been changed. The new laws came into effect on January 1, 2000. According to the old laws, citizenship was conferred by the blood of at least one German parent, and not by place of birth. To become German—that is, to become naturalized—was a very lengthy, complicated procedure which involved the renouncing of previous nationality. Dual citizenship is not welcome in Germany unless one parent is German. A major problem with regard to renouncing nationality was—and to some extent, still is—the fact that over 2 million of the foreigners are Turks, and although they have been around the longest (many since the 1960s, see above and below), they have strong emotional and religious reasons for not wanting to give up their Turkish citizenship. For many other foreigners, dual citizenship is not so much of an issue. Another 2 million or so are from European Union (EU) countries, and theoretically at least, European integration has made us all into citizens of Europe. Our passports all look the same, and the actual country we come from is irrelevant. Yet another 2 million foreigners are from other, i.e. non-EU, European countries such as Switzerland, Romania, ex-Yugoslavia and the Russian Federation (and let's not forget the 12 men and 19 women from San Marino); around 200,000 are from the United States—and to the best of my knowledge, only Shere Hite, author of *The Hite Report*, has renounced her U.S. citizenship to become German—and the rest are mainly refugees and asylum seekers.

A MINI HISTORY OF GERMANY'S FOREIGNERS

"Germany is not an immigration country," is the oft-heard official cry, not just of Kohl's conservative government, but also of its Social Democratic/Green successor. The fact is that de facto, Germany is Europe's leading immigration country and has been for a while. In the boom years of the "Economic Miracle" at the end of the 1950s, Germany discovered that it didn't have enough able bodies to fill the labor market. So it looked to the poorer countries of southern Europe—eastern Europe being sealed off behind the Iron Curtain—and started actively recruiting. Turks, Yugoslavs, Greeks, Italians, Spaniards and Portuguese poured in and were dubbed "guest workers." The idea—if indeed anybody gave the matter any thought—was that the "guests" would leave again when work ran out. The reality was that the guests settled in for the duration, sent for their families, and formed their own colorful, polychronic and decidedly un-Germanic sub-cultures. Integration did not take place for many reasons, not the least being the leave-again fiction. By the early 1970s, the German economy was in decline, and the guests were no longer needed. Not only was the come-to-work-in-Germany invitation retracted, but the government, anxious to get rid of the now unwelcome residents, actually offered monetary incentives for them to leave. No matter that these incentives came from the social security payments the guests themselves had contributed and were therefore entitled to anyway—the majority were not about to go home nohow. Over the following years, they flourished and multiplied, for the most part continuing to keep much to themselves outside the workplace. In the case of the largest group, the Turks, religion has played a major role here, since intermarriage is problematic, and the Islamic culture practiced by the older generations has put severe social and integrative restrictions on the generations born in Germany—thereby causing considerable internal conflict. Although public authorities on all levels (local, state and federal) have created offices to oversee "foreigner affairs," the Germans have been unwilling or unable to integrate the Turks and occasional well-meaning projects to promote better intercultural relations have often proven frustrating. Now, with the new citizenship laws in place, meaningful integration may be facilitated.

It is, however, not the guest workers who are generally considered the "problem" foreigners. These are mainly the asylum seekers and refugees, who until 1993 were able to enter Germany fairly freely under Article 16 of the Basic Law, which guaranteed each individual the right to apply for political asylum—a long process—and in the meantime, live in Germany at the expense of the state. Even after being turned down for political asylum—and the vast majority of applicants were—the rejected were rarely ejected, and almost all of the asylum-seekers ended up remaining in the country. The unprecedented generosity of Article 16 led to an ever-increasing number of the politically and economically disadvantaged of this world flocking to Germany—almost half a million in 1992 alone. Of these, around 5 percent were considered to be genuinely politically persecuted. By 1993, the situation was held by much of the population and by most politicians across the political spectrum to be untenable, and it became possible to muster the necessary two-thirds majority of parliament to alter the Basic Law and effectively limit the entrance of asylum-seekers into the country. Only those who come straight to Germany from a country which Germany recognizes as guilty of political persecution—and there aren't many of those on the German list—are remotely eligible for asylum. The rest, should they ever make it onto German soil, are immediately turned away. Unsurprisingly, the number of asylum seekers dropped radically after 1993, and is now down to about 100,000 a year. Refugees (as opposed to asylum seekers) are sometimes let in during a period of crisis in their home countries, ex-Yugoslavia, for example, but they are given only limited residence permits and after the crisis is deemed over, they are sent home as fast as possible. That said, Germany remains far more hospitable to people in distress than other western countries.

Right-wing extremists and more conservative Germans fear multiculturalism is responsible for rising unemployment and crime rates as well as a loss of core German values and norms. Younger and more progressive Germans are more welcoming of these changes, seeing in them the opportunity to create a more diverse and open society.
Greg Nees: *Germany: Unraveling An Enigma*

Despite the 1993 amendment, there are still 1.5 million asylum-seekers and refugees living in Germany, housed in special quarters throughout the country. Most of these foreigners are not allowed to work, not allowed even to stray far from home—a trip to a neighboring town may be illegal. They are often extremely "foreign," and have little chance to be anything else. They tend to be feared and disliked by the local residents, and unpleasant incidents are not uncommon. All too easily branded as "criminals"—and the crime rate is high, but some of the minor crimes are understandable—they are convenient scapegoats for more indigenous social unrest. In the new Länder, former East Germany, where foreigners were virtually unknown before unification, and where the economic situation is not yet comparable to that of the old Länder, tensions run high. Unscrupulous politicians of the far right deliberately foster xenophobia. Some communities have simply refused to accept asylum seekers or refugees, claiming that they endanger social harmony and ethnic homogeneity.

FOREIGN GERMANS

Who are the German foreigners? They are mainly one-time Germans who for political reasons—the carving up of the map after the war—found themselves, usually unwillingly, in some other country in Eastern Europe. Some managed to trek back to one of the Germanys after the redrawn boundaries, but many could not, especially after the Iron Curtain descended. Only after the fall of communism could these "Germans"—after four decades, very foreign Germans with lit-

Green Cards for Indians?

Germany's ambivalence to its foreign population is once again in the lime-light. Fearful that Germany is losing ground to other countries in the field of high tech, the present chancellor, Gerhard Schröder, recently decided that he'd better do something to "reverse the brain drain," as he put it. So he proposed relaxing immigration requirements for IT whiz kids from Asia. Of course, he didn't want to repeat the mistakes of the past, and al-low an uncontrolled stream of foreigners into the country . . . the new "guest workers" would be invited for a strictly limited time, and without their families. Concretely, he came up with the idea of offering 20,000 temporary Green Cards to the high tech specialists earning over $50,000 a year (a way to keep out the unemployed riff-raff . . .).

The announcement caused a furor, and reactions ran the whole spec-trum. Some called the proposal "racist and discriminatory"—the very idea of exploiting the knowledge and expertise of people who were basically un-welcome in the country was considered outrageous. Others pointed out that Germany needed experts in a number of fields, not just in IT, and wanted to extend the Green Card idea. Yet others worried that if Germany opened its doors to a bunch of foreigners—bright ones, at that—the flood gates would cave in to a never-ending wave . . . And so on. One prominent member of the opposition launched a campaign called *Kinder statt Inder*, children rather than Indians—which provoked another outcry and back-fired. The government was forced to modify its original proposal, but managed to get it approved. Green-carders (with families) are on their way. The story simply illustrates just how ambivalent Germany is about its foreigners. But it has re-opened the immigration debate, and a commis-sion has been set up to investigate the situation.

tle or no knowledge of German culture or language—"return" to Germany. However, German law recognizes them as German citi-zens. Called *Aussiedler*, well over 3 million already live in Germany, and they continue to arrive, despite government attempts to have them stay where they are. The upper ceiling on admittance is cur-rently 225,000 per year.

JEWS FROM THE EX-SOVIET UNION

I've already mentioned this group in the section on Jews in Germany (see p. 82), and I mention them again here only because these immigrants are, in fact, the only immigrants Germany "welcomes," provides with start-up help in the form of housing, German language lessons and other social benefits, and who are able to become German citizens relatively easily (this was the case even under the old naturalization laws). Indeed, the Russian Jews are treated in much the same way as the Aussiedler. It is yet one more irony of history that many non-Jewish Russians who want to immigrate to Germany are now willing to pay a high price on the black market to have the once-despised word "Jew" stamped into their passports; the trade in forged passports is apparently flourishing. Many Jews in the ex-Soviet Union apply for a visa to Germany (a visa must be obtained before departure) without any definite intent to emigrate—they consider the visa a safeguard against outbreaks of anti-Semitism. There are apparently 150,000 visa applicants and visa-holders still living in the countries that once made up the Soviet Union.

SINTI AND ROMA

There are one or two small but integrated ethnic minorities living in Germany. The Sorbs, descendants of Slavic tribes, the Friesians, descendants of a Germanic tribe, and a minute population of Danes all settled in northern Germany at some point in history, and have remained there, trying—with varying degrees of success—to preserve their distinctive languages and cultures. There is no stigma attached to belonging to one of these minorities, and discrimination is not an issue.

The opposite is true of the largest (dual) ethnic minority living in Germany. The Sinti and Roma, better known in Germany by the derogatory label *Zigeuner* (gypsies), are said to number around 70,000—and are therefore roughly comparable in number to Germany's Jewish population. (I should add that the population figures are hard to verify because the Sinti and Roma are not counted as a distinct ethnicity, and many do not take part in official census reports.) Like the Jews, the Sinti and Roma were more or less wiped out during World War II: around 500,000 European Sinti and Roma were killed by the Holocaust. (Again, figures here differ—the *Encyclopedia Britannica* estimates the number killed at 400,000, while some Sinti and Roma sources put the figure at 1.5 million.) But whereas the Jews have become a privileged minority in contemporary Germany, the Sinti and Roma are not officially recognized as being a national minority, and they remain unpopular, misunderstood, feared and often simply dismissed as vagrants or common criminals. In Bavaria, the police are known to categorize the Sinti and Roma as an ethnic type—this is illegal and contravenes international conventions on the protection of minority rights—because they consider all Zigeuner to be potential criminals and potentially, a public danger. Sinti and Roma have a long history in Germany—they have been around for about six centuries. Today, they are German citizens, Christian (most of them are Roman Catholic), their family names are often typically German, they live primarily in the urban areas of western Germany (only a handful live in the new Länder), and they lead much the same lives and practice the same professions as mainstream Germans. If they deny their heritage, they can blend into the landscape and avoid discrimination and hassle. However, if they let the world know that they are Sinti and Roma, if they use their language— German Romany, a German derivative of a language which can be traced back to Sanskrit—outside their homes, then they are more than likely to encounter dislike, rejection and mistrust. It is not politically incorrect to bad-mouth the gypsies and make them into scapegoats for all of the myriad petty crimes endemic in urban areas. And it is petty crime which earns contempt; major crime—for which the Sinti and Roma are rarely blamed—is apparently far more honorable.

In April 1999, a full-page ad appeared in the *New York Times*, appealing to German authorities to put an end to the Bavarian racist databases. The ad, designed to draw U.S. attention to discrimination against the Sinti and Roma, was supported by a long list of internationally well-known personalities. Personally, I am not absolutely sure that the majority of readers of the *New York Times* will have understood who the Sinti and Roma are, since the ad did not make this entirely clear, so I have my doubts about the effectiveness of the ad. However, there is no doubt in my mind that the public in general, whether in the United States, Germany or elsewhere, should be made aware of the massive prejudice against this ethnic minority, which is desperately in need of a good lobby.

I do not want to leave the impression that Germany is alone in not welcoming the Sinti and Roma with open arms. On the contrary— and this is important—they probably live better here than anywhere else. They are very much second-class citizens to the east of Germany, in Hungary, in the Czech Republic, in Slovakia . . . and are generally considered to be untrustworthy vagabonds in the other countries of western Europe.

5 PEOPLE WITH DISABILITIES

The disabled and/or the chronically ill are part of our society—therefore they do not have to be integrated into society. Rather, society must be helped to view disabilities and chronic illnesses as something natural and to deal with them as such.

Aktionsprogramm 2000

AN UPBEAT VIEW

Not surprisingly, in the literature put out by ministries and agencies of the German government, the situation of the disabled and the chronically sick is upbeat: it would appear that in the past decade, considerable progress has been achieved on a variety of fronts—social, legal and medical—with regard to bettering the lives of people with handicaps and integrating them into mainstream society. And indeed, there have been a number of breakthroughs, the most significant of which, leaving medical progress aside, being the 1994 amendment to the Basic Law asserting that "nobody may be disadvantaged because of a disability." This long-debated, highly controversial prohibition against discrimination essentially removes all legal barriers to the full social integration of a group of people who throughout history have been seen as an unimportant minority, a fringe group, inferior to their non-disabled fellows and therefore not deserving of equal treatment.

A LARGE MINORITY

This minority is, in fact, much larger than many people think. There are currently around 6.6 million people in Germany who have registered themselves with the state as severely handicapped, and another possible 5 million who have some form of disability but who have not made this officially known—among other reasons, to avoid the stigma of being labeled "disabled." Since in many cases there are very good reasons for registering, such as eligibility for a range of benefits which, depending on the degree of disability, include tax reductions, special job protection, extra vacation, reduced or free public transportation and special parking permits, bureaucratic "outing" is not an altogether bad idea.

SOCIAL DISCRIMINATION

The disabled may be equal in the eyes of the law, but in the eyes of society they are definitely not. Laws cannot regulate how people feel and even how they act towards their fellows when the acts are subtle enough to slip through the statute book clauses and paragraphs. Acts as simple as crossing the road to avoid having to confront a person in a wheelchair, or moving away from a gathering of mentally handicapped children on a station platform so that the group ends up isolated. Discrimination is all-pervasive, despite considerable efforts on the part of both the public and private sector—and specifically, of course, the numerous associations of the disabled and their friends—to make the public aware what it means to be disabled. And the sad fact is that the disabled are excluded from many areas of life because their fellow citizens, consciously or unconsciously, create insurmountable barriers to their participation.

INSIDIOUS BARRIERS

Barriers are partly attitudinal, partly physical. Without going into too much detail, I would say that the most serious attitudinal barrier is the unwillingness of many employers to hire people they consider "unwell" or "ill." So they would rather pay fines than comply with a law that requires employers of over 16 employees to give 6 percent of their jobs to people with severe disabilities. Paradoxically, it does not help that the law gives particular job protection to people with disabilities; the way employers see it, once hired, the disabled are next to impossible to lay off. And discrimination starts early. Although the education ministers of the various German Länder decided in 1994 that separate schooling for handicapped children was not necessarily a good idea, and that in future, handicapped children should be sent to regular schools whenever possible, integrated classes remain rare. Not only is there a lack of qualified staff and adequate facilities at "normal" schools (and special schools, *Sonderschulen*, exist for disabled students whose needs cannot be met at "normal" schools), but the will to integrate is often lacking, especially on the part of parents with non-disabled children. They think their own kids will be academically disadvantaged or somehow "infected" by close, daily association. What we have, then, is a rather perfidious separate-but-equal system.

I did a short study recently on the subject of the disabled in Germany, and I was taken aback by what I found out. There are strict building codes, for example, requiring new buildings to be "handicapped friendly." But buildings continue to be constructed with no regard whatsoever for people in wheelchairs or the blind. In the worst case, there's a fine to pay, but that is frequently calculated in from the start. Older buildings are very rarely modified unless their owners are threatened with court action. Public transportation is supposed to be accessible to people in wheelchairs, but most of it isn't. I have rarely been in an elevator with buttons that could be reached by people in wheelchairs, or with raised digits for the blind. Moreover, having the

Action Mensch

One tiny but significant indication that the attitude towards the handicapped may be undergoing a change is the very recent, March 2000, renaming of an organization which had the very best of intentions, but the most unfortunate of titles—*Aktion Sorgenkind*. A *Sorgenkind* is a problem-child, or a child that causes worry. A *Mensch* is—well, a mensch; a sensible, mature, decent human being. Originally established in 1964 to help babies with birth defects caused by the drug thalidomide, the organization has since expanded its activities, and put the DM3 billion it has raised primarily through a TV lottery show in the years since its founding into around 33,000 projects. One such project, *Aktion Grundgezetz*, was to make the public aware of the 1994 addendum to the German Basic Law (see above) and turn the legal phrasing into concrete action. In recent years, even before changing its own name, the organization confronted the problem of sympathy versus respect for the handicapped, and tried to increase public sensitivity to the difference. One of its ongoing campaigns is to mobilize the public to take to the streets on May 5, the day on which Europeans show their solidarity with the handicapped. Around 35,000 people supported the cause in Germany on that day in 1999—about as many people as regularly show up for a Galaxy Frankfurt American football game. Still, progress is definitely being made.

occasional wheelchair-friendly elevator in hub stations does not make it possible for wheelchair occupants to get on or off a train, bus or tram, or exit at other stations, where there are frequently no escalators, let alone elevators. Some television programs have subtitles, but very few live broadcasts are accompanied by aid to the hearing-impaired, despite many appeals to those responsible. And so on.

THE GOOD NEWS

The good news is that things are definitely improving. Ramps, toilets and other facilities for the disabled are definitely more part of the landscape than they were a decade ago. The disabled themselves are becoming more active in demanding their rights, and are becoming less dependent—at least psychologically—on the people that care for them. The barriers I talked about above are slowly being surmounted. And Germany is certainly relatively generous in its financial support of the disabled. Moreover, the number of private initiatives to assist the handicapped is growing. For example: In mid-2000, an entrepreneur in Hamburg started up a website with job listings (www.kein-handicap.de). To get around the negative attitude towards employing the handicapped because of the extra job security they "enjoy" under the law (see above), the creator of this Internet job market suggests that the handicapped offer their services as freelancers. Not an ideal solution, but a practical one. Although equality is not around the corner, it is not beyond the horizon.

6 THE LEGACY OF THE WAR

With Germany's defeat in the Second World War the German people said goodbye to the aggressive, militaristic chauvinism that had characterized German policy-making for the two preceding generations— a goodbye that was, one is tempted to say, irrevocable.
Peter Pulzer: "Model or Exception—Germany as a Normal State?"
in *Developments in German Politics* (ed. Smith, Paterson, Padgett)

TENTACLES OF GUILT

I have already referred once or twice to the lingering effects of the war (World War II) on the German psyche. The Germans have their own particular identity problems, and carry their own particular burden of history. Of course they do and of course they must, say many non-Germans self-righteously. But is this so self-evident? For how many Brits ever think about, let alone agonize over, the havoc they have wreaked and the deaths they have caused over the centuries? How many Spaniards flay themselves for the horrors inflicted by their forefathers during the Spanish Inquisition? How many Americans walk on thorns to atone for their ancestors' treatment of the Indian population? And so on. Not even the peoples who are actively slaughtering each other around the globe these days seem to feel much remorse. That the Germans continue to feel a whole gamut of emotions with regard to a war and a genocide which took place over half a century ago and which practically none of them had anything to do with should perhaps not be taken for granted. The fact is, however, that few Germans are completely immune to the "Great German Guilt Syndrome." The recent heated controversy sparked by the remarks of a German writer, Martin Walser, to the effect that he was fed up with having Auschwitz "instrumentalized" to make the Germans feel bad, is an indication that the Germans do feel something, be it guilt or responsibility or simply resentment that there are still those who think they should feel guilt and/or responsibility.

A FRESH START?

The democratic parties (in Germany) are fully conscious of the responsibility that has devolved to them as a result of Nazi history, and they have also accepted their share of responsibility for that era. Recently, however, there have been signs that a minority of the population would like to confine the Nazi era to the history books and allow it to be forgotten. This must never happen.
Ignatz Bubis in *Speaking Out—Jewish Voices From United Germany* (ed. Susan Stern)

The turn of the century provides a good excuse for stock-taking, and nowhere is it more tempting and perhaps even appropriate to do this than in Germany. In 1999, the seat of government moved from sleepy Bonn, the provisional capital of the Federal Republic until unification, to the post-unification capital, Berlin. This move is more than just geographical; it is highly symbolic. Berlin, the largest city in the country, was once capital of Prussia, then the capital of the new German Empire in 1871. After WW II, the city was divided up between the victorious Allies, and then physically divided through the middle when the Allies fell out with each other, and the Russians consolidated their communist bloc. Then East Berlin became the capital of the newly created German Democratic Republic, in 1949, and West Berlin found itself an island stranded in enemy territory, kept alive through supplies flown in from the West. And so it essentially remained—an enclosed city with special status—until the Wall came down (see pp. 63–67).

This city is now, at the turn of the century, the largest construction site in the world. Everybody, it seems, and certainly those with jobs in the *Regierungsviertel*, or Government District, is working in temporary quarters, on computers balanced precariously on piles of boxes. And this too is symbolic. Will a Berlin government—any Berlin government, not necessarily just the present one—be the same (read: amenable and dependable) as the Bonn government? Or, to rephrase it in the language of many political commentators—what can we expect from the Berlin Republic as opposed to the Bonn Republic, which incidentally was never known by that name during its 50-year existence? Are its political aspirations as monumental as its brand new architecture? Is it to be feared? In a recent orgy of Germany-bashing, the British press has surpassed itself in devising horrendous scenarios, and, as the *Washington Post* put it, "hinting at an evil Teutonic gene that will strive to channel a secret power lust into leadership of a new European super-state." More reasonable—sane—observers are not much concerned about Nazi ghosts, but foresee that Germany, government and population alike, may become a bit cockier and assertive than it has been in the decades since the war.

In terms of a rebirth of national pride, a new sense of patriotism, this may be the case—and I for one, a Brit and a Jew, would not consider this to be a necessarily worrisome development. On the contrary. I don't think that it is very healthy for young people to feel so uncomfortable with being members of a national group that they have to downplay or even apologize for it. Or claim to be first and foremost Europeans—a hybrid, cop-out identity if there ever was one. I believe quite strongly that if you tell people often enough that they should be ashamed of what they are, they will eventually become angry, and if they become angry enough, they may become as ugly as they are accused of being. That is one of my theories for the rise in popularity of the extreme right. Martin Walser is probably correct in saying that his "enough of the guilt" comments were perceived as liberating. However—and this is important—a sense of patriotism American-style does not, of course, release anyone from remembering history and feeling responsibility, not just for what cannot be changed in the past, but for the present and the future. Walser, with his own personal agenda, neglected to make that clear.

THE FUTURE OF MEMORY

I doubt if any nation knows as much about its recent history as the Germans. This was not always the case in the new Federal Republic: in the 1950s, 1960s, and into the 1970s, the war was a subject that was talked about as little as possible. Schools glossed over it. Then came a breakthrough with the showing of the U.S. television film *Holocaust*. Young Germans were stunned. Many confronted their parents and grandparents with the war and their part in it for the first time. Family fights broke out; kids left home in hysterics. I was already teaching at Frankfurt University, and I can remember realizing clearly for the first time how much easier it was to be the child/descendant of survivors than the child/descendant of so-called perpetrators. Many of my students refused or were unable to distinguish between the hardcore perpetrators and the bystander perpetrators—they were merciless with their relatives. Since that time, it seems almost as if the nation cannot get enough of the gory details; the war and the Holo-

Political Correctness

A true story: A few years ago, I received a phone call from a journalist from the Catholic News Agency. He wanted to know if I was the author of a booklet published by Inter Nationes called *Jews in Germany Today: Dynamic Growth, Dramatic Change*. I told him I was. Then he asked me if I had written the sentence, "The German media [allots the Jews] considerably more coverage than their numerical presence [in Germany] would seem to warrant ." I said I had. Then he told me that the head of the Berlin-based Center for Research into Anti-Semitism had found my statement to be offensive and that he, the journalist, wanted to know if I had anything to say before he turned the item into a news story which would be distributed to the media through his wire service. Well, I certainly did have something to say. I said I stood by every word I had written in the offending paragraph: that some aspect of Jewish life made it into the German media practically every day in practically every newspaper and on practically every TV channel, and that considering there were only 43,000 Jews living in a country of over 81 million people (today, only five years later, there are between 80,000 and 100,000), I thought that this coverage was remarkable— that is, worthy of remark. I went on to say that we Jews living in Germany were accorded so much attention and indeed deference in the media that it was hardly surprising that most non-Jewish Germans thought that there must be millions of us living in their midst. The journalist at the other end of the line was silent for a moment. "You're Jewish?" he asked. "Sure," I replied. "Oh, then I'll check back with Professor Benz." A few days later, he called me again to say that the "story"—presumably about my anti-Semitism—had been dropped.

caust are omnipresent. Not only is the period thoroughly covered in schools as part of the required curriculum in every *Land* (federal state), but the media continue to feature it daily. The country is dotted with memorials, monuments and museums. And, of course, concentration camp sites, which are visited regularly by school classes.

Holocaust education has been part of the (West German) school curriculum since the 1950s, but has been revised and vastly improved in the meantime. Brought up at required intervals throughout the period kids go to school, the Holocaust syllabus is now taught throughout the united country with Teutonic thoroughness. As I see it, however, there is one problem with Holocaust education in German schools which is remarkably difficult to tackle: the inability of many teachers to adequately convey a chapter in their history which they themselves are unable to comprehend, and to which they lack distance. Most teachers have never consciously met a Jew—how could they in a country which has practically none? The contemporary Jews they "know" are media faces, or Jews they have met in Israel or the United States. The Holocaust is so unspeakably dreadful . . . that many simply don't know how to speak about it in front of their classes. They stand there with their own complicated gamut of feelings which they cannot articulate. I have talked to teachers about this on countless occasions. They tell me about their feelings of unease—especially in the face of young students who, still blessed by the innocence of youth (!), are not about to take the information lying down. In face of some of the questions and challenges of these young people, teachers are called upon to find answers that they don't have. And since teachers in Germany perhaps more than elsewhere are supposed to be authority figures (see pp. 40–41), it is harder for them to say "I don't know, I can't explain it." So it is entirely possible that for entirely understandable if regrettable reasons, Holocaust education is not accomplishing what it ideally should be . . . As a result of the Holocaust Conference in Stockholm in early 2000, a new task force has been set up in the German State Department to reconsider Holocaust education in Germany. My own suggestions would include teaching teachers how to teach the Holocaust . . .

What, then, is the future of memory in Germany? Will Germans continue to remember when the old century becomes past as opposed to present history? Will the 20th century simply be written off as an "unfortunate" one? The 10-year debate over the planned Holocaust monument in Berlin got most of the country arguing about whether a gigantic construct—the size of several football fields—was in the interests of the future memory of the Holocaust, or whether it would serve as a *Schlussstrich*, or final shut-off line, relegating memory to stone and to the past, and releasing future generations from responsibility. My personal feeling was that the debate itself was the real memorial, and that we could have done without the stone pillars—mine was a dissenting voice. However, I am entirely optimistic that the memory of the past will continue to make a recurrence of the nightmare impossible in Germany in any foreseeable future.

THE
WAYS

PART ONE

Doing Business with the Germams

THE GERMAN WAY

Like so much else about Germany, the German way of doing business is enigmatic.

Greg Nees: *Germany: Unraveling an Enigma*

TAKING OVER

You'll find an ever-increasing number of interesting books on German business on bookstore and library shelves, and this is hardly surprising. Not only is Germany the world's third-largest economy and Europe's biggest consumer market, but it also plays an increasingly pivotal role in global trade as the world's number two exporter. Moreover, German companies are flexing their corporate muscles in a way which only a few years ago would have been unthinkable. Mega-mergers are making

international impact, and even the least business-minded among us are probably aware the Germans have become highly acquisitive and that the likes of Rolls Royce and Bentley are no longer the British flagships they used to be; that Daimler and Chrysler are now locked in a transatlantic marriage; that Deutsche Bank has swallowed up Bankers Trust; that Bertelsmann now owns Random House. The list is long. Not that the ball is always on the German's side of the court: Mannesmann did everything it could to thwart a hostile takeover by the British company Vodafone, and when it failed, was left with egg on its face.

In fact, German companies are increasingly finding that putting up effective defenses against takeover attempts is becoming quite difficult, if not impossible. For one, the traditional bugle call, sounded usually by the firms targeted by a foreign competitor and calling on other German corporations to ring-fence the victim against the predator, falls these days on deaf ears. Gone are the times when the German car makers stood shoulder to shoulder to ward off an attempt by Italy's Pirelli to buy the tire maker Continental; or when the German insurers blocked the French financial group AGF from taking over the then second-largest insurance company, Aachener und Münchener. Gone too are most of the legal and semi-legal intricacies of German corporate law, which helped keep foreign competition at bay. Nowadays, corporate transparency serves as a much-desired ticket to the capital market, and the concept of Germans fighting off non-Germans has been squeezed out by the market dictum "think globally, act locally."

And act they do. Merged or unmerged, German companies have gone global with a vengeance and are to be found worldwide—partly because staying home is too expensive, and partly because it makes a lot of sense to produce goods where they are wanted rather than to export them. It takes just a couple of giants to start up production plants in, say, South Carolina, and a hoard of small supply companies follows. So now there are Germans, Germans everywhere. Conversely, there are plenty of foreign companies in Germany, especially in highly skilled, capital-intensive sectors—banking and IT, for example—where high labor costs (and Germany has among the highest in the world, see below) are not a crucial factor.

MUTANT DINOSAURS

So how do the Germans do business? Certainly not enigmatically, as suggested by Greg Nees (see quote above), but the answer is becoming more complex by the month, and appears full of contradictions. On the one hand, the Germans are becoming more confident in their own business skills and acumen, and more aggressive in preaching "their way;" on the other, they are hungry to learn from others, primarily from the Americans, and American business schools are enjoying an unprecedented vogue. An MBA—from a top school, of course—is rapidly becoming a passport to job success, well, at least to landing a job. Whereas in the old days, Germans who went into business and ended up climbing the corporate ladder did not necessarily have a university degree at all, but rather a training qualification—and those who did go to university as often as not chose to study law rather than business. The traditional German way of doing business was—well, very German, and if you have waded through parts one and two of this book, you could probably make some accurate guesses about it, even if you have never had anything to do with German business. In the preface to a section on business Germany in his book called *EuroManagers & Martians* (1994), Richard Hill includes the following quotes: "'We need drastic changes in the way the dinosaur is run, and we need them fast' (Board member of a major German corporation); 'Our firm has been functionally organized for the past 95 years' (answer to an industrial survey)." A marvelous book called *Understanding Cultural Differences* by Edward T. Hall and Mildred Reed Hall, published in 1990, concentrates on the Germans, French and Americans. Part of each national section deals with the business mores of the particular culture. The following is taken from the table of contents under the heading "The Germans:"

> *German Time: Precise Scheduling, Slow Pace*
> *German Space: Inviolate*
> *The Door As Symbol: A Solid Barrier*
> *Power: The Name of the Game*
> *Order in All Things*
> *Compartmentalization: Airtight*
> *Possessions: Having vs. Using*
> *Formality: Politeness and Distance*
> *The Negative Image of German Business*
> *German Management: Authority and Control*
> *Labor: Bottom-Up Power*
> *Negotiations: Power in Action*

I realize it is hardly fair to give the headings without the accompanying text, but I think a skeleton picture emerges which is not unhelpful. Traditional German business in the Old Economy is based very much on a rather rigid structure, where ambiguity is avoided like the plague—of course: ambiguity, probably the greatest single cause

Trade Unions and Works Councils—Ingredients for Consensus

(I've extracted and adapted the following from an article written for Meet United Germany *by a German lawyer, Karsten Schmidt, a good friend who recently passed away. Karsten made the German system comprehensible to me, and he put it so much better than I could . . .)*

It was an Englishman, Sir Stafford Cripps, who is said to have reintroduced the trade unions to the British zone and from there to the rest of Germany after World War II. He conceived of a different form of trade unionism from that which later proved to have a less than beneficial influence on the British economy. With Cripps's aid and assistance, West Germany developed around 20 industrial unions which organized the labor force for the whole country. A metalworking factory, a carmaker, for instance, would have the Metal Workers' Union and a chemical plant, the Chemical Workers' Union, regardless of the specific skills each worker possessed. Demarcation disputes between the unions and skills became yesterday's emotions and thus irrelevant. Moreover, the industrial unions were and are organized on an area-wide basis with the area membership deciding on industrial action by ballot. Closed shops are not permitted and the lockout is the accepted counterweight to the strike.

The membership of labor representatives on the supervisory boards of the major German companies has played its part in achieving industrial peace. The board frequently serves as a safety valve for local complaints, grievances and other pressures; the labor representatives on the board can and do use their contacts with the other board members and, through them, with management to find solutions. Strike action, which requires a

of angst, leads to illness and days off work—and everybody has to know exactly where (s)he is in the hierarchy or scheme of things. This understanding of one's function and place, incorporated into a system which was, and indeed still is, extremely worker-friendly in terms of social benefits and holidays, has given rise to a tremendous loyalty on the part of the workforce. It is still not unusual to find employees who started out in one company when they went through their on-the-job-training and end up retiring from the same company some 45 years later. The situation of German workers is uniquely German, in that they have two separate organizations going to bat for them: the works council and the trade union. This "dual system of interest representation" is thoroughly confusing to outsiders, but is very effective in giving workers negotiating power—and thereby minimizing industrial conflict, because all sides know well in advance what the out-

secret ballot conducted on an area-wide basis, not per plant or company, is taken only when there seems to be no other way out of a given situation. The labor force in any sizeable enterprise is organized plant-wide into works councils, irrespective of union membership. The council members are elected by those in the labor force they will serve, and when in office, cannot be fired by management—except for cause. In large enterprises the works council has its own offices and members perform only council work at their former plant salary. They are, however, paid by the firm. The works council is in some instances of immense influence in the plant. Its agreement to shift and working hours, to hirings and firings, to health and safety measures, is frequently sought and sometimes required. For major operational discussions, such as plant relocations, changes of products or new plant, the economic council—a subdivision of the works council—must be given the opportunity to comment. Significantly, however, wage bargaining is industry-wide, not plant by plant, and thus does not directly involve the works council.

The type of consensus resulting from the infrastructure described above—the absence of major strikes or other industrial unrest, admittedly with some dramatic exceptions, especially in the 1980s—contributed to the postwar economic miracle "as much as did the Teutonic obsession with work ethic and careful and delicate management tactics" (Karsten). Many of the strikes that occur these days are so-called "warning strikes"—strikes that take place during the annual wage negotiations between unions and employers, and that, together with worker demonstrations and fiery rhetoric on the part of union leaders, are as much part of a ritual as anything else. On the whole, the German system of cooperation and consensus works remarkably well.

come of any dispute is likely to be. Minimizing conflict and reaching consensus are important keys to understanding the philosophy of German business. Consensus is a state of mind. Everybody along the line, however low on the totem pole, has a say—usually delegated to an elected representative—in at least some stage of the decision-making process. A most German word *Mitbestimmung* contains the notions of "joint" and "voice" and translates as co-determination; it describes the complex participation relationship between the employed and the employers. The process is lengthy and can be extremely exacting along the way—but it works effectively.

THE PACE OF CHANGE

I keep moving from the grammatical past to the present, because I am describing a system in flux. The past decade has wrought so many changes—and given the dinosaur's pace at which change usually takes place in Germany, this is revolutionary in itself. Quite simply: part of what is changing in German business is the very pace of change itself. Why? Confronted with a global economy driven by business cultures more agile, more flexible, more entrepreneurial and more willing to take risk than its own—and that at a time when its own economy was teetering on the brink of recession—corporate Germany reassessed its options and did some serious juggling with its strengths. If traditional, conservative, regulated-ad-absurdum thoroughness was no longer the key to success, it had to make room for another German virtue: a truly remarkable ability to react fast and effectively when threatened with catastrophe.

> **Germany can't change, right? Wrong. Smart, aggressive companies are breaking the old rules—and thriving.**
> *Fortune* magazine cover story, Aug. 2, 1999, Vol. 140, No. 3

There are many theories doing the rounds to explain both the catastrophe and the quantum-leap reaction on the part of the business community. Right after the fall of communism and the political and economic opening up of Eastern Europe—in other words, the sudden emergence of magic numbers of brand new suppliers and demanders—the country went through a brief economic upswing, since it was generally assumed that Germany, with its traditional ties and affinities to the countries to its east, would provide a convenient stepping-stone and entrée to the new markets. That Germany was perhaps in bad shape to deal with a future which was already demanding ever-accelerating speed in innovation was not immediately clear. Germany had more or less ignored the information technology (IT) revolution which was raging all around it, and at the beginning of the 1990s, was one of the information-poorest countries in the Western world. Kids in school, including my own daughter, born in 1978, were still learning to type on conventional typewriters. The Internet was considered to be a newfangled and entirely unnecessary game toy, an adult's version of Nintendo. The New Economy was an idea which invoked fear, not a sense of opportunity.

THE MONEY SHIFT

By the mid-1990s, things were no longer going so well in Germany. The heady times of the early years of German unification, when the appetites—and the pockets—of the over 16 million East German

Fear of Failure

In Silicon Valley, bankruptcy is viewed as a necessary and inevitable cost of innovation, and this attitude encourages people to take chances. If you can't fail, you won't start . . . In Europe, bankruptcy carries a lifelong stigma. Whatever you do, do not declare bankruptcy in Germany: you, your children and your children's children will all carry a lasting mark of Cain in the eyes of German society. If you must declare bankruptcy in Germany, you are better off leaving the country. (And you'll be welcomed with open arms in Palo Alto.)

Thomas L. Friedman: *The Lexus and the Olive Tree*

One reason that the Germans have traditionally been so conservative in their attitude towards risk-taking and innovation is their overriding fear of failure. Since the Germans are not traditional face-savers in the manner of the Japanese or even the Spaniards, this may seem surprising. But the fact is that few Germans can bear the thought that they could lose their job, be forced to accept a lesser one, not perform up to scratch—in short, be disgraced or humbled not just in the eyes of others, but in their own eyes as well. And to make things worse, the list of what constitutes a failure in the eyes of many Germans is very long. There are women who won't even try to get a job because if they were gainfully employed, it would look as if their husbands were unable to support them—a disgrace for both partners. (In case that sounds far-fetched, I know from my afternoon-school lobbying days that it isn't!). There are teachers who cannot admit to their colleagues that they are having problems with a particular class because this would be an admission of lack of control or loss of authority. There are students who never graduate for fear of not passing their exams. And in a curious twist, there are people on the rolls of the unemployed who would rather stay that way than have to face a new challenge they might not be up to—an even worse failure than being unemployed.

But again here, I believe that the culture is undergoing a vast change. The venture capital lesson—that you are only worth investing in once you have learned the hard way how not to do things—is one that is spreading to other areas of life. The need to innovate and thereby take chances is becoming a categorical imperative: as people from all walks of life are being forced to act with uncharacteristic disregard for the possible consequences, they wish the same behavior on others, if only to minimize the disgrace of their own possible "failure." And as the notion of failure becomes less disgraceful, so does the general mind-set toward writing off an unsuccessful venture as "valuable experience" and starting up again. This positive attitude is already prevalent in the New Economy: young e-commerce entrepreneurs have little problem going out on a limb, and regard possible failure with relative equanimity. They are dealing with funny-money, after all—and if one company goes bust, they have the next one up their sleeve. And even Old Economy giants who are toppled—Klaus Esser, ex-head of Mannesmann, for example—bounce up the next day in their role as "experts" in precisely the area where they came a cropper.

consumers seemed inexhaustible, were over. Exports to Eastern Europe, which for a few short years had swelled the coffers of German companies, slumped. Some speculative deals in the eastern states came crashing down, forcing the government to clean up the mess with even more taxpayer money. The German public, struggling with the staggering costs of rebuilding the East, grumbled loudly. Public opinion soured and turned ugly at times. And the German economy, out of synch with the rest of Europe, was facing recession. Money became tight.

But not for long. What helped dispel the gloom was a remarkable shift of wealth that was quietly transforming the western German society of the 1990s and is still continuing to do so. In conservative western Germany, a generation of thrifty hard workers has been slowly dying out. The accumulated wealth—an estimated DM2 trillion ($1 trillion, which is 1 followed by 12 zeros for those of you who, like me, have difficulty with numbers over a million)—of these successful, aging money-makers, the creators and beneficiaries of the postwar economic miracle, is being passed on to the next generation at the present annual rate of DM180 billion ($90 billion) in the form of under-the-mattress cash, property, goods and, of course, family businesses. And here comes a vital fact to bear in mind: Despite the high visibility of a few corporate giants, it is small and medium-sized businesses, those with under 500 employees and an annual turnover of less than $55 million, that made and still make up the backbone of the German economy. These SMCs, called *Mittelstand*, were traditionally family-run, at least until the death of the last patriarch. So there's fortune aplenty being transferred into the hands of quite a number of the relatively young.

However, the businesses they are inheriting are often strapped for operating cash, badly needed to expand the business. Worse: the businesses are often no longer viable in this new borderless business world which has a plentiful supply of free-moving capital and cheap(er) labor willing to forego costly social benefits. Indeed, faced with fierce competition, the new owners of *Mittelstand* companies in Germany are finding the costs of their highly developed social market economy prohibitive. And whereas the company founders often felt considerable personal responsibility for their employees and their welfare, many of their heirs have harder hearts and fewer personal ties to the workers than their founding fathers. One of the few ways to get rid of employees is to simply go out of existence. Either that or sell out, which has led to businesses changing hands, being bought, sold, streamlined, consolidated, merged, restructured, revamped (and whatever) at an unprecedented rate. The alternative—to hold on and find ways to raise money to keep going profitably and humanely—can be an uphill task, and not worth the struggle if the heirs are as personally wealthy as is often the case.

The banks, hit by the depressed economy of the mid-1990s, have not exactly rushed to the rescue. Little wonder, since by then, the banks were increasingly facing a rather tough choice: on the one hand they often owned considerable chunks of the companies they had been financing, so they felt pressure to prop up their shaky investments; on the other, corporate lending simply became less profitable for the banks than, for example, investing in bonds or stocks. Other sources of corporate credit were hard to come by in Germany. For years, the Bundesbank (the German version of the Fed) frowned at companies which tried to raise money by issuing bonds, so corporate paper became such a rarity that its market in Germany never grew beyond a fraction of what it was in the United States. So it was almost inevitable that companies both big and small, when pressed for cash, started looking at the stock market. That previously moribund institution, viewed by the general public as a club for thieving speculators, began to look more attractive. Even the option of going public seemed not so bad after all. Of course, it did impose certain unpleasant and thoroughly un-Germanic obligations such as transparency and making complete strangers privy to entirely confidential information about profits and losses—but still. It was/is another option. It was/is worth considering.

THE IT REVOLUTION

Parallel to all of this, during the 1990s the IT revolution took Germany by storm—and none too soon. The nation of computer illiterates as late as the mid-1990s became a nation of Internet addicts. It was as if Germany, chronically constipated with regard to information, had received a miracle laxative. (I apologize for that image, but can't find a better one.) Information—at least, the sort that is transmitted by IT—started speeding from computer to computer, and a generation of Germans became—and remain—galvanized. Communication became all the rage—and don't forget: the Germans have never been hot on communication. E-mails started to fly—from office to office, company to company, and so on. Of course, this has been happening all over the world, but the impact in Germany has probably been greater than anywhere else, simply because the Germans started out so late and were so far behind. All of which is not to say that today Germany is a world leader or anything close to it when it comes to IT. It barely makes it into the top 20 in many of the league tables: numbers of computers per thousand people, computer processing power, number of Internet hosts, and so on. But this is changing quickly as costs to connect to the Internet decline—high connection costs being the number one reason more Germans aren't yet online. Telecommunication liberalization only just started at the beginning of 1998 and the Germans still pay by the minute for local calls. Not exactly the ideal wave for surfing the web. But the trend is clear.

In the meantime, the ordinary Germans, those less-fortunates who have not gotten any significant chunk of the DM2 trillion and have not had to worry about financing an undercapitalized company, have also been catching up with technology. They too have been discovering the Internet and the delights of online banking, online discount brokers, shopping and spending funny-money. And they have taken to fast information the way they took to fast food in the 1980s. Almost everybody under 25, it seems, has a cell phone—and the system is compatible throughout the whole of Europe and most of the rest of the world, so transnational mobile phone communication is far easier than in the United States. Information delivery has become almost instant—including access to real time stock market prices.

And the temptation to gamble—uh, speculate—uh, invest—has become all the greater since interest rates have been hovering around an all-time low, so there is little temptation to stick any extra cash into a savings account, which is what almost all Germans used to do. What's more, during the 1990s, the government decided to impose a 30 percent automatic withholding tax on interest income above a low minimum, so a savings account became just about as profitable as a mattress. At the same time, the Germans' propensity to worry about the future was exacerbated when the nation's social security system showed a rapidly widening deficit and the demographic prognoses became ever gloomier. Germany's population, like the population of the rest of Europe, is getting older and those of working age who pay into the social security system are rapidly becoming too few to bankroll the elderly. Already by the mid-1990s, it had become clear that those who hadn't won the lottery or inherited a fortune would have to find better ways of providing for their own old age than relying on their pension or on a pittance savings account. Enter the "German Market Marvel."

INTRODUCTION TO EQUITIES

One illustration of how all these seemingly unrelated factors—the fall of communism, the generational transfer of wealth, the IT revolution, population trends—came together is the Deutsche Telekom Story. Deutsche Telekom used to be a state-run monopoly, universally disliked for its outrageous rates and quite appalling service. Along came unavoidable deregulation—and it must be said that Deutsche Telekom neither quickly nor willingly gave up its monopoly. Ultimately, this new competition meant that Telekom simply had to shape up or lose its once-captive market to nimble, aggressive start-ups. To raise the money to compete in the post-monopoly world where profits are not guaranteed by the state, it decided to go public (privatization is a relative term: the state still owns a major stake in Telekom). Knowing that the average German was leery of buying shares in anything, let alone in unpopular Telekom, the company launched a massive advertising campaign. Buy shares in Telekom and watch your money grow overnight was the tenor, if not the actual substance, of the message. The public, assaulted from all sides by this IT-generated media campaign, succumbed and bought Telekom shares at around $15 a share. The day the shares were sold on the Frankfurt Stock Exchange in the fall of 1997, the entire country followed the trading on the Internet or on business news television. In the meantime, the shares have risen and fallen again—certainly, no modest investor has made a fortune. But Telekom seems to have broken the taboo on playing the stock market and even though it was, and still is, disliked by many, Telekom and its partial listing represented a safe initiation to the stock market. The former monopolist wasn't going to fold overnight and more likely than not, would provide more return than a savings account. Germany has joined the modern world—and being Germany, will probably join the world-class league. It won't take long before we'll be reading that the Germans own more stocks than anyone else—right now, the Americans and Brits are still the leaders. It is perhaps no coincidence that the Frankfurt Stock Exchange has global pretensions and is actively forming partnerships with other European bourses. In one such move, the Frankfurt exchange is trying to link up with London and possibly with Madrid and Milan to form a common market for European blue-chip shares. These would be traded in London, while a growth and venture segment, in conjunction with Nasdaq, would handle all European and U.S. high-tech and Internet stocks in Frankfurt. While it is unlikely that Frankfurt will unseat London as Europe's top financial address in the foreseeable future, it is certainly striving to take on a leading role.

This won't be easy, since the German bourse is still a pygmy compared to London. By one yardstick, namely the comparison of the value of the stock market with the gross national product, Germany's ratio is about one-third of that in the United Kingdom. To catch up, Germany needs to attract big foreign institutional investors, such as U.S. and U.K. pension funds. This means it has to move decisively from catering to the interests of its stakeholders—usually German banks—to creating value for minority owners. This it could do, for instance, by paying higher dividends to the shareholders instead of keeping these funds under the corporate mattresses. Or by going public with its non-core businesses, thus giving outside investors a reason to hope for a quick rise in the share price. It was hopes such as these that fueled the boom which changed the nation.

THE *NEUER MARKT*

The *Neuer Markt* (new market) is—to quote *Fortune*—Germany's highly successful answer to Nasdaq. Started up only a few years ago as an off-shoot of the Frankfurt exchange, it lists so-called "growth" companies that would not make it onto the DAX (Germany's Dow Jones) because they are too small, too young, too volatile, too risky. But these companies, mainly high-tech and telecommunications start-ups, are nimble, flexible, innovative—although occasionally not quite as promising as they initially made themselves out to be.

For a time, in fact, it looked as if the Neuer Markt was a miracle money-machine which was defying the laws of the market economy. A number of inspired, often penniless dreamers who went public became paper millionaires overnight. Since the German IRS taxes the pants/skirts off those who cash in their speculative winnings within 12 months, the newly paper-rich are obliged to watch the fortune of their fortunes rise and fall with the whims of the market. Nevertheless, an impressive number of these start-ups survived their first year. Everybody was happy: the inspired dreamers, the banks, who cashed in hefty commissions, and the buyers of the stocks, who, like the company founders themselves, saw their initial investments shoot through the ceiling, and often remain there. In one year alone (1998), Neuer Markt prices rose by 174 percent. In the six months between the fall of 1999 and the spring of 2000, they rose by 220 percent.

An old saying quips that if something seems too good to be true, it probably is. The Neuer Markt was starting to resemble the pyramid game: "send \$5 to the next person on the list and receive a \$1 million within a month." By early 2000, the money-machine became less predictable—and probably a lot healthier. As high-tech stocks took a drubbing worldwide, many of the German dreamers saw the market value of their companies drop by half—which in some cases meant the loss of paper billions. This was in part because of a few bad apples among the genuinely high potentials; completely unrealistic expectations on the part of less-inspired dreamers; ungrateful (or foresightful!) speculators who jumped off the bandwagon even before the 12-month qualifying period when prices were still in heaven. The Neuer Markt menu is now being more carefully scrutinized by all involved, including the *Zulassungskommission der Deutschen Börse*, the authority responsible for weeding out unsuitable market hopefuls and ensuring a standard of quality. But most of all, of course, by the investors, who, better informed thanks to their IT toys, are becoming more picky in placing their bets.

The above should not lead anyone to suppose that the Neuer Markt is not a success story. It has spawned a new generation of stock market investors, injecting much-needed capital and excitement into the German high-tech sector. It is one of Germany's most impressive success stories of the decade.

The Day the Deutschmark Died

If there was one thing that the Germans were hugely—and rightfully—proud of, it was their currency, the Deutschmark. This heavyweight was the payment of choice in much of Europe and the underpinning of most Eastern European economies. Was. But is no longer.

On January 1, 1999, the euro (€) came into being. Eleven European countries, together referred to as Euroland, adopted the euro as a common currency in lieu of their national monies. To ease impact on the public and to give the euro time to gain the confidence of the international financial community, the euro will remain legal tender but not a physical currency until January 1, 2002. Only then will euro coins and notes become real money and for another six months circulate together with all of the other currencies in Euroland. Come July 1, 2002, however, and Germans will have to part with their precious Deutschmarks (as will the French with their francs, the Italians with their liras and so on), exchanging them for euros at a rate of €1 for every DM1.95583. In the meantime, during this three year warm-up period, Germans are forced to live in a currency limbo: goods and services are physically paid for with D-marks; German workers get their pay stubs with a sum in euro but withdraw D-marks from their ATMs; grocery stores post prices in euro and D-mark; electronic transfers are done in euro sums. Confused? So are the Germans.

Although the German population has never approved of this changeover—during the adoption debates, public opinion polls showed that around 80 percent were against the euro—the German government pushed ahead with setting up the European Monetary Union and the phasing out of the D-mark.

The shift has created a lot of uncertainty, naturally abhorred by this nation. The D-mark has represented 50 years of a stable and powerful currency—years preceded by three German currencies in three decades. A decline in the euro against the dollar has made travel-happy Germans fear that maybe they can't make that trip to Disney World, while those with more money at stake are racing down the autobahn to one of the friendly Swiss banks to switch their funds into Swiss francs, dollars or pounds.

INSIDE THE COMPANY

2

PLUS ÇA CHANGE . . .

The times they are a-changing: this is the message of the previous chapter. And yet—have the fundamental changes mentioned above really altered business style, the way Germans conduct their daily business? To some extent of course, yes. Secretaries, investment bankers and journalists while away their time in front of computers. Because so many people have mobile phones, they are more easily reachable. Theoretically. In practice, they are not, because as in other civilized countries, calls can be vetted and transferred to answer machines. More and more secretaries are becoming redundant and replaced by computerized voices. In fact, there is reason to suspect that entire companies have been replaced by computerized voices, because after pressing button after button "to help us direct your call to the appropriate department" and listening to interminable music, the caller very often gets chucked out of the system, and is left holding a bleeping receiver. Germany has indeed joined the IT world. The irony, of course, is that the United States is discovering that customers don't much like automated telephone systems and the like, and is moving back to the human touch—real, live operators and service personnel. This is one instance where Germany might do well to resist the call of technological change.

There have been other changes, too, some that have already been mentioned in other contexts. The traditional German office building of individual offices, and offices-accessible-only-through-other-offices, where privacy is close to holiness, and inaccessibility a sign of seniority, is not as common as it used to be. The American open-plan layout is making inroads, and younger Germans, especially in fields associated with IT and media, are becoming used to working in a loud, bustling environment which would have driven their predecessors quite mad and unable to hear themselves think.

> *Business organizations are oligarchic. Power is concentrated in a small number of people at the top. . . . The organization and the individual's role within it are logical, methodical and compartmentalized. . . . Germans look for strong decisive leadership from someone who knows what he is talking about.*
>
> John Mole: *Mind Your Manners*

However. All of the above notwithstanding, I still maintain that a very great deal has not significantly changed. The German way of doing business remains essentially as it was: hierarchical, compartmentalized and task-oriented, characterized by top-down, need-to-know communication; a direct approach which can knock the breath out of the unprepared; cautious, lengthy decision-making based on reams of carefully prepared written material, interminable discussions eternalized—in anticipation of eventual legal action—in reams of written notes and minutes, and not concluded until consensus has been reached—and confirmed in writing, of course.

LOGICALLY DESIGNED TO BAFFLE

There are hierarchies and hierarchies—and the German variety is confusing. (Edward T. Hall suggests that this is deliberate.) To begin with, the larger German companies are run by two boards, the management board and the supervisory board. Without going into detail, the supervisory board supervises the management board, but it is the management board which wields most power over practical operations, and the chairperson or speaker of the management board is the company kingpin—albeit not exactly the CEO, since he is answerable to the supervisory board. The supervisory boards of the large corporations and banks are made up primarily of a handful of Germany's business and banking elite, men—always men—who may sit on up to 10 boards at a time, and who are not too inclined to interfere in the running of someone else's company, since . . . The buddy system works well. To be fair, supervisory boards are required to include in their membership a percentage of company employees, but the real power of these employees is mysteriously less than it might first appear to be.

The company itself is made up of hierarchical fiefdoms, with the heads reporting upwards. Interestingly enough, none of the managers on any given level necessarily have any formal training in management. The German system promotes highly-qualified, skilled technicians into technicians who manage, a practice which has its pros and

Angst Management

Change management? Crisis management? In Germany, we have a variation on the theme: angst management. No kidding. There are even books on the subject—one of them is called *Kostenfaktor Angst* (*Cost Factor Angst* by Winfried Panse and Wolfgang Stegmann). Researchers at a business college in Cologne have worked out that over DM100 billion ($50 billion) are lost each year to German business for work-related angst reasons such as absenteeism and alcoholism. Amazing. Angst, we learn, knows no hierarchical boundaries. Nevertheless, it is particularly troublesome in management, where it is a strictly taboo word. Taboo or not: managers admit that they experience the most angst at the thought of losing their jobs (68.2 percent); of getting sick or having an accident (67.1 percent); of making mistakes (59.1 percent); of losing prestige and recognition (52 percent).

- Angst management is obviously needed here. The Cologne researchers have come up with a few suggestions to help angst sufferers:

- Accept the feeling, don't try to sublimate or suppress it.

- Being pushed into a corner causes angst. Allow your employees maximum possible maneuverability within defined parameters.

- Don't try to be an omnipotent boss. Acknowledged mistakes can be better avoided in the future than ones you have hushed up.

- Recognize the fact that even your own superiors may experience angst; show understanding for the difficulties and responsibilities that accompany top management positions.

- Keep in touch with colleagues through regular person-to-person talks. This way, you'll find out what others are doing, and they will become more predictable.

- Make sure that the tasks you assign are completely clear, otherwise your subordinates may end up feeling insecure.

- Make sure you give your colleagues the recognition and praise they are due.

- I've culled the above from an article in *Welt am Sonntag* (18 June 2000) called "Look Angst Straight in the Eye."

I, for one, will be sure to do that from now on.

cons. On the pro side, the guys who manage really understand the business they are managing and the technical difficulties involved. They are highly task-oriented, and know how to produce top-quality goods. On the con side, many of the former technicians know nothing about managing people, team building, negotiating—in short, about being managers. Moreover, they often have little or no overview of the business functioning—read: financial situation—of the company as a whole. The structure of the organization is a complex puzzle best left to the board. That the cons can have serious negative consequences on company efficiency has become very clear to some of the board members, as well as to many of the technicians-become-managers themselves, and that is why more and more companies are not just hiring MBAs, but are simultaneously paying a lot of money to top business schools to conduct custom-designed executive programs to help their present personnel meet their managerial responsibilities, while encouraging their most promising young employees to enroll in executive MBA programs. Since, however, international business school practices are going to take a long time to make a significant impact, one can expect the German task-oriented, up-from-the-ranks management style to persist for a while.

LINES OF AUTHORITY

Germans are sticklers for form, and there is always a clear line of authority—the *Dienstweg*. No open door policy here—not only are there literally no open doors, but if a subordinate were to bypass his immediate superiors to get to someone higher on the scale, he would not be popular. In fact, if a person low in the pecking order finds himself in the presence of someone higher, in an elevator, for example, conversation will be limited to *Guten Tag* and *Auf Wiedersehen*, and eye contact is studiously avoided. For every eventuality, there is a proper procedure, the channels are provided and employees are expected to follow them. Curiously, however, top management often appears to want a security back-up system—a way of checking on what is going on down below, as well as obtaining independent counsel. Consequently, there is often a shadow line of authority which, because it is semi-hidden and not subject to normal controls, is immensely powerful and keeps everyone on their toes. This was demonstrated in the Kohl government: there were gray eminencies in the chancellery who were rumored to wield more power than the members of Kohl's own cabinet.

FACE-TO-FACE 3

Germans are indeed very sincere people and assume that others are too. They are often disappointed, as other people who prefer a casual or flippant approach to life do not always give serious answers to serious questions. Germans tend to search long and deep for the true meaning of life and like to spend their time profitably, whether it is to enrich their coffers or their soul.

Richard D. Lewis: *Cross-Cultural Letter to International Managers*

BRAINSTORMING

As I have stated earlier in this book, the Germans are not natural brainstormers. This is hardly surprising, given the way they feel about knowledge being power. Brainstorming requires sharing ideas, and this is hard for people who hold on jealously to whatever they feel is theirs. Brainstorming could lead to others taking the credit, and perhaps even the material reward, for something they could not have come up with without your input. Or so goes the logic shared by many Germans.

Many, but by no means all. The Germans are learning that they, too, can profit from brainstorming, and that the advantage of pooling knowledge can outweigh the disadvantage of relinquishing copyright on one's own ideas. Within closed groups—teams, departments, committees and boards, etc.—members are more inclined to brainstorm these days, perhaps in part because competition is fiercer, and outdoing the competitor usually requires more than one brain. Nevertheless, brainstorming sessions will often be recorded, so that credit can be given where credit is due . . .

Because of the hierarchical nature of the system, brainstorming works best among peers. In a session involving different ranks, factors such as the pecking order, desire to impress, fear of making a fool of oneself, etc., can be a serious hindrance. The most fruitless sessions I have observed have been with mixed-rank participants.

NEGOTIATING: THE MEETING

(The assumption here is that the German negotiators have not been to a U.S. business school, participated in American-run executive management programs, nor otherwise been indoctrinated into more Anglo-Saxon ways of conducting business.)

Count on it: your German negotiators—we'll assume there are more than one—will expect to start procedures on time. Impeccably attired, they will expect the other team (henceforth referred to as you) to conform to similar sartorial standards. Introductions will be formal, and the use of surnames and titles the rule. If you are visiting them on their home turf, they will have given prior thought to the seating, which is likely to be hierarchical. It is not a good idea to change places, or to move your chair to be closer to your neighbors.

The Germans will get down to business immediately. More than a few minutes of preliminary chit-chat is not on the agenda. The Germans have no need to get to know you, or to like you. The American desire to overcome uneasiness between strangers is not germane. You are all assembled for a specific purpose, no frills or niceties needed or wanted. If you are a person who likes to add a bit of humor to ease the atmosphere, forget it. It's not that all German businessmen were born humorless, there just is no room for humor in the German board room.

Prior thought is the name of the game—the Germans will have given considerable thought to all aspects of the business at hand. Inevitably very well prepared, usually armed with stacks of material, they will have planned their strategy meticulously. Left to themselves—that is, if they were dealing with their compatriots rather than with foreigners—they would first agree on an agenda or order of business, the *Tagesordnung*, which, once approved, would be written in stone. However, when negotiating with non-Germans, they are usually aware that their Tagesordnung may have to be sacrificed on the alter of flexibility, and most German teams are resigned to this, even though it goes against the grain—the discomfort is sometimes tangible.

Each member of the team will have a role, and know when to contribute his two cents—his own particular area of specialization. The arguments will be compartmentalized, solid, and supported with sta-

The German Manager's Guide to a Successful Meeting
(*Adapted from advice to managers in the*
German newspaper, Die Welt*)*

Preamble: A meeting is only as good as its leader

1. Avoid routine. Do not hold unnecessary meetings just because there is a precedent—weekly meetings, regular updates, etc. Remember, there is some truth to the adage, "Experience is the end of creativity."
2. Keep the number of participants to a minimum (not more than 10). Do not confuse quantity with quality.
3. Prepare the meeting meticulously. The agenda, distributed in advance, should be comprehensive and detailed, with an exact amount of time allotted to each item.
4. Set clear goals. The absence thereof costs time and money. If possible, state the main purpose of the meeting with a question: Should we shut down our plant in Bavaria?
5. Get down to the business at hand immediately. Any social chit-chat prior to the meeting is harmful. Start the proceedings with a friendly greeting, but then make sure that you are well into the first item on the agenda within 15 minutes.
6. Be up-beat. Any indication of pessimism demotivates personnel.
7. Be extremely organized. Announce the game rules at the outset. Make sure that all present are aware that they have a fixed time— recommended: up to 2 minutes—to make their opening statement, and 30-60 seconds to make a contribution during the discussion. Make sure that these times are adhered to from the start. Adhere to them yourself. Tell the participants at the beginning that personal attacks will not be tolerated. Mediate in controversial discussions. Do not lose control of the meeting.
8. Give the participants regular breaks for coffee or a cigarette. However, set a strict time limit to the breaks, and enforce it.

tistics, hard facts and the full weight of whatever authorities are appropriate, and these represent definitive voices, not to be disagreed with. In anticipation of your counter arguments, they will come prepared with their second line of argument . . . and third and forth.

Germans are very much enamored of their own rhetoric—as are quite a number of other nations—and it can take some effort to get them to listen. Do not assume during periods of polite silence that your words are necessarily registering—your German counterparts are quite likely to be wrapped in their own thoughts preparing their next speech. A good way to ensure their attention is to ask unexpected questions. When you do manage to get through to them, it may take a while to get them to change gear, but if they can be persuaded that your arguments have some merit, they may be willing to look for a compromise, and even make decisions during the course of the discussion.

This will all take time—time the Germans consider well spent as opposed to wasted. Do not confuse German thoroughness with pedantry. They will tend to go over the same points several times, to make sure there is no room for misunderstanding. They will look for areas of weakness in your presentation or argumentation, and if they find deficiencies in whatever you are offering them, they will let you know—without any attempt at being diplomatic. It is important to remember that German compartmentalization permits them to be breathtakingly blunt with their business counterparts— they are not attacking you personally when they lay into you, but rather, your logic, your product or your price. Many Germans will freely admit that they deliberately avoid getting to know business acquaintances well—how, they ask, can we negotiate effectively with people we like?

At the end of the meeting, they will go away and write copious notes on the proceedings. They will expect you to do the same. They do not consider that verbal agreements are binding, and they have been known to wreck delicate negotiations through their insistence on pinning everything down. A top manager at J.P. Morgan told me recently that it was the younger team members rather than the older, seasoned ones who were the worst offenders in this respect, perhaps because they are unproven and are interested in simultaneously preventing misunderstandings, being thorough, and covering their own backsides. Remember, responsibility is taken seriously so pinning down details can help to delineate fault rather clearly if something goes awry.

TIPS

The trouble with trying to anticipate how your German negotiating partner is going to behave is, of course, that (s)he may well have tried to anticipate how you will behave. The confusion resulting from both sides bending over backward to accommodate each other is mind-boggling. Ideally, then, you should start out by establishing some ground rules. You can talk about what you are hoping to achieve within a certain timeframe, and discuss how you think you are going to get there. At the very least, you will probably end up with an idea of the extent to which your negotiating partner is going to try to play along with your strange foreign ways, if indeed (s)he has any understanding of them. If your German counterpart is unwilling to enter into such a preliminary sounding-out, and fails to appreciate why it might be helpful, you can figure that you are dealing with a diehard case, and proceed with the following in mind:

- Be as direct as you can. Germans are not concerned with face-saving or appearing rude, so you should state your position clearly without regard for personal sensitivities.

- Be prepared for your German partner to be blunt or even outright impolite. Remember that any attack on your product or your approach is not meant personally.

- Take into account the paramount importance of rules, regulations and laws in the mentality of your German partner. Rules exist in the abstract—that is, they are seen as absolute—and therefore can seldom be waived or adapted to the situation.

- Since the Germans are low on the context scale and need to have everything spelled out, your partner is likely to state the obvious, i.e. appear pedantic, and far more importantly, rely on explicit verbal communication to interpret what you are saying. Never assume that anything which has not been put into as many words will be understood. The language barrier, while often not a major issue, makes explicitness even more important.

- Never underestimate the tendency of Germans to compartmentalize.

Business Wit

According to Dakota Indian wisdom, "If you discover you are riding a dead horse, dismount." German business wisdom is slightly different:

1. Get a stronger whip
2. Change the rider
3. Maintain that you always ride dead horses
4. Summon a committee to analyze the horse
5. Investigate how other companies ride dead horses
6. Change the criteria for proclaiming horses dead
7. Form a task force to revive the dead horse
8. Set up a training unit to instruct in the riding of dead horses
9. Make a comparison of a number of dead horses, create a benchmark
10. Hire expert support to ride the dead horse
11. Harness several dead horses together to increase speed
12. Order a study to find out if there aren't cheaper consultants to be had
13. Announce that your dead horse is better, faster and cheaper
14. Look for other uses for dead horses
15. Revise the service requirements for horses
16. Establish an independent budget position for dead horses

WOMEN IN GERMAN BUSINESS 4

The people who are least likely to make it to the top are women . . .
There are some structural reasons why they may find it harder . . . but
the fundamental reason is that German males are chauvinist.
John Mole: *Mind Your Manners*

WHERE ARE THEY?

Women, women everywhere—except at the top. Women in high places in German industry are a rarity. Women in high places in German academia, the administration, the media, are slightly less exotic, but not much. Women in high places in politics are becoming more common, but largely because of party-imposed quotas—indeed, absolute parity in the case of the current governing coalition party, the Greens. The conservative CDU, the opposition party, recently appointed a woman to its top post, much to the chagrin of some party insiders and the CDU's even-more-conservative sister party, the CSU.

Yes, of course there are women in Germany who have beaten the system, broken through the glass ceiling and made it up the corporate ladder. I interviewed one such lady shortly before she died not long ago—she had made it onto the management board of Deutsche Bank, and was the only woman on any board of any of the top ten German companies. Indeed, she was one of the top 50 most powerful businesswomen in the world. Her secret? I was brought up as a boy, she told me, and I was taught to think and act as one. There are other successful businesswomen, most of them running their own companies. But the overall figures tell a sad story—sad, that is, if you happen to think it desirable that women should ascend freely in that once exclusively male domain.

Too close for comfort

FACTS AND FIGURES

Today—or at least by last count in 1999—around 57 percent of 15 to 65 year-old women are employed outside the house, making up 43 percent of the workforce in Germany. Of these women, over 70 percent work in the tertiary (service) sector, usually in low-ranking positions. Of the more than 15.6 million women in employment, about one third have part-time jobs. Well over 2 million, or close to 15 percent of all working women, have jobs which pay less than DM630 (about $315) a month. In industry, women receive between 64 and 74 percent of what men in equivalent positions earn.

It's lonely here at the top; the only other woman I have any contact with is my secretary.
Birgit Gantz-Rathmann, Head of Personnel
for the Cargo Division of Deutsche Bahn

Although women make up over 53 percent of high school students and 43 percent of university students, they are vastly under-represented in all professional walks of life. In business, they hit the glass ceiling at around the middle management level. A recent study (*Hoppenstedt*) shows that in large companies, women make up 3.2 percent of top management, and 5.5 percent of middle management; in small and medium-sized companies they make up 8.8 percent of top management—partly because enterprising women circumvent the glass ceiling by starting up their own businesses—and 16.2 percent of middle management. Other recent studies show even lower figures. In comparison with other countries, the best of figures are remarkably low; women occupy 43 percent of management positions in the United States, 33 percent in Britain, and 28 percent in Switzerland. Hoppenstedt reports that of the 600 board members of Germany's top public companies, only 12 are women—a meager 2 percent. There are no women on the management boards of the top 30 German companies. In the ivory tower world, whereas women make up 70 percent of the non-academic staff and occupy 73 percent of the part-time jobs, only 6.9 percent have professorial rank, and only 2.9 percent are full professors with the German ranking of C4.

This of course is not a situation unique to Germany. The Old Economies of most industrial nations are still almost entirely run by men. Other nations have shown a tendency towards more liberalization, sometimes because of natural social pressures, sometimes because of quotas. Particularly in the high-tech sector in America, women, often in their forties, are guiding billion dollar companies through the changing corporate landscape. The more German business comes into contact with these other cultures—and we know that is already happening—the more open they will be (well, may be) to accepting the necessary and inevitable change in their own society.

WHERE ARE THEY HEADING?

It is always dangerous to make predictions; nevertheless, I am about to do just that. I believe that German women are on the way up corporate ladders, albeit in their own way, which may not make complete sense to outsiders (men). More women, I believe, will start up their

Money Is Male

A recent study by financial journalists Bodo Schäfer and Carola Ferstl and quoted in *Die Welt am Sonntag* on June 11, 2000, throws depressing light on the relationship of German women to money. It appears that 50 percent of all assets belonging to women are to be found in savings accounts—which, as I have pointed out elsewhere, are just about as profitable as mattresses. Around 80 percent of women have a pension of less than DM800 ($400) a month; the study doesn't mention that many of these women must have other sources of income—husbands, for example—or else they would be starving. Almost 30 percent of—presumably married—women don't know what their husbands earn. More than 80 percent of married women leave all financial matters to their husbands. Of all the women who get married, less than 10 percent insist on a marriage contract which removes some of the financial disadvantages that are built into German law with regard to women. And most German women (no percentage given) claim to be saving for something they want to buy or for their children, not simply in order to make money.

The study claims to be based on a questionnaire sent out to a million women—hard to believe, but still. It seems that women are family-oriented (surprise); that they are more concerned about others than about themselves (huh); that they don't have much self-confidence. They just don't seem to like having to deal with money. Strange. And yet, when they do invest, they get 5 percent more return on their money than men do. There's got to be a moral in there somewhere.

own companies and create their very own ladders. More women will venture away from traditional female areas of business—from human resources to hairdressing—and create their own niches. By this I mean that while I am not sure to what extent they will challenge men on male territory, I think they will simply carve out new territories in the New Economy.

When a male manager has a family, it enhances his image; when a female manager has a family, it ruins her career.
                    Ursula Männle: *Frauen in der Politik*

The family structure and traditional roles I talked about in the section on Gender Roles (see p. 71 on) will probably continue to exert a strong influence, so that ambitious women will continue to feel they need to choose between children and career. Consequently, they will be less likely to push hard for infrastructure improvements which would make it easier for mothers to work and the birthrate may sink even lower. Let's hope that the biological imperative makes itself felt before it's too late and the German population dwindles away. However, German women are waking up to the fact that there are other possibilities and other ways. It's clearly happening; they are already breaking out of their traditional roles, and finding the courage to compete.

5 A BUSINESS ABC OF THE GERMAN LEGAL SYSTEM

The German legal system is a civil law system based on central codifications which cover nearly all aspects of German business life . . . The great codes—the Civil Code, Commercial Code and Criminal Code, to name only a few—were inspired by the codifications of Napoleon Bonaparte, who created (without realizing it) a lasting and positive memorial to himself in a country which he thoroughly despised, because only few Germans could speak French, and none, to his knowledge, Corsican.

Karsten Schmidt: "Doing Business in Germany"
(in *Meet United Germany*, ed. Susan Stern)

STATUTE LAW AS OPPOSED TO COMMON LAW

Since I've referred so often in this book to the German love for Rules and Regulations, it is only fair that I add a few words about the German legal system. For all that the system is often the butt of jokes because it has acquired a reputation for being inflexible, with its laws written in stone and its verdicts unresponsive to previous decisions, many preconceived ideas about the way it works are far off the mark. The German system does not operate on the same case law and precedent principle as Anglo-Saxon common law, but instead is based on the Napoleonic Code. It is true that the body of German law, most of which is federal rather than state, is made up of more than 1,900 acts and 3,000 statutes. But these can be interpreted beyond the written text; judges and scholars are free to delve into parliamentary history and seek out the original intent of the act. This will then be taken into consideration, so that in fact, decisions issuing from the courts do reflect current conditions and changes within society, and no doubt just as effectively as those issuing from common law. In the end, the various law systems probably arrive at much the same conclusions, albeit for different reasons and in different ways.

The German court system is comprehensive and characterized by its specialist courts—labor, administrative, social, finance—all in addition to the so-called "ordinary" courts, the vast majority of which (around 75 percent) deal with criminal and civil matters. There are federal and state courts; all of the lower courts are administered by the *Länder*, and only in the final instance does a case come before a federal court. Most courts have their own lines of appeal which lead to their own supreme court. The individual Länder all have their own constitutional courts, and the country as a whole has a Federal Constitutional Court, in Karlsruhe, the only court whose findings in the form of rulings or opinions have the force of law. Practically all German judges—in all, over 20,000—are professionals: they are not popularly elected, but appointed for life. The only judges who are chosen differently are those who serve on one of the two senates of the Federal Constitutional Court; here, half of the judges are elected by the *Bundestag*, the lower house of parliament, and half by the *Bundesrat*, the parliamentary chamber of state representatives. These judges serve for 12 years and cannot be reelected. Certain lower courts admit lay judges—experts with specific expertise—who sit with the professionals and help make judgements which are supposed to be more in line with "real" life.

Of particular note to Anglo-Saxons: the German legal system does not have a jury system—there is no such thing as a civil jury at any level, and in the criminal system, there is a jury of selected laymen only in capital cases. Court decisions are therefore made by independent, but nevertheless civil-service judges. The prosecution too—there are over 4,000 public prosecutors in the country—is also part of the civil service; public prosecutors establish the facts of the cases and in court proceedings, act as prosecuting counsel.

Not all Germans who study law have the intention of going into the legal profession. After they finish their university studies and pass the first state examinations, they are qualified *Juristen* (not quite the English word "jurist"), which does not mean that they are lawyers. Many Juristen go into business, become company administrators, managers, whatever. To become bona fide lawyers, after leaving university, the Juristen have to go through a compulsory course of practical training and then pass another set of tests, the second state examinations. Only then can they practice law. Some choose to add a doctorate or an Anglo-Saxon LLM to their qualifications—this is no doubt very wise in a system which has the highest respect for degrees, but often leaves the recipients with gray hair before they get their first real job. This is part of the German eternal-student dilemma (see p. 141 on).

ADVICE TO BUSINESSPEOPLE

Get yourself a competent German lawyer who knows your culture well, speaks your language, and understands exactly what your needs are. The legal situation is complicated enough without further confusion caused by unnecessary cultural communication problems which have nothing to do with the law. Be aware that like their counterparts in other countries, German lawyers work by the billable hour, minute and second—that is, they can be expensive. Their services are, however, indispensable for the businessperson unfamiliar with German procedures.

There are many legal entities to choose from in Germany. One of the most commonly used corporate vehicles is the GmbH; it is a relatively flexible limited company which often proves to be the most convenient for the foreigner, simply because it accommodates most of the requirements for a foreign entity to operate in. The articles can be drafted in fairly straightforward language; there are no shares as such, but quotas; no nationality requirements for shareholders or managing directors; no compulsory board (except for larger units); and the lengthy purpose clauses in common law jurisdictions, carefully drafted to include all possible applicable corporate activities, can be replaced by short general language. When the company is first set up, fiscal years can be freely chosen to suit the company's organizational convenience but must not exceed 12 months.

It took Germany a long time to discover the practice of having shelf companies, available to be used and activated at will. Today, shelf companies do exist, although every GmbH and other corporate vehicle is supposed to be tailor-made and with its own set of articles. One problem with the creation of shelf companies for eventual sale to potential investors is the minimum capital of DM50,000 required for a GmbH; however, this hindrance, so I have been told by people more knowledgeable than I, can be overcome. As I said, you need a good lawyer!

There are, of course, many corporate entities other than the practical GmbH—I will not attempt to list, let alone describe them. For anyone considering setting up a business informally—that is, attempting to by-pass the tedious and expensive legal entities and formalities—banish the thought from your mind. Any business unit, be it a limited company, a corporation, a partnership or even a sole proprietorship, must be registered in the *Handelsregister* (commercial register) at the local municipal court. Tedious as this might be, it is the only way to limit liability—and unlimited liability is not anything a sane person would want.

GERMANY AS AN INDUSTRIAL LOCATION 6

An expensive industrial location can hold its own only as long as it is a good location—an exigency reflecting the fierce competition stemming from world economic integration.
Facts About Germany, German government publication

STANDORT "D"

Standort "D"—the German formula for expressing "Germany as an industrial location"— slips off the tongue far more smoothly than the cumbersome English expression. Anyone with any interest in business will sooner rather than later become involved in the Standort "D" debate—the ongoing discussion about the pros and cons of Germany as A Good Place To Do Business. Or even a possible place to set up shop. On the pro side: Germany undoubtedly has a lot to offer the potential investor in almost any sector of industry, banking or commerce. It's a modern, efficient country with a well-trained work force; what it lacks in natural resources, it makes up for in human skills. The Germans are hard workers, reliable and efficient—in fact, almost all of the Germanity characteristics I talked about in earlier chapters of this book make for the kind of workforce most employers would give their right arm for. A highly monochronic culture is not just one of the most successful by-products of the industrial revolution, it goes a long way to ensuring that the industrial revolution can continue unabated.

So where's the rub? Well, in a nutshell, it's the fact that this dream workforce is very expensive. Not only do Germans—and I'm now talking specifically about those working in the manufacturing sectors in western Germany—earn more than most in terms of the money they are paid directly, but the employer in Germany has to pay another huge sum—up to 82 percent—in additional wage costs, the employer's mandatory contribution to retirement and unemployment insurance, health insurance, extra pay for vacation and a Christmas bonus . . . The sum of the direct wage and the additional mandatory costs make German workers into the most expensive in the industrial world—almost twice as expensive as workers in the United States. To aggravate the situation, western German workers work less hours than workers anywhere else in the industrial world—not just because the working week averages out to less than 36 hours, but because the Germans have over 41 fully-paid days off per year. On average, Germans work 118 hours less per annum than their U.S. counterparts. Then again, German laws make it difficult to keep a plant running around the clock—workers may only work at certain times. Come 5 P.M., machines have to be turned off—well, not quite, but you get the idea—and this has led to plants being run at low efficiency: lower than anywhere else in the industrial world. On the plus side: since strikes are not a frequent occurrence, fewer hours are lost in Germany than in most other countries, except in Japan, Austria and Switzerland. In terms of taxes, as far as the workers are concerned, income tax is high, although not quite as high as in countries such as

Between vacations ...

Japan and Denmark. But since each worker has to match the social and health costs paid by his/her employer, take-home pay is about half the gross wage. From the point of view of the employer, taxes are pretty horrendous, especially corporate tax, which alone can amount to over 40 percent of profits—the total tax on profits amounts to around 60.4 percent. This was after the minor tax reform of 1997 lowering the wealth tax, but before the latest tax reform of 2000 which will soon lower corporate tax to 25 percent. Indeed, the general Standort "D" situation should improve considerably after the introduction of the new tax reform, due to go into effect in stages as of 2001, not least because the capital gains tax of about 50 percent on the sale of company cross-holdings will be abolished. Since banks and insurance companies have traditionally held huge stakes in companies, this measure is likely to produce a spate—some are hoping for a tidal wave—of mergers and business activity.

Germany has a qualified and motivated workforce, stability which is relatively social, a sophisticated transportation and communications infrastructure and a high potential for innovation . . . If we point out the weaknesses of Germany as an industrial location, it is not in order to badmouth it, but rather to improve the situation.
From the 1998 *Institut der deutschen Wirtschaft* report on Germany as an industrial location.

Productivity in Germany is very high—it's higher only in the Netherlands. However, this considerable plus for Standort "D" is to some extent counterbalanced by the fact that through direct investment, a high level of productivity is highly exportable . . . What you gain on the swings, you lose on the roundabouts. Foreign investment in Germany is much lower than in Britain, for example: between 1990 and 1996, it accounted for only 0.6 percent of gross fixed capital formation.

I culled most of the above information from the highly respected *Institut der deutschen Wirtschaft*, an organization in Cologne which monitors the state of the German economy. To sum up: there's good news and bad news, and as far as the future is concerned, the good news (particularly in view of the 2000 tax reform) seems to predominate. Potentially, Germany is an excellent industrial location, hampered primarily by its price tag. This is not an insoluble problem, and is being tackled fairly actively by those in a position to change things—politicians, trade unionists, and of course, industry itself. In short, the prospects look healthy.

PART TWO

Understanding the System

CHANGE-RESISTANT EDUCATION

Even Germany's hallowed education is showing signs of fatigue and is currently the subject of loud criticism. Calls for reform are rampant, but to date all parties involved—government, faculty, administration and students—have done little beyond attempt to place the blame elsewhere.

Greg Nees: *Germany: Unraveling An Enigma*

THE APPRENTICE SYSTEM: A MODEL WITH FLAWS

This book is not the place to go into the intricacies of the German education system—for more information, just take a look at the government publication *Facts About Germany*, or pull it up on the Internet under www.government.de and check under Education and Science. Suffice it to say that the Germans have a highly complex and differentiated system which in recent decades has been considered a model for the rest of the world. In particular the vocational training system—practical on-the-job experience combined with theoretical instruction at a part-time vocational school—has earned international kudos; the Germans require that practically all of their workers, be they automotive technicians, plumbers or hairdressers, go through an apprenticeship. The better the qualification, the higher the worker can aspire—and a top vocational qualification may allow the holder to become a *Meister* (master) and run his/her own business. This remarkable apprenticeship tradition has helped to keep German industry ahead—not without reason are the Germans considered superior technicians and craftsmen.

However, the apprenticeship system requires that companies invest in future generations, and provide supervised temporary "jobs" or internships for the trainees. Not all companies are willing or able to do this, especially when business is not as booming as it might be. One major structural problem therefore is a lack of sufficient *Lehrstellen* (literally—learning places) for young people, especially in the new eastern states or *Länder*. The prospects for those unable to find a Lehrstelle are dismal, because without any qualification, only the most menial jobs are attainable—and then it actually may be more profitable to throw in the towel altogether and collect unemployment or social welfare.

UNIVERSITIES: YOU GET WHAT YOU PAY FOR

A nation with an exceptional tradition of scholarship has been having great difficulty, more than most others in western Europe, in adapting its distinguished system to the needs of today.
John Ardagh: *Germany and the Germans*

The university system, designed by Wilhelm von Humbolt in the early 19th century, is paid for by public funds (read: taxes). A university education is guaranteed by the Basic Law (the German constitution) to all those who get an *Abitur*, the high school diploma which students receive if they can pass the tough examinations at the end of the 13th class—in the new eastern Länder, after the 12th class—at which point they are usually already sprouting their first gray hairs. Students still tend to go to the university or some other higher education institution nearest to where they live, and a large number of them continue to live at home into their mid-twenties. The Abitur alone does not automatically allow a student to study whatever (s)he wants: some departments require a higher grade point average on the Abitur than others. Hence, medicine and law—both undergraduate fields of study in Germany, to the extent that a student enters law or medical school straight out of *Gymnasium* (high school)—as well as psychology and economics, for example, are normally what are called *Numerus Klausus* (NK) subjects: courses of study restricted to a limited number of better students. The natural sciences don't always have to resort to NK: they require so much of their students that only the hardiest persevere.

Keeping the number of students down—therein lies a joke. Despite the fact that the Germans are slow to multiply—and they have one of the lowest birth rates in the world—the antiquated German university system is completely overrun by students. This is partly because more students go to high school and end up with an Abitur than in former times, and partly because there are not enough Lehrstellen to go around, so high school graduates who have no desire to study but can't find an apprenticeship can park themselves at a university for an almost indefinite number of years and do odd jobs on the side (see *Eternal Students* section below). Many of these students never graduate; some departments of some universities—mine, for example—have a drop-out rate of over 70 percent. Nevertheless they swell the statistics, and, if they bother to show up, the classrooms as well. Even the departments which supposedly restrict their intake are hopelessly swamped. Rooms designed for 50 are packed by hundreds. Truly dedicated students will show up to a lecture hours in advance, just to make certain they get a seat. Many less dedicated give up in the first semester, and resort to the most ingenious methods of getting through the required courses. These methods include getting together in groups and having different people go to different classes, and either record the lecture, or take copious notes, which are then shared by all. Or hiring more advanced (and with any luck, brighter) students to write the required paper or take the exam (it is rare that both a paper and an exam are required). Or again, turning up at the exam and cheating (cheating is rampant, but there is no moral stigma attached to it—on the contrary, it is viewed as a game). Or finally, never attending a regular class, but instead, paying for cram classes taught by entrepreneurial graduate students (*Repetitoren*) who focus on the examination topics, which, incidentally, often have nothing whatsoever to do with what was taught in the regular classes. Indeed, many law students consider the *Repetitorium* to be the only meaningful activity at university.

I should hasten to add here that in my opinion, the students are victims in this system. The vast majority are certainly not lazy, morally reprehensible spongers looking for an easy ride. On the contrary. They are short-changed as far as higher education goes, and most of them simply try to get by as best they can. Many catch on early that higher education at a mass German university is not likely to equip them for their later careers, but that a university degree—the piece of paper rather than the accumulated knowledge it is supposed to represent—can be useful. So they devise survival strategies and they learn what they need to know outside the hallowed walls of the institution. To the extent that young Germans are remarkably well-informed compared to many young people elsewhere, they obviously succeed despite the system.

NO MONEY, NO MOTIVATION

> *Perhaps no institution in Germany has been more resistant to change than the university and, until the 1970s, more successful in preserving its traditional forms of internal governance.*
>
> Gordon Craig: *The Germans*

It is bad enough that the universities are overrun by students; what makes matters worse is that they are underrun by everybody else, in particular by the teaching staff. There are a number of reasons for this. Firstly, the Länder education ministries are dependent on the Länder finance ministries for money, and education does not always run high on the cash-strapped finance ministers' list of priorities. The priority lists vary from *Land* to *Land*, so some university systems are better off than others. However, whenever public money is tight—and it usually is—teaching jobs, particularly in the "soft" areas such as the humanities and liberal arts, get slashed. And public money for education is practically never supplemented by private money—endowments, huge gifts from grateful alumni—because education is the responsibility of the state, and not of private individuals. It is not part of German thinking to pay for anything that their high taxes are supposed to be taking care of. So universities are chronically hard up.

Then again, there aren't that many grateful alumni anyway. The huge, impersonal state universities seldom inspire much loyalty on the part of their graduates. There are no university sports teams to inspire enthusiasm. (Tom Wolfe's novel, *A Man in Full*, caused great confusion among some of my students.) Although I should mention that alumni clubs do exist, set up in the past two decades for the most part by graduates of economics departments (surprise, surprise) and regarded as networking groups rather than as fundraisers. And it was a private business college—The European Business School, (see p. 150)—that started the trend, followed by the smaller state universities such as the one in Freiburg.

Another reason why universities are underrun by the teaching staff has to do with the status of most university teachers, from lecturers to professors. They are all civil servants of one kind or another—there are essentially two kinds, *Angestellte* and *Beamte*—and as such, they enjoy tenure. This is a simplification—not all Angestellte are permanent employees, but at a German university, most are, unless they are the most junior academics, in which case they aren't.

Dimido Professors

Many—well, some—members of staff at German universities show up on campus only on Tuesdays, Wednesdays and Thursdays—*Dienstag, Mittwoch* and *Donnerstag*. This phenomenon has long given rise to the expression "Dimido professors." Federal Minister of Culture Michael Naumann brought this issue up at a meeting of representatives of the German Academics Association (*Deutscher Hochschulverband*) early in 2000; he accused academics of having little else on their minds than retirement in Tuscany after the age of 52 and went on to remark that the professor who was supposed to examine his daughter hadn't bothered to show up at the appointed time. Well, the room exploded. Calumnious, shouted the outraged delegates, who claimed that most of the 17,000 professors in Germany put in 60-hour weeks, and if their colleagues in the humanities sometimes stayed home on Fridays, well, that was to read books, correct papers and maybe even do some writing. The cultural minister said that he was not suggesting that professors were lazy, rather that they were "melancholy" on account of the awful situation at mass universities. And that's the fault of you politicians! retorted the delegates. The meeting ended with vague promises of compromise on all sides. In the meantime, several of German's most eminent professors have broken ranks with their colleagues and are firing off broadsides in national newspapers. Political scientist Bassam Tibi describes the situation as catastrophic— "particularly in the humanities, where the scientific debate doesn't go beyond the 'blah-blah' level." He socks it to his peers, who have "small minds, lousy publications and cannot measure up to their counterparts elsewhere." Ernst-Ludwig Winnacker, one of German's foremost scientists and head of the prestigious *Deutsche Forschungsgemeinschaft* (DFG), a national research foundation, expresses the situation more diplomatically but no less forcefully on the front-page of *Die Woche*, July 14, 2000.

Melancholy, indeed.

Anyway, the bottom line is that most people who teach at German universities can do—or not do—more or less whatever they like, they are "lifers" and essentially can't be fired. No pressure to publish, no pressure to teach. Certainly no pressure to teach well. No pressure to even show up. Which is not to say that the vast majority of them are derelict in their duties . . . it's just that the work ethic often leaves something to be desired. Since there is no way to be promoted without leaving the university you are at and applying for a better job elsewhere—in other words, there is no ladder to climb, no tenure track, within one institution—after the initial euphoria of being an academic has worn off, there is little incentive to actually do anything at all. Teaching can be a thankless task, for all the reasons given above. Some members of the faculty are therefore forced to resort to their own ingenious methods to ward off sheer boredom. It is not unknown that a member of the teaching staff is not sighted by his/her department for semesters on end. This can, of course, be due to serious illness—a broken arm in the recent case of a member of my own department—or simply the pressure of other responsibilities, such as appearing on TV talk shows or the like.

Then again: since the students don't fit into the packed classrooms anyway, and can often get through their studies without attending lectures, it often makes little difference whether the teaching staff shows up or not. Students complain more about the unavailability of faculty during their posted office hours than during their scheduled classes—and most students consider it advisable to have eye-ball to eye-ball contact with the person with whom they plan to do their final examination at least once before they take the final exam, hence the need to show up at an office hour. Only very occasionally do the students get so fed up that they take legal action—which, as far as I know, has never ended up with a professor being more than slightly embarrassed.

Ah, the woes of the German university system. I have not even touched upon such other problems as the quite incredible bureaucracy compounded by a complete lack of caring on the part of the administration. Students at my university claim that degrees are awarded for sheer persistence and bloody-mindedness—a "f____ you" attitude—when confronted with the litany, "It doesn't matter what you want to do, it is simply not possible."

None of the above is likely to endear me to my colleagues, and I apologize to the many who are extremely conscientious and hard-working despite the far-from-ideal work conditions. Smaller universities are better off than the larger ones; certain departments—economics and business studies and certain esoteric institutes with no students at all—get more money than others; some of the smaller, new universities in the new Länder are leapfrogging into the 21st century and do not deserve my nasty remarks. However, as I see it, the greatest hope for the German university system lies in the fact that we are just about to witness a wholesale generation change, as the '68ers retire—many of them are giving up at around 60, when they first become eligible for a state pension, and even the diehards have to leave by 65. Then we'll see. Maybe things will improve . . .

ETERNAL STUDENTS

The turn-of-the-millennium figures indicate that around 1.7 million students are officially registered at one of Germany's finest, but only 700,000 can be considered "serious"—that is, ones who actually show up for classes and show signs of working towards a degree. Around 1 million students have been registered for ten years or longer without ever passing Go—or perhaps that should read, "Go!" The following comments are about the "serious" students:

It takes the average student six-and-a-half-years to get a degree. Since students are pretty long in the tooth when they enter university simply because it takes them so long to get the Abitur, this means that most new university graduates are at least 25 years old. To the extent that the degree they emerge with (a *Staatsexamen*, a *Magister* or a *Diplom*) is more than an Anglo-Saxon BA, but possibly less than an Anglo-Saxon MA, it is not entirely fair to compare American or British grads with the Germans. However, "many students would benefit from the introduction of a three-or-four year BA course so they could enter the world of work before they got close to retirement" (*The Economist*), and indeed, some German universities are thinking about offering three-year BAs. Alas, German universities don't think fast.

Why do German students study so long? Partly because although they have to take relatively few required classes—this varies from department to department—these classes may not be offered for semesters on end. The way faculty interpret academic freedom makes it very difficult to get any given person to teach any given class, so a class may be officially required, but if nobody feels like teaching it . . . Or several required classes will always be offered at exactly the same time—probably on Wednesday from 10 A.M. to noon, since this is the favorite teaching time—so the students can only take one a semester. Or the information given to the students by the Examinations Office (*Prüfungsamt*) turns out to be completely incorrect, but the student doesn't discover this until his 10th semester, when he presents his papers to graduate and finds out he has another few semesters to go.

Another reason why students take so long to get their degrees is, curiously enough, financial. Many of them have to work part-time during their studies. This is curious, because the university itself is practically free—the student pays a nominal administration fee of about $100 per semester. Moreover, parents in Germany are required by law to support their offspring until they are 27, get a degree, get married, or earn enough to support themselves, whichever comes first. But somehow, students always seem to need more money than they get from their parents, and end up doing what the Germans themselves call "jobbing"—working part time at temporary jobs. This takes time away from studying. There is a student loan system, but parents have to submit to a means test, and many students don't even bother to apply. The idea of running up debts is anyway distasteful.

And here we come to a controversial topic: student fees. Most students are vehemently opposed to the idea. It does no good to point out that if they were to pay, they could make demands. They have been raised with the conviction that education is a right, not a privilege, and this principle is enshrined in the Basic Law. The very idea of elite, private schools goes against the grain—and here I should add that few German students have any understanding of how the system in the United States functions. They don't realize—and don't want to be told—that the different U.S. states have state university systems, some of which are outstanding. They simply believe that the U.S. system is for the rich, and that only kids with wealthy parents can afford a good education. Serious student loans—loans of many thousands of dollars—which can take many years to repay are unthinkable for most young Germans. And this inflexible

Commencement

"we want, we are owed" attitude in searching for solutions to the German university crisis—and it is generally recognized as a crisis—is one of the reasons why a nation-wide student protest movement in the late 1990s fizzled out, and the striking students returned meekly to their universities without having accomplished anything. They were unable and unwilling to negotiate.

Finally, a compelling reason for a student to remain at the university for years on end is the same reason for him/her to become a student in the first place: a lack of jobs, a lack of prospects. Since "real life" is not very appealing, it is put off for as long as possible. Moreover, life at university is not unpleasant—on the contrary. As I mentioned above, many students live at home and have their basic needs (laundry, etc.) taken care of, so their cares are relatively few.

PRIVATE SCHOOLS, BUSINESS SCHOOLS AND CORPORATE UNIVERSITIES

Since a university education is practically free and guaranteed to all who graduate high school, there has been little demand for an "alternative" system of private institutions of higher education in Germany. Those few students who are sufficiently dissatisfied with what the German public universities have to offer simply go abroad, often to England, where until recently there were no fees for EU members. (There is now a minimal charge of around $1,500 a year for a regular three-year BA course.) For the vast majority of the discontented, a four-year undergraduate program in the United States was and is way beyond their financial means, and it is extremely difficult for Europeans to get financial support for an entire *Studium*, course of studies leading to a degree. Within their study program in Germany, students can quite easily spend a semester or even a year at another European university at minimal cost on such European programs as Erasmus/Socrates. The courses they take at the foreign university may count towards their studies at home, but the stay abroad generally slows down the graduation (although certainly not the learning) process. Only at the graduate level does financial support for U.S. universities become more—but not readily—available.

There are, however, a few—very few—private universities in Germany, most charging annual fees that by U.S. standards are pretty reasonable—from $3,000 to $10,000—with most coming in under $8,000. An "established" school, 15 years old, in Witten-Herdecke, for example, offers a number of disciplines including business, medicine and dentistry, and costs just over $3,000 per year. It has almost 1,000 students. The European Business School outside Frankfurt charges around $8,000 per year and offers a diploma in business to around 800 students. A school specializing in management and accountancy, WHU in Koblenz/Vallendar, has only 288 students, and costs $5,500 per year. Its two-year executive MBA program costs a total of $30,000. EAP in Berlin, the German branch of a French school, offers management studies for a handful of students—around 50—and charges them $4,000 per year.

Schools for the very few. The trend, however, is catching on. In Bruchsal, the International University in Germany has made a recent debut, and offers a range of degrees, from MICT (Master of Information and Communication Technology) to an MBA and a BSc; the price tab is about $9,000 per year. The new International University Bremen, a cooperation with Rice University in Houston, will soon be offering courses for scientists and engineers as well as for social scientists at about $7,500 a year, and in Stuttgart, an Institute of Management and Technology, costing $5,000 per year, is about to open its doors with a flagship MBA program. The Stuttgart venture is a cooperation between three German universities and 44 companies. The Northern Institute of Technology, a private university which has been announced for Hamburg, is going to be relatively pricey—about $20,000 per year including accommodation—and in the same city, the Gerd Bucerius International Law School (less expensive at $7,500 per year) is also due to start up in the near future. Other such institutions are springing up elsewhere. In almost all of the private schools, a percentage of students are eligible for scholarships and student loans. The demand for what the Germans have always regarded as an elite system is clearly making headway.

Nowhere is this more apparent than in the field of business studies or economics. Students who, eventually, emerge with a Diplom in *Betriebswirschaft* or *Volkswirtschaft*—both variations of business studies or economics, with no exact translation into English—often claim to have the equivalent of an MBA. This, however, is definitely not the case, and more and more German companies are anxious to employ "real" MBAs. As a result, ambitious German Diplom graduates seek out good "B" schools to supplement their German education. Since the domestic private schools are not essentially for post-graduates, these smart graduates look abroad. There are a number of excellent "B" schools in Europe, mainly in Britain, but also in France, Switzerland, Spain and Italy. Germany is now moving to get into the act—the Stuttgart school mentioned above—but in the meantime, U.S.

business schools are rushing in to fill the German vacuum. Purdue (Krahnert) is descending on Hanover, Duke (Fuqua) on Frankfurt, and other such deals are in the offing. Some German state universities are actively seeking out U.S. partners—the University of Frankfurt, for example, is planning an MBA program together with NYU (Stern). Some of the courses will be taught in Germany, others will be transmitted from the home base via Internet-based online learning technology.

Another buzzword in German companies these days is "executive education." Many companies have contracted with leading business schools in Europe and the United States to provide their potential high-flyers with management courses which do not lead to an MBA degree, but which nevertheless are supposed to impart invaluable knowledge and count heavily in an employee's favor—and at little or no extra expense to him/her either. Occasionally, the companies with an extensive exec. ed. program will claim to have a "corporate university," a boast which can be confusing. Among those making such claims are Lufthansa, Deutsche Bank and DaimlerChrysler.

POSTSCRIPT

I am glad to report that the furor surrounding the appalling situation in many departments at many large German state universities—see how careful I am being—has come to such a head that new models and modules are being proposed right, left and center. There is now general agreement that in the sciences, at least, "something has to be done fast." As a result of the crying need for young experts, 10,000 computer scientists are being imported from India (see *Green Card* box, p. 91) and more young scientists in other fields are bound to follow. Thus, it is entirely possible that things in academia have gotten so bad that they can only get better, and as we have seen in the Business section (p. 105), Germany is capable of finding solutions and bouncing back fast when backed up against the wall. However, I am less confident about the foreseeable future of the "soft" sciences—the humanities in general, the "parking lots" for many of the non-academically inclined. After countless years of debate as to whether students entering the English department of my university should be required to know any English whatsoever (most courses are taught in German), the matter has once again been effectively shelved. After all, if minimum standards of English were required of the students, they might be required of the teaching staff as well. In economics and the sciences, English is already a sine qua non.

2 SEX AND SUCH

Sex in the Sixties was very much a body thing, but now it's more emotional and romantic. The young can have sex whenever they want, so they no longer have to prove it.
John Ardagh: *Germany And The Germans*

MIND-SET AND *MORES*

Germans are generally far less hung up on sex than are many Americans. Most Europeans—at least the ones I know—are amazed at the American preoccupation with sex in all its forms, from simple nakedness to outright pornography and from sexual orientation to so-called deviant practices. Americans appear to be easily shocked—I'm tempted to say they *are* easily shocked—and camouflage sex whenever possible, for example as art in the case of nakedness, or as love in the case of sex acts. Germans, on the other hand, are a broadminded folk who have pretty effectively overcome whatever puritan heritage they may have, even though the church has always exerted a strong influence (see p. 76 on). Their

"I wonder if those senior citizen sex tours are covered by health insurance?"

easy "anything goes" attitude strikes the visitor the moment (s)he walks past a newsstand before even leaving the airport and catches sight of the numerous magazine and newspaper covers decorating the racks. Nudity is rampant, and the poses are not always modest. And it's not even as if the magazines were necessarily tabloid rags catering to salacious appetites; on the contrary, they often belong to the serious press—news magazines, literary journals and thoroughly respectable publications containing recipes and knitting patterns for the German *Hausfrau*.

NUDITY

Nudity in Germany is something many kids grow up with. It often happens that families wander around at home with nothing on—no big deal. This took me—a once-inhibited Brit—completely by surprise when I first visited my future in-laws in a small town in southern Germany. There is no automatic connection made between nakedness and sex. Moreover, talking about the body and its functions may not be dinner-table conversation, but it is otherwise acceptable and unadorned. By that I mean that the Germans see no need to employ complicated euphemisms. Women go to the toilet and mention that they are having their period—no need to talk in hushed tones about little girls' rooms and difficult times of the month.

Interest in sex (with or without nudity) is . . . well, I was going to say healthy, but that is a value judgement! Lively. It is certainly a lot less shameful, embarrassing or downright prurient in Germany than in the Anglo-Saxon cultures I am familiar with. Sex is generally regarded as fun, and people of all ages—even your own parents and your friends' parents— admit to enjoying it, and that's not even an appalling thought! Sex can be and is talked about freely, over the dinner table so to speak, and between the generations—so much so that some Americans I know here think that it has become depersonalized. Not that it doesn't sometimes have its seamier side, but even that is taken with a shrug. Now that private television has become firmly established in Germany, and there are plenty of channels to choose from (see *The Almighty Box*, p. 219), sex programs are prime fare— and often at prime time, although the really explicit material is supposed to be shown only after the kiddies are in bed. Some of it, the really explicit stuff, is packaged as "documentaries"—for example, as a program on the making of hardcore porno films, complete with interviews of the main actors, and close up shots of the action being shot . . . But resorting to subterfuges is not really necessary. Sex programs are as much part of the television menu as are soaps in the United States. On some channels, the evening programming revolves almost exclusively around sex, and there is one station that carries one telephone-sex advert after another, complete with a sample of the wares. Well, sort of. I don't consider myself particularly uptight as far as sex is concerned, but when my daughter was growing up, I used to worry—uselessly of course—about what she would be exposed to. But she—and as far as I can tell, most of her contemporaries—seem to have ended up with a pretty cool attitude. I was surprised at how blasé she and her friends were when they had sex education at school: although the lessons were graphic and the "instructions" explicit, the kids of both genders seemed as interested or as uninterested as they were in anything else in biology.

AIDS is a concern among young Germans and there are quite clever safe-sex ads in the media and elsewhere . . . Nevertheless, I have it from reliable sources—my students—that Germans, particularly young German men, don't see AIDS as their personal concern, and will use protection only if they are given no choice. I wonder if this is culture specific? However, in the only country in the western industrialized world where smoking is actually on the increase, a careless attitude towards AIDS strikes me as consistent, and I conclude that maybe young Germans consider themselves immortal. On the other hand, AIDS is certainly not rampant in Germany.

Many young German women are on the Pill, and in fact, often start taking the Pill before they become sexually active. Young women, adolescents, are urged to have regular gynecological check-ups, paid for by their health insurance, and many gynecologists recommend starting early. In some cases, health insurance may even pay for the Pill. If a young woman does not want her parents to know that she is going on the Pill, her doctor will usually cooperate—ironically, if there is a problem here at all, it usually arises over health insurance, because normally the bill is sent to the parents. On the other hand, few parents are likely to object, unless they have strong religious views, for example.

My own observations apart, a number of studies on teenage attitudes towards sex, dating, fidelity, love, marriage, and so on, show that today's young Europeans have a more mature approach to sex and mating than their 1968 generation parents, who tried to throw off the taboos by going to extremes and lumping so-called free love together with drugs, political activism, pacifism, feminism, and other "isms." Today, attitudes to sex, drugs and politics are differentiated.

"So, what's to see around here?"

Sexual relations among teens are generally accepted and acceptable, and parents' worries, if they have any in this regard, are not so much about promiscuousness—which appears to be very out these days—as about AIDS and unwanted pregnancies. Early pregnancies in Germany can be terminated fairly easily; although there is some hassle involved and counseling is required, anyone determined to have an abortion can get one. However, abortion, like promiscuousness, is not what a lot of kids want.

You Goofed, Ms. Minister

The federal minister for family affairs, currently a female social democrat, recently got herself into trouble. It turns out that her homepage contained a number of links which, if pursued, led to a whole series of porno sites. A few clicks, and the female or youthful homepage visitor—who else would check her page in the first place?—would land on "Callboys," "Cybersex," "Erotic Pages" and even "Pornoteens." Nobody at the ministry had ever bothered to take the minister's advice and explore what was described as "a treasure trove for women." This was going a bit too far, even for the Germans. The conservative opposition parties howled with outrage—the web page was a scandal, a disgrace. Suddenly, though, the furor died down. It appears that other parliamentarians were carefully checking their own homepages. Links are tricky things . . .

In an article in a recent issue of *Time* magazine, a Dutch sociologist is quoted as saying that most European teenagers are "serial monogamists." She goes on to say that they are good at "negotiating" both with themselves and potential partners on whether they are ready for intercourse. This, she says, is different in the United States, where the dating system defines behavior: you are expected to kiss on the first date, caress intimately on the second, and so on. She adds that the continental European kind of openness does not lead to sex at an earlier age, and that in the United States, where there is a much more repressive attitude, the average age for first having sex, 16, is younger than in most of Europe.

THE DATING GAME

My German students who have dated Americans tell me that they are both amused and confused by American dating habits. First of all, it took them a while to catch onto the notion of "dating," since there is no equivalent word in German, and indeed, Germans don't date in the American sense. They agree with the Dutch sociologist's description of prescribed dating behavior, but they add that their American partners often think it necessary to "justify" sexual behavior with professions of great love. "The Americans seem to feel that only if we first establish that we are not only going steady but intend to get married and spend the rest of our lives together can we have sex without it being 'cheap.'" The German attitude is far more that sex is no huge deal, experimenting is fine, but relationships can be transitory and professions of undying love are superfluous. German women typically get married in their late 20s, men in their very early 30s—if they get married at all. Millions simply cohabit. There is little stigma attached to being an unmarried parent, although single working mothers are still often considered to be poor mothers (*Rabenmutter*), whereas single working fathers are considered to be veritable paragons.

Young Germans tend to do things in groups rather than in twosomes, with couples as well as singles hanging out together, going to cafés, movies, discos, clubs, and whatever is "in." A night out often

Sex, Sex Everywhere—But Not in German Bedrooms

A meeting of the European Federation of Sexology in Berlin in June 2000 provided the German media with another reason—uh, excuse— to feature sexual mores in as much graphic and minute detail as possible. Never, it turns out, have we been so bombarded with naked, or leather-clad, seamed-stockinged, stiletto-heeled sex as we are now. Surprise, surprise. Sex is being used to market just about everything these days: a recent addition to the German billboard scene includes a picture of a lascivious young woman, legs wide apart, exhorting viewers to "Buy me." Buy shares of a pop music channel is what is meant in this particular ad. Another ad for cigarettes features two sides of a church confessional box: on one side, a female sex-bomb, on the other, a laughing priest. Both are smoking. Curiously enough, all this sex-on-every-street-corner is doing nothing for real sex, the body-to-body kind that used to take place between regular German burghers in the privacy of their homes. Sex, it appears, has moved out of the bedroom to wherever the television is—usually in the living room in German households—and even then, it takes place almost exclusively on the screen and not on the couch. Funny. The Germans, says the latest research presented in Berlin, have sex less often than the Americans. And when they do indulge, they are pretty quick about it—quicker than the reputedly unsexy Brits. The head of the Frankfurt Institute for the Science of Sex explains that the so-called "new sexuality" concentrates more on the spiritual aspects of sex, on love-of-self rather than on old-fashioned coitus. Could this be a new version of medieval Courtly Love? The famous—or perhaps infamous—annual Love Parade in Berlin is more a self-love show, says the Frankfurt expert. Well. As a member of the elderly 1968 generation, I am truly shocked.

starts off around midnight and continues until early morning. Many cities have special night owl public transport—buses and trams that are rush-hour crammed at 4 A.M. If one of the crowd has a convenient room or apartment, others often "crash," regardless of gender, and if necessary, share mattresses and beds quite chastely.

There is a song recorded in the 1970s by Meat Loaf called "Paradise by the Dashboard Light." It's a wonderful satire on American dating habits. It was my American students who told me about it, and they tell me that nothing much has changed in terms of ritual. "We date seriously," they said. "Marriage is always on the horizon." They—the Americans—find the German more casual attitude towards sex and marriage to be foreign, slightly intimidating, but liberating. "It's difficult at first to admit that you just want to have a good time with someone you like, get some sexual experience, but without any commitment. You feel guilty! But when you realize that your partner—male or female—wants the same thing—hey, it's great! And when it ends, no broken promises, no unfulfilled expectations, no hard feelings—just thanks for the good times and the giggles."

ATTITUDES TOWARDS GAYS

Not very long ago, I witnessed the picketing of a restaurant in Atlanta, GA. The owners were two gay men, and some members of the community found their running a restaurant offensive. At the same time, I've been told that Atlanta is the gay haven of the American South. I don't think the gay ownership of a restaurant would be an issue in New York or Los Angeles, but I know that gays marching in the St. Patrick's Day Parade has caused a problem in a number of U.S. cities. The San Francisco or Provincetown gay communities are perhaps unique, but the very fact that so much is made of them indicates that they are not accepted as normal. I understand that the situation is changing in the United States and that some states such as Vermont are beginning to recognize gay relationships, but I also know that there is a strong counter movement.

In Germany, being gay is not perhaps a complete non-issue, but in most cases it is not a major one. Society in general, but particularly urban society, seems to have little difficulty accepting alternate life styles, and the era of social stigma is very much on the wane. Some gays I have talked to would have outed much sooner if they hadn't been worried about their parents' reaction. However, once they have overcome that hurdle—and around half of Germany's outed lesbians and 60 percent of outed gay males claim that at least one parent re-acted negatively to their coming out—they can live the way they want without public censure. Around 70 percent of Germany's gays say that they have achieved a positive self-image.

That said, discrimination does exist, and the suicide rate among young gays is higher than among young straights. Gays sometimes feel that they have been passed over for a job or some other opportunity because of their sexual orientation, although this is always hard to prove—the law certainly does not permit this kind of discrimina-

New Status for Same-Sex Couples

The German government is currently proposing legislation which would enable registered homosexual couples to qualify for most of the same benefits—tax breaks, "family" health insurance and social security, rights of inheritance, for example—as those claimed by married hetero-sexual couples as a matter of course. This kind of "partner" legislation is becoming common in Europe. France, for example, has already intro-duced a marriage-like legal institution, a "solidarity civil covenant" for couples of any sex combination, and this institution, PACS, has become very popular not just with homosexual couples, but also with heterosex-ual partners who are not attracted by fully-fledged marriage—and the far more complicated divorce proceedings if things don't work out. The German proposal is not as radical as PACS in some ways, but it would give gay and lesbian partnerships legal status similar to that of couples joined by holy, or just plain civil, matrimony.

Inevitably, in a Christian country such as Germany, where family values are considered sacred despite the obviously dwindling numbers of families (see p. 71 on), a controversial proposal such as this is rally-ing all of the conservatives—those who seek to conserve—who fear that legal recognition of homosexual couples will destroy the core of society and cause the birth rate to sink still further. Well, such opposi-tion is to be expected. Interestingly, the opponents (with the exception of some diehard Catholics) are making every attempt to be politically correct and not to appear homophobic. Few claim to have anything against homosexuals, it's just that the state has a constitutional duty to protect the family and encourage couples to have children.

The proposed legislation is not yet law, and the outcome is uncer-tain. However, the very fact that the government is doing its best to meaningfully recognize homosexual couples and will certainly make some headway is, I think, an enormous step in itself.

tion. I asked a friend—ex-student and now a teacher—whether his homosexuality caused him problems at school, where most of his colleagues know that he lives with his boyfriend, and he said no. But other gay school teachers say that they would be worried about the reaction of some of their students' parents if the word got out.

POLITICAL CORRECTNESS AND SEXUAL HARASSMENT

The Germans are moving up on the scale of political correctness. Until not very long ago, PC was more or less unknown. The Germans, with their propensity for being direct and calling a spade a spade, used to say what they thought without worrying about the feelings and sensibilities of their fellows. To some extent, that has not changed. The handicapped are still the handicapped, and not the differently abled. Old people are pensioners, not senior citizens. Euphemisms are rarely used, certainly not the exaggerated ones—a toilet is not a powder room as I have mentioned elsewhere. However, PC has certainly crept into the language as far as women are concerned. German is a language in which masculine and feminine are clearly differentiated. It used to be that when a group of people (mixed sex) were referred to, the masculine form would be employed: students, for example, were *Studenten*—the masculine plural. No longer. Students are now *StudentInnen*, a word that combines the plural of both genders.

Sexual harassment is something else again. The Germans, like the Americans and many other Europeans, have definitely changed their attitude toward sexual harassment in the past decade or so, and have made significant moves to identify it and remedy it. There are laws in place, especially in the public sector, which are supposed to protect women from harassment and give them possibilities of redress. However, what counts as sexual harassment? An off-color remark? An accidental fleeting touch? Accusations such as these would not get far in a court of law, unless they were so crass that they could not be overlooked. If, however, a person could prove that she (probably she) had been promised a benefit—a job, a promotion, a grade—in return for sexual favors, and that the withholding of such favors had had a prejudicial effect, then she might have a case. Then again, the legal process is long and humiliating, and few would be tempted to face it.

My own observations at universities in Germany and in the United States indicate that male American teachers feel themselves far more vulnerable to accusations of improper behavior by students than do their counterparts in Germany. Practically none of the people I spoke to felt at any risk at all. Since Germany is a closed-door culture, university office doors are closed at all times, even—perhaps especially—when a student is present within. It is very rare to hear of a case of a student complaining of improper behavior, let alone suing.

SEX (SCANDALS) AND PUBLIC FIGURES

Sex scandals are not unknown here in the tabloid press, but they cause little more than passing interest, and have no apparent effect on the career of the person involved. It is often generally "known" or rumored that a particular married prominent politician, banker, pillar of industry, etc., has a mistress, but this barely causes a shrug, and doesn't make "news." I can't recall ever having heard of a prominent married woman having a lover—either women are more discreet, or there just aren't very many prominent married women. It is not unusual for top government leaders to have had several wives—consecutively, of course—and for prominent men to father children at an advanced age. In fact, in the late 1990s, the top three German politicians boasted 11 (or was it 12?) current and ex-wives between them.

Sexual Abuse or an Intercultural Misunderstanding?

Very recently, the following incident took place: an American female student who was participating in her American university's junior year in Germany program called her father, a lawyer in the United States, and told him she'd be sexually abused. The previous night at 4 A.M., she'd accompanied a young man, a German student, to his room. They had spent the evening together, and he said he wanted to show her something. Once in his room, he had come on strong. What actually took place, I don't know. At any rate, her father immediately screamed attempted rape and threatened dire consequences. In the meantime, unaware that anything at all was wrong, on the same morning-after that the girl was crying to Daddy, the young man left a note under her door, thanking her for a really nice evening, and asking her out to a movie that night.

The story is so recent—it was told to me by the faculty member in charge of the program right after it happened—that I don't know the final outcome. It seems fairly clear that a major cultural misunderstanding took place, and that both parties misinterpreted signals. In the meantime, a great deal of damage has been done.

Germans in high places don't seem to go in for the kinky sex sometimes indulged in by the Brits in similar professional positions—uh, occupations—so the sensational press has less to work with. Show biz personalities are expected to do outrageous things, and they sometimes do, but this more often involves alcohol than sex. The Germans did follow the "Monica Story" fairly avidly, but not, it seems, because of the sex (who said sex?) involved, or even because of the swearing-under-oath aspect; what fascinated the Germans was the mileage that the Americans—media, politicians, man-in-the-street—got out of what they, the Germans, considered was a non-story.

OTHER SEX-RELATED ATTITUDES: A SHORT LIST

Nudity: As I pointed out above, nudity is no big deal in Germany, and is not confined to the house. Children run around naked in the summer, on beaches, in parks and gardens. Nude beaches and nudist colonies (called FKK) are common throughout the country—and in areas not specially designated as such, many young women sunbathe topless. At swimming pools and in city parks, bare(d) breasts are part of the scenery. One of the funniest scenes I have ever witnessed was in a large public park in the middle of Frankfurt: a number of naked men on their lunch break were standing around reading financial newspapers (recognizable as such because they were pink) each slowly revolving on his axis to get an even tan.

Body Hair: German women are not under quite the same societal pressure as American women to shave their legs and armpits. Nonetheless, the under-30s do shave more than many other European women do, especially southern Europeans, many of whom do not shave at all. It's all a question of what men find sexy.

Sweat: Germans are not as sensitive to sweat and body odors as Americans. Deodorants are used—and are easily obtainable in supermarkets and drugstores—but a personal "aura" can be a turn-on, or so I am told. Germans shower regularly, but not necessarily every day. Not long ago, a national news magazine looked into the national myth that Germans are super-clean and discovered that they weren't—more like ordinarily clean. Vaginal douches are not commonly used or sold; they are considered to be destructive of natural flora, and therefore conducive to bacterial infections.

Sex Shops: These are all over the place, even in small, conservative Bavarian towns, and often decorate their windows with their wares.

They are frequented quite openly by both men and women. Compared to sex shops elsewhere (Amsterdam, for example), the German ones can be quite tasteful! One of the most successful German businesswomen of recent decades—she's still going strong—is Beate Uhse, who is into the sex business in a big way; her company is listed on the stock exchange and has been doing well.

Hardcore Porn: Most large video rental stores, which can be found on almost every street corner, and unlike shops, can remain open until late at night, have a special hardcore porn section, where kids under 18 are not supposed to browse. They do, of course.

Condoms: These are available everywhere: in supermarkets and drugstores, both places where you can pick them off the shelf yourself; in pharmacies (*Apotheken*), where you will have to ask for them at the counter; in public toilets, where they are dispensed by machines. Women often carry them as well as men—and are not particularly reticent in insisting on their being used.

With Love: The Germans don't end letters with Love unless they mean it. Many a misunderstanding has been caused by that Anglo-Saxon endearment. Germans expect a more literal ending: best wishes, regards, etc. And on the subject of love: the Germans distinguish between *Ich liebe Dich*, literally "I love you," and *Ich habe Dich lieb*, which means "I like you or fancy you." The former is a strong statement which should be reserved for special relationships—it is not the currency which is needed to initiate sex. Overuse of "I love you" leads Germans to think of Americans as superficial.

A WORD OR TWO ON DRUGS . . .

The drug culture is, I suppose, pretty universal. Until recently, most officials at the German equivalent of junior high and high schools were still claiming that they had no substance abuse problem . . . well, not a serious one anyway. These days they openly admit that they do have a problem and that it starts early. Many schools have a drug counselor—not a professional, but a member of staff appointed to keep an eye on the situation and periodically tell the kids how dangerous drugs are. The fact is, pot, hashish and the designer drugs somehow manage to find their way onto school campuses, no matter what measures are taken. Some schools turn a relatively blind eye, others expel caught offenders. Off campus, drugs are easy to get for anyone looking for them. They are available in the many clubs (formerly discos) which dot the urban landscape. They are a prime feature at the raves that can go on non-stop for days. Prices for drugs vary from *Land* to *Land*, and I hear that they are highest in the more conservative Länder such as Bavaria, where the police are not as permissive as elsewhere. In general, the law goes after dealers, not users: this means that in cities, junkies are very visible, often in the area around the main train station, which is also frequently the red-light district. It is common to see people huddled in doorways shooting heroin or smoking crack pipes in broad daylight. In some places, the state or local authorities have set up supervised centers where certified addicts can be weaned off hard drugs; this policy has been implemented in other European countries with considerable success. All in all, the drug scene is sad, but by no means unique to Germany.

THE STATE KNOWS BEST 3

The relationship between authority and citizen in a country [can be shown] to be modeled after the relationship between boss and subordinate, teacher and student, and parent and child.

Geert Hofstede: *Cultures and Organizations*

IN THE INTEREST OF SOCIETY

It often comes as a surprise to Americans that Germans accept so easily what Americans see as interference by the state. Whereas Americans, individualists to the core, oppose almost any infringements of their personal rights whether or not guaranteed by the Constitution, Germans are more collectivist in their outlook. That is, the Germans give greater consideration to the interests of the group—the entire society—than do the Americans. Which in turn is not to say that on a world-wide scale of individualist versus collectivist nations, there is all that much difference between Germany and the United States—introduce a country such as Singapore or Guatemala, and the differences pale. However, the Germans do allow the state to make a surprising—at least to Americans—number of decisions which curtail their individual freedoms; they live in what is sometimes referred to as an authoritarian democracy, and they are quite happy on occasion to leave it to the state to act in their best interests. So, for example, they have little problem accepting curtailment of their freedom of speech if the state decides that certain opinions are dangerous to the society as a whole. Nazi propaganda is banned in Germany, and it is illegal to disseminate it, although the all-pervasiveness of the Internet has made this difficult to control. For a time, the Internet book distributor Amazon.com was offering Hitler's *Mein Kampf* on its list of available books, and Germans put in their orders, the book being unobtainable here. Amazon was later persuaded to remove the book from its catalogue—but in the long run, such Internet commerce is unavoidable. Ultra-extreme right-wing parties—the neo-Nazis—considered by the state as subversive, are banned. Shades of McCarthyism, say some Americans. Perhaps, but the Germans as a whole can live with such benevolent authority from above.

They can also live with a far more comprehensive social system than exists in most other countries—and which requires them to participate whether they want to or not. Thus, nobody who works as a private or state employee—and over 50 percent of the workforce is employed in some area of so-called public service—can choose *not* to be part of the state pension system, not to have health insurance, not to contribute to unemployment insurance, etc. Only the self-employed can escape mandatory contributions. Normally, the employer, private or state, pays half the contributions, the employee the other half—although some contributions of certain state employees, *Beamte*, are paid wholly by the state. Because public coffers are so empty these days, there is much talk about a private pension scheme to supplement the state system; current proposals, however, are for a *mandatory* private scheme—in other words, the decision to pay into a private pension fund will remain that of the state.

Taxes—well, the Germans pay a lot, more than many—and many includes the Americans and the Brits. These taxes, which are about to be progressively lowered from the present maximum of 51 percent on private income to 42 percent, are spent not just on nitty-gritty necessities such as education, research, defense, justice, public safety, economic development, public construction, autobahns etc. etc., but also on culture. Or rather, Culture. Theater, opera, ballet, symphony (and other) orchestras, museums, monuments—all of these receive major public support. Not all Germans appreciate that their hard-earned taxes subsidize Culture for the very few—many Germans figure that those who go to the theater, opera, and ballet should pay the full price themselves. These are expensive pleasures, and income from the tickets sold does not come close to covering costs. Again, the state knows what's good for its people.

Father State

BEST FOR BABY

One example of state intervention in the private sphere is found in the laws concerning pregnant women and women who have just given birth. Pregnant women are protected from doing almost anything that could potentially harm the unborn child—and employers must spare them from hard physical activity, allow them to stay home if they are experiencing problems, etc. Pregnant women essentially cannot be fired, no matter how much time they have to take off work. Four weeks before the baby is due, the expectant mother is supposed to stop working—at full pay—although she can insist on working up to the last minute. However, after she gives birth, the law requires that she give up work, still at full pay, for between 8 and 12 weeks depending on the type of *Mother Earth* birth: single/multiple, easy/problematic. This "state interference" is generally regarded as positive and beneficial for mother and child, although it is yet another reason for employers to hesitate before hiring a woman of child-bearing age (see pp. 72–74).

Education is the responsibility of the federal states—the Länder—but is coordinated on the federal level. It would be impossible in Germany for a Land to decide that children could be educated by their parents at home in lieu of being sent to school, or that evolution should not be taught, to give just two examples.

THE NEWS IS GOOD FOR YOU

I mention elsewhere in this book (p. 220) that the state demands a fee for the possession of televisions and radios. This money goes to the public broadcasters, of which there are quite a number. Until the 1980s when private television channels were given permission to operate, the state had a major, if slightly indirect, say in what the viewing public could watch. And the state felt—and still feels, but nobody cares much any longer—that its citizens should be educated. Consequently, the programs are traditionally heavy on Culture, documentaries and news programs. Since there is a lot of competition now from the private channels which provide the entertainment that viewers want—and it's quite amazing how many solid, upstanding burghers prefer sex and violence to wildlife in Outer Mongolia—the public channels are lowering their standards and catering to popular tastes. Talk shows are giving way to game shows, news programs to film thrillers. But—and this is something I personally am happy about—there is still an excellent offering of world news at regular intervals throughout the day and evening.

GUN CONTROL

Gun control is not an issue in Germany. The normal citizen may not possess a gun, and doesn't. Most Germans view the ongoing American debate as incomprehensible, especially in view of the violent crime rate and the gun deaths at school. Papa State in Germany knows that guns are bad for you—and that's all there is to it.

THE RUGGED INDIVIDUALISM OF THE GERMANS

Nothing if not contradictory (see p. 50 on), the Germans occasionally refuse state intervention precisely where it might be expected. Whereas there are speed limits on just about all American roads and highways, the German state has been unable to come up with a nationwide ban on speeding on the hundreds of autobahns which crisscross the country. If local conditions require limited re-duced-speed areas, these will be imposed by the authorities and en-forced—quite rigidly. But the car lobby is extremely strong and has successfully prevented German car drivers from being victims of mad ecologists or road-safety nuts. Although gas in Germany costs a bomb—and is rising steadily because the Green governing coalition party managed to impose a progressive ecology tax—rugged individ-ualist German drivers are not to be put off. And while motor vehicles have to prove their road-worthiness every two years, German drivers do not: once they have obtained their driving license, they can drive forever—if they live that long.

Another contradiction: the Germans brook little interference with their right to smoke, and thereby harm themselves and their en-vironment. Cigarette smokers do not pay extra for their health insur-ance and mothers are not jailed for smoking during pregnancy and thereafter; of all the very few rules in Germany that can be broken with impunity, the occasional "no smoking" signs in public places head the list. Germans smoke almost everywhere.

PART THREE

Practicalities: Everything (Else)

HELLO, NEWCOMERS

1

Germans have a world-famous penchant for order, and nowhere is this more evident than in their rules and regulations surrounding residency permits, work permits and taxes. For newcomers to Germany—especially those unfamiliar with the language—these regulations can be both daunting and confusing.

Main City Magazine, Newcomers Guide, 1999

EXPECTATIONS

I've written the first four chapters of this section with newcomers to Germany in mind—visitors who intend to live in the country for a while as opposed to short-term tourists. The last three chapters are for both groups. However, I am not very consistent, and some of the advice in the first chapters—on what to bring along, for example—is for anyone.

Living in Germany, or in any other unfamiliar culture, takes some getting used to, and it can take years for foreigners to feel halfway at home. Too many westerners just assume that this won't be the case—Germany isn't China, after all, where we know from the start that everything will be quite different. Funnily enough, the conscious or unconscious expectation that the transition will be relatively easy is likely to make it harder, and more confusion, leading to frustration and irritation, can be caused by apparent similarities than by obvious dissimilarities.

So—be prepared and be patient. Patience is probably the most sanity-preserving quality you can bring along with you. Accept "German Ways," no matter how much they may confuse and frustrate you at first—and here I'm referring specifically to the hassle of getting established and physically settling down in your new environment. Relax and be yourself. The Germans are not going to hold it against you if you don't do things their way. As long as you don't come over as arrogant and condescending, you'll be forgiven for almost any cultural *faux pas* you could make.

WHAT (NOT) TO PACK

What should you bring to Germany? Nothing special. That is, whatever personal effects you want to have along of course, but that's about it. Germany is an affluent, western civilized country, and I can't think of anything of vital importance (other than non-fat, calorie-free frozen yogurt or fruit-flavored douches) that you couldn't get here if you needed it. You may not always find exactly the same brands you use at home, but if you are willing to be minimally adventurous and try out local varieties, you may be in for a few pleasant surprises. German tissue toilet paper, for example, can be a lot softer and thicker than the standard 2-ply kind you get in the United States (because German toilets are less prone to clog up, or so I'm told).

If your household is being transferred to Germany by a moving company, you may not be too concerned about volume. However, if you are moving yourself, although you may feel an almost over-whelming compulsion to bring along suitcases full of familiar items, my advice is: don't bother. Be nice to yourself—travel light! And don't worry about the embarrassment of having to explain over the counter in halting German that you need intimate items: tampons and condoms are as easily identifiable in Germany—and throughout Europe—as they are in the United States and can be found in vending machines in public toilets as well as on the shelves of any drugstore (*Drogerie*). In Germany, the pharmacy part of an American drugstore is a separate shop (*Apotheke*) and here, you usually have to ask for what you want, even if it is not a pharmaceutical, prescription item. But here too, intimate products are readily available. If you need prescription drugs, you can almost certainly obtain them, but you'll have to go to a doctor before you go to the Apotheke, and give him the generic name of what you need, since brand names differ. Take along the list of ingredients of the home product, printed on the bottle or packaging. Some products available over-the-counter in the United States—DHEA, for example—have not yet been approved in Germany.

APPLIANCES AND APPAREL

Make sure that any electrical appliances you bring along work on 220 volts—these days, most small items such as hair dryers, curlers, tooth-brushes and travel irons are on convertible voltage. So are most laptops and other computer equipment. German plugs—which serve only as socket adapters, not as voltage transformers—can be purchased either at home or here. Lugging along heavy transformers for larger appliances makes little sense if you are not planning to set up home here—and even then, it may be more practical to buy electrical equipment here. Video recorders and televisions, for example, work on a different system in Europe. They operate on a format called PAL as opposed to the American NTSC or Asian SECAM. What this means is that not only can you not use American machines in Europe, but you can't watch the American video films you bring over with you on the European system. Don't worry, though; almost all commercial U.S. films can be rented here on the PAL system from video rental stores in the more cosmopolitan towns. German washing machines—European washing machines in general—take forever to complete a cycle, but they actually clean clothes very satisfactorily without the addition of bleaches and other additives. Standard German refrigerators are small—the U.S.-sized monsters are available, but cost the earth—and are often supplemented by a larger, separate freezer unit kept in the basement or storage room.

The only things you might have trouble finding in Germany are very small clothes and shoe sizes. About the smallest regular German size (34/36) is roughly a U.S. size 4/6, and the smallest shoes available in regular shoe shops are for relatively large, wide feet. Incidentally, beware of any charts giving you "European" clothing sizes, because this is one area where the Europeans have not yet harmonized, and British, French, Italian and German sizes are significantly different. So a

Unpluggable

U.S. size 8 is a British size 12, a German size 38, a French size 40 and an Italian size 42. Europeans know to ask what the labels really mean.

2 CULTURE SHOCK TIMES TWO

In a way, the visitor in a foreign culture returns to the mental state of an infant, in which he or she has to learn the simplest things over again. This usually leads to feelings of distress, of helplessness, and of hostility towards the new environment. Often one's physical functioning is affected. Expatriates and migrants have more need for medical help shortly after their displacement than before or later.

Geert Hofstede: *Cultures and Organizations*

THE FIRST SHOCK

The following does not normally apply to tourists or short-term visitors. It is not Germany-specific—it applies to any move abroad. It's something any potential ex-pat needs to know.

Most people expect some sort of culture shock when they move abroad for any length of time, even though they don't always anticipate how hard it can hit, and how disoriented and depressed they may become at first. The fact is, living away from home in a foreign environment, where everything, not just the language, is different and strange, can drain a lot of energy. You feel like an idiot much of the time. You start missing things you never dreamed you'd ever miss—your neighbor's noisy late-night jam sessions, T-bone steaks and prime ribs, even TV commercials—and wish you could just relax and be yourself instead of worrying whether you are doing the right thing or making a fool of yourself. What struck you at first as "cute" can end up driving you nuts: the local shops lose their quaintness when you find yourself being ignored; the narrow, winding streets can become a nightmare when you have to park in them in a hurry. And so on. The problem often starts when you move, and that wonderful German efficiency you had heard so much about turns out to be a myth. Nothing goes right, nothing you order is delivered on time.

You can't even scream at the unhelpful salespeople because you don't speak their language—and when it suits them, they don't speak yours. After a while, you become desperate. To make matters worse, none of your good friends are around to commiserate with you, and if you are an accompanying partner or spouse, your other half is tremendously busy at work, and has no time to listen to your domestic woes. The children miss their mates, are going through their own culture shock and spend the day whining and complaining. Life becomes unbearably lonely, and to make everything much worse, you begin to have relationship problems because you are so uprooted and unhappy. You decide you want to leave—and your relationship problems become worse.

This is a worst-case scenario, but it is not infrequent. The good news is: if you can stick it out, it is almost always just a temporary phase. Culture shock is not to be taken lightly, but there is a pattern to it, and this pattern can be described in what Geert Hofstede calls an acculturation curve.

THE ACCULTURATION CURVE

When you first find out that you are going abroad for an extended time, you're likely to be very happy and excited. You start making plans, your friends are all envious, and you are very busy. This is the so-called euphoria or honeymoon phase, and it normally lasts until you get to wherever you are going. However, as soon as you are faced with real life as described above, depression sets in. How long the depression lasts, or how severe it becomes, is not predictable—if it is not understood as what it is, a temporary phase, it can lead to your returning home. But if you can ride it out, it slowly fades as you become acculturated, or accustomed to your new surroundings. You make friends. The strange ways of the people around you become less strange, and you find you can cope better. Eventually, you feel back on a more even keel. Hofstede says that when you have become thoroughly acculturated, you are likely to end up with one of three mental orientations: your refound stable state of mind may be negative compared to what it normally is at home, but still acceptable; it may be the same as it was at home, and you have simply become biculturally adapted; or it may be better than it was at home, and you've "gone native"—in this case, become more German than the Germans.

THE SECOND SHOCK

The second shock is the less expected one. Most expatriates eventually return home. At first, the prospect—and then the reality—of moving back to familiar places and faces can seem pretty good, and although you may feel sad at leaving your new home and friends, the prevalent feeling is excitement and euphoria. Once you are truly back, however, these good feelings may—and often do—pale. Everything at home is so . . . well, the same. Boring. Your friends are still the same people they were, but they haven't moved ahead, and you have. You are full of experiences and images that have enriched you—but your friends don't really want to know. They are not really interested. You become annoyed, then angry and resentful. You start going through reverse culture shock, and find it difficult to readjust to your old cultural environment. You are somehow stuck between worlds. It may take a while to go through the necessary reacculturation phase—and some people never really fit back in. These are the ones who often decide to emigrate. Funnily enough, these same people report that if they emigrate to yet another culture, they go through the entire culture-shock process again. Apparently, as Hofstede points out, culture shocks are environment specific, and for every new environment, there is a new shock.

TIPS

Forewarned is forearmed: The best preparation for culture shock is understanding what it is, and knowing that as tough as it may be, it doesn't last forever. The more you know in advance about the culture you are planning to become part of for a while, the less intense the culture shock is likely to be. So do some homework before you leave home. Read as much as you can on the history, culture and customs of—well, in our case, the Germans. Seek out people at home who have lived in Germany themselves. They are often better informants than actual Germans, who don't really know what to tell you about their country in terms of what you will find strange or difficult because they themselves take it all for granted. And above all—be prepared for a difficult time at first and be patient. Accept from the start that initial depression is an almost inevitable stage of acculturation and don't blame yourself or consider yourself a failure when it hits. Seek out other expatriates. Above all, don't let yourself be sucked into a lethargy which has you sitting at home feeling miserable.

HASSLES AND HEADACHES 3

The Germans clutter up their little landscape with lots of little signs, most of which warn you that something is prohibited (verboten), *not permitted* (nicht gestattet), *strictly prohibited* (strengstens untersagt) *or punishable* (strafbar).

Bob Larsen: *Getting Along With The Germans*

SERVICE WITH A FROWN

To give an upbeat start to a downbeat topic—customer service, or what passes as such in Germany, is getting better. Or, in case that is an exaggeration, I'll rephrase it: there are firm intentions on the part of many organizations to give some thought to service and consider whether it could or should be improved. Task forces are being set up to investigate the notion of service, and the relationship, if any, between the quality of service and economic return. Until very recently, service in Germany—or lack thereof—was a non-issue, mainly because the general public did not demand it. They simply accepted that as a customer or client, they would be treated with the contempt that such status conferred. They expected to have surly, rude cashiers, superior, unhelpful (un)civil servants—and don't forget, about half of the German working population are public employees of some kind—belligerent, complaining taxi drivers. The mistreated general public didn't complain, they didn't write letters to the management, they didn't boycott the offending establishment. Germany was not a *Dienstleistungsgesellschaft* (a society concerned with service) and that was all there was to it. When they went abroad and salespeople, officials, restaurant staff, etc., were pleasant and cheerful, many Germans were extremely put off—they thought they were being made fun of. They complained that Americans (in particular) were phony and superficial, because they would greet complete strangers with a dazzling smile and, "Hi honey, how are you today?" or worse, "Hi, I'm Greg and I'm your waitperson tonight. I'd be happy to walk you through our specials . . . ." The Germans knew that the people serving them didn't give a damn how they were, and they felt much happier if they were treated accordingly.

Well, things have changed a bit. Maybe enough Germans found it more pleasant to be greeted with a friendly smile, no matter how phony, than with a disdainful frown. Maybe enough became irritated at the sheer amount of time they wasted getting nowhere with stubborn salespeople and officials. Maybe they got fed up with omnipresent negativism—the "it can't be done, it isn't possible, we've never done it that way and we're not about to start" attitude. I don't know. More likely, some smart entrepreneurs realized that in a highly competitive market place, the only added value they could give was service. So—not only did existing institutions, from supermarkets to public offices—even the internal revenue service!—instruct their personnel to be nicer, but a whole new service industry came into being—businesses whose sole business it is to make life easier and pleasanter. Well, let's say easier. The pleasanter part is harder, but they are getting there. And now the Germans are beginning to ask for better service. Ask, mind you; not go to the barricades for. That is still to come.

Again, I am not suggesting that Germany has made a quantum leap in terms of service. But a quantum hop is noticeable. I fly into Frankfurt airport a lot, and it has become a slightly friendlier place. Passport officials are now known to look up at you with a smile and occasionally—I swear this has been known to happen—welcome you to the country. Lufthansa, appreciated for its safety record, has never been known for the friendliness of its personnel—on the contrary. However, even this is changing. Both Lufthansa and Deutsche Bahn (DB), the German railway system, have set up information booths and are encouraging personnel to answer questions politely. Both companies have recently acknowledged that they have become unacceptably unpunctual. Lufthansa blamed its customers and sent them letters telling them to show up at airports on time; DB fired its chief executive. This is what happens when service becomes an issue. (Both Lufthansa and DB are in the process of becoming privatized. Maybe this too is playing a role . . . Just a thought.)

As far as attracting foreign business is concerned, service is now being taken very seriously indeed by all concerned in any way—especially by the myriad organizations and institutions promoting economic development. Germany, as I have pointed out in a number of places in this book, is not an easy country to penetrate, simply because the rules and regulations appear insurmountable. Just trying to establish a legal entity is enough to drive all but the most determined away (see p. 136). But Germany is suffering from the lack of foreign investment and is desperately trying to woo foreign companies. So the public sector—agencies on all levels, from the federal to the municipal—is anxious to assist wherever possible, and so is the private sector—law firms, relocation companies, and the countless "consultancies" that have sprung up—which sees a nice income to be made out of being helpful.

So—all in all, I predict that as a result of turbo-globalization, service in Germany is about to improve at an amazing rate. Soon, we'll be greeted at airports with bunches of flowers and champagne, or rather *Sekt*, the German version of the latter. And one of these days, serving personnel in affordable German establishments will introduce themselves with a smile (not with their first names, though) and walk you through your choices.

BE PREPARED

If you want to live and work in Germany and you are not a member of the European Union, be prepared for seemingly endless red tape. In addition to a residence permit, you'll need a work permit, for which you need a written offer of employment sufficient to convince the powers-that-be that only you—and no European with the right to work in Germany—can do the job. You should be aware that the stiff requirement prevents most accompanying partners from being allowed to work, no matter how good their qualifications may be. Because of all the bureaucratic hurdles involved, it's best to contact your local German diplomatic representative before you leave home; that way, you'll find out in advance where you stand, what documents and photos you will need to produce, whether you'll be required to undergo a physical examination, and so on. Once you arrive in Germany, you'll find yourself trekking from one permit-issuing office to another, and if you go to the wrong office first, or don't produce what you're supposed to produce, you'll be sent back to Go. And that's not even the end of it—the formidable formalities remain to torment you, since permits usually need to be renewed at set intervals.

RENTING

Renting places can be a mighty tricky business in Germany. First of all, finding suitable and affordable accommodation is very often a major headache. There's a shortage of good housing in most German cities, and whenever something really nice becomes available, the word gets round—funnily enough, this is one area in which information flows fairly freely—and it is often snapped up even before it appears on the market. Local newspapers carry housing ads (usually on Wednesdays and Saturdays, with some Saturday editions appearing on the newsstands on Friday afternoon), and suppliers are sometimes swamped by demanders within minutes of publication. If you use a real estate agent (*Makler*), you'll end up paying between one and three months rent in commission. Note: this fee is not due until a contract has been signed. No contract, no commission. Note too that once a real estate agent has shown you a property—for private or business use, it makes no difference—that agent is the one entitled to bag the commission, even if other, perhaps more helpful or sympathetic agents later show you the same property. There are exclusive listings, but often, all the agents in town scramble over the same places. In other words, you can't choose who gets the commission—and you can't bargain either.

Another way to go about finding accommodation is to place an ad yourself in one of the local newspapers, many of which have a substantial housing-sought section. You can then specify your most unnegotiable requirements. Landlords, often driven mad by people phoning in answer to their ads, sometimes prefer a quick way out—calling a likely candidate themselves. So your ad should be as appealing as possible. Get a German friend to help you formulate it—or simply insert it in English.

Accommodation is described in terms of the number of rooms it offers, and the number of rooms includes all rooms except the kitchen, bathroom(s) and toilet(s). A three-bedroom apartment which has in addition a living room, separate dining room and den or study appears as a six-room apartment.

Contracts (*Mietverträge*) may include a lot of complex clauses which, if you don't understand them, can end up costing you a lot of money—in renovations, for example, or in the amount of money you are asked to put up as a deposit or *Kaution*. It is therefore a good idea to get help from knowledgeable friends, from the Makler or from a lawyer (*Rechtsanwalt* or *Notar*). The services of these last two do not come cheap, but they can be invaluable. Another good source of information on the rights and responsibilities of renters is the local Tenant's Association (*Mieterschutzverein*) and similar organizations, listed in the Yellow Pages under *Mieterschutz*. One way or another, you should find out what is included in the rent and what is not. You may have to pay extra monthly *Wohngeld* (literally "living money") for such conveniences as a janitor, garbage removal, building maintenance and the like. Heating may be included in the rent or Wohngeld, but other utilities are almost always extra. You should also check on how to get out of the contract if you should decide to leave before the expiration date. And remember—when you do leave, cancel everything in writing, from your phone to your water bill. Otherwise, you may end up paying for future generations of tenants.

The good news for the renter—once the signed contract is in his hand—is that there are a number of laws in place making it very difficult for the owner to dislodge him, or even to raise the rent on him. These laws are changing all the time, but the trend in recent years has been in favor of the tenant.

When you rent an apartment or house, be prepared for the fact that an empty place is just that—completely, echoingly, empty. Unless otherwise specified, there is often nothing in the rooms but bare walls, ceiling and floor (and bathroom/toilet fixtures where appropriate). No built-in or other closets, no drapes, no wall-to-wall carpets. Kitchens normally contain nothing but plumbing connections and electrical outlets—no counters, no cupboards, no electrical appliances, not even a stove, range or even sink. If the previous owners or renters are leaving some of their old fixtures behind, they will ask you for money (*Abstand*). Since new renters are often willing to take over built-in kitchens and the like for the sheer convenience, the amount asked for is often very high. Be prepared to bargain. If you are able to take over a phone line from the previous tenant, it is advisable to do so, just to save yourself the hassle of ordering a new connection (number), which can take weeks to install. The partly federally-owned Deutsche Telekom still has a monopoly on telephone lines and local calls, so although you can use another private company for long-distance calls, you can't bypass Deutsche Telekom entirely.

Be warned: Furnished apartments and houses are not common, although they are becoming easier to find these days in the larger cities. They tend to cost a bomb, however, and on an occupancy of more than a year, it often makes (far) more economic sense to rent an unfurnished place and buy the necessary furniture—which, however cheap, is likely to be nicer than what you'll find in a furnished place.

And with any luck, the bought furniture can be passed on to the next tenant—the *Abstand* mentioned above works two ways.

REGISTERING

German officialdom has a need to keep track of where everybody is. So, for example, within a few days of getting or changing a "permanent" address, you have to register yourself at the appropriate office—the *Einwohnermeldeamt* or the *Ordnungsamt*, which translates loosely as the office in charge of order. This registration requirement applies to Germans and non-Germans alike. I won't bother you with what you have to do and have in hand in order to register, because if you're a tourist you don't need to know, and if you plan to stay, you'll find out soon enough. Suffice it to say that the process is time-consuming and frustrating, and since you don't exist if you aren't properly registered, I'm sure quite a few people spin off into limbo along the way.

Registering your car is as bothersome as registering yourself—and

Civil Registration

In his chapter, "Doing Business in Germany" (in *Meet United Germany*, ed. Susan Stern), German lawyer Karsten Schmidt has the following to say:

The registration process is of some importance in Germany and amazingly does not lead to serious thoughts of civil unrest. Everybody, within 48 hours of arrival, must hold a tryst with the local authorities and register him/herself. The authorities will then send a copy of the registration certificate to the local birth registry office if the new arrival is German or to a central registry if he is not. Deregistration is also a must and for tax reasons can be valuable proof of departure. It would be unthinkable for such general registration to be introduced into Britain or the United States where registration is required, if at all, of foreigners, but not of nationals, and the very idea of a comprehensive registration system is considered a serious threat to civil liberties. In Germany, however, universal registration is part of life and nobody thinks badly about it. It is a tedium, to be sure, but who cares. And through it, people can be easily traced. This is of importance as much for families looking into their roots as for the creditor whose debtor is moving about . . . All-comprehensive registration has not created an administrative nightmare. It is well-organized and serves many useful functions. It is one of the basic units of the ecosystem of public life in Germany. It helps the state function—and function it does.

if you change your address during your car's lifetime, you have to re-register the car after you have re-registered yourself. What's more, you have to clear your car through the motor vehicle inspection department (commonly known as *TÜV*) before you can register it—and thereafter every two years. TÜV, comparable to but more thorough than emissions testing agencies in the United States, employs officials who are among the most implacable and heartless in Germany—which is why most cars on German roads are in pretty good shape. And since the German police are equally implacable in checking the validity of the TÜV symbol displayed on each car, it is expensive to "forget" to put your car through the inspection procedures.

RELOCATION SERVICES

The German penchant for regulating every aspect of existence makes practical life difficult enough for the Germans themselves, and almost impossible for foreigners, who are completely overwhelmed and baffled at the seemingly senseless obstacles to getting anything done, be it getting themselves legal status, setting up a business or a household or buying a car. However, there's some good news. A service industry has come into being simply to help people—usually foreigners—move. Called relocations, it does everything for expatriates, from showing them around town and introducing them to the surroundings, finding suitable living quarters, taking them through all the formalities of buying or renting, getting everyone and everything (TVs and radios included) properly registered with the appropriate authorities, signing the kids up in kindergartens or schools—to providing them with intercultural training seminars to prepare them for culture shock caused by all the "Strange German Ways." Relocation companies are expanding their services as both competition and demand increase; some now offer property management, insurance plans, legal services—and will even set up business entities.

So—there's help for those that can afford it. The rest just have to muddle through themselves, with a little help from their friends. The good news is that some cities such as mine, Frankfurt, are making a concerted effort to make life easier for expatriates. Frankfurt has even set up a help line in English to assist the desperate. We now have an annual "Newcomers to Frankfurt Day," a huge fair-plus-happening in City Hall where large and small businesses, churches, schools, clubs—just about every individual and organization with an interest in introducing themselves and their wares to the newly-arrived—set up booths and give out information. Moreover, there are quite a number of expatriate groups—women's clubs, business clubs, cultural clubs—in or around most urban areas, and they provide various forms of support, from networking to helpful publications.

FINDING THE RIGHT SCHOOLS

Some of the first questions that many potential expatriates have when their company asks them to spend time in Germany concern their children: what about schooling for my kids? Will they suffer from being taken out of their home environment and put into a different school system? What about the language? How will they manage when they return home? There are many questions, reflecting many fears.

If you are planning to stay in Germany for a long or indefinite time, you can, of course, put your children into regular German schools. There is a lot to be said in favor of this: young children pick up the language incredibly fast when they are thrust into an all-German environment, and that goes for the culture, too. So you may be doing them a big favor by allowing them to integrate into their new environment as quickly and painlessly as possible. At the same time, there are disadvantages to sending your kids to a local school. Americans expect not just the academic life but also the social life of their offspring to revolve around school-organized activities. They are used to having a whole gamut of sports, cheerleading, bands, clubs and dances, etc., included in the school program. For the most part, if such activities exist at all in Germany—cheerleading doesn't, except in the rare cities where there is an American-style football team— they are extramural and arranged by private institutions such as sports clubs, dance and music schools. School itself is primarily academic; there is little school spirit, and school plays no real role in the life of the community.

Another disadvantage—at least to mothers, (see section on Women, pp. 72–74)—of German schools is that classes are concentrated into the morning, and school lets out by lunchtime. Lunchtime, however, is a movable notion, and varies from day to day. Sometimes classes are over by 11 A.M., other times not until 2 or 3 P.M. On a long morning, by the end of the 7th class kids are exhausted and hungry. There is no school lunch. Afternoons, whenever they start, are "free" for homework and non-school social activities.

An alternative to a local German school is a European or International school. European schools are springing up mainly in those towns which have a large expatriate European community—Frankfurt, for example, home of the European Central Bank. These schools have a varied curriculum which does its best to provide the kids with some measure of their home language and culture. The International Schools are based more on the American model, and serve the families of expatriates who want their children to have a more all-around, English-language, American-style education (complete with extracurricular activities) and to end up with the International Baccalaureate—the school-leaving examination which makes it easy for them to get into universities in most countries of the world. There are already quite a number of International Schools throughout Germany, and their customers come from all over the world—the schools are not American enclaves. The kids receive highly personalized teaching in small classes. Since the International Schools exist all over the world, it's not a bad idea to put your kids into the system if you know you're going to be moving a lot. However, there are also definite disadvantages to sending your children to an International School. Unless your company pays for tuition (many companies do), you will be burdened with stiff fees—to the tune of many thousands of dollars per year. International School children are not well-integrated into German culture, many never really learn the language. So they grow up in an international limbo culture.

Any decision as to schooling should be based on a thorough investigation of the possibilities in the particular area of Germany you end up living in. The message here is that there is a reasonable choice in most urban areas, and overall, schooling of all kinds is pretty good. Children almost inevitably profit from a period of living abroad, and that certainly applies in Germany.

DOCTORS AND HOSPITALS

A short word about medical care. The German health insurance system is comprehensive and makes health care, including dental care, accessible to just about everybody. And medical standards in Germany are very high. But while German medicine is probably as good as in any other country in the world, including the United States, the attitude of doctors towards patients often—certainly not always—leaves something to be desired. The attitude of doctors to other doctors leaves a lot to be desired, too; the rigid pecking order, particularly in hospitals, does not make for warm collegial relations.

This, plus the tendency to compartmentalize—view the patient in bits and pieces and treat each part separately—make for an entirely unholistic approach which is disturbing. A surgeon may be unwilling to pass his patient on to an oncologist simply because (s)he, the surgeon, doesn't interact with the oncologist and doesn't know what's going on in the oncologist's field. Large hospitals in big cities—often the best equipped in terms of the latest machines—can be as dismal as a morgue. Many hospitals have no private rooms for anyone, not even for the most highly insured patients. This can lead to inhuman situations in, for example, the cancer ward, where relatively healthy patients who are being given chemotherapy have to share a room with someone who is dying.

In former East Germany, doctors and medical personnel were considerably more concerned with the psychic health of the patients. There were—and still are in the eastern Länder—hospital-organized support groups for the sick and their close relatives. This is relatively unknown in the western part of Germany, where support or self-help groups are increasingly coming into existence, but are not part of the hospital system.

To close on a positive note: if you should be unfortunate enough to get sick while you are in Germany, don't worry. The medical attention you get will be state-of-the-art. Just don't stick around too long if you need Tender Loving Care—that is in sort supply.

DEALING WITH PEOPLE IN OFFICES 4

Many government offices, especially those open to the general public, close for the afternoon. It is also often difficult to reach someone after three on Friday afternoons, because many companies close early.
Greg Nees: *Germany: Unraveling An Enigma.*

THE OFFICES WE CAN'T AVOID

This short section is not just for business people, but for any of you who have occasion to deal with people—employees and managers—who inhabit German offices. Germans may or may not work hard, and they may or may not work efficiently—but they do manage to make themselves rare to the so-called client or customer. And once you get a foot in the door, unless you play the game their way, you may not get far. I have therefore included my comments in this part of the book on *Practicalities* rather than in the part on Business.

You might assume that office life had become pretty standardized in this modern world of e-commerce, globalization, telecommunications and jet-setters. You would be wrong. Office life is still highly culture-specific. Assuming that you ever manage to reach the people you want to reach, the wrong approach to office inhabitants—bureaucrats, businesspeople, secretaries—is likely to cause you frustration and do great harm to your cause, whatever it might be. There are a few things you should know in advance.

HARD TO REACH

Not surprisingly, in a country as bureaucratic as Germany, it's difficult to avoid having to deal with people in offices. I've already mentioned that many public-sector offices—the places where you register yourself and your car for example—have very limited office hours, i.e. hours they are available to the walk-in public. Doors are open three mornings a week if you are lucky, and just occasionally for a couple of hours on one afternoon. Other public-sector offices such as the internal revenue service have similar visiting hours. But non-availability to the public is a German disease (see section on Shopping, p. 203 on) and extends beyond the notoriously un-service-oriented public sector. Banks, for example, keep cutting back on their open-for-business hours, since telephone banking and ATMs are effectively doing away with face-to-face banking. Whole companies have cut themselves off from the live public almost entirely, and are not even reachable by phone: their communication is exclusively electronic.

While it is certainly true that much of the above could be said about other western countries, what is particular about Germany is that so many people are not in their offices so much of the time. The standard working week is from Monday to early Friday afternoon—Friday afternoons after 2 P.M. belong to the weekend. However, office personnel are only at their work-place (*Arbeitsplatz*) when they are not somewhere else—on vacation, for example (between five and seven weeks a year, see p. 138), or on a *Kur* (a sort of health farm or spa vacation which employees are entitled to go on and which is paid for by a generous health insurance system), or simply enjoying the numerous national or local legal holidays that relieve the tedium of work. Or, of course, they could be off sick—in 1999, the average number of days missed by employees because of illness-plus-Kur was a staggering 16!—or on fully-paid maternity leave—a mandatory 4 weeks prior to delivery and 8–12 weeks thereafter—or simply otherwise indisposed.

HEAVY PROTECTION

Employees are well-treated under German labor law, benefits are bountiful, and it is not surprising that non-wage labor costs are extremely high—46 percent. Germans are (in)famous for working fewer hours a year than any other industrialized nation (see p. 138). Management, however, does not share (or take) the same benefits; during the office season (see p. 138), most managers tend to be around quite a bit, and many work late into the evening. However, their physical presence on the premises does not necessarily make them accessible to anybody but their personal secretary. This particular secretary's job is first and foremost to prevent her (yes, her) boss from being disturbed, and most such secretaries are very good at this. They sit in a room which guards the only entrance to the boss's lair. The sentry-secretary is known as a *Vorzimmerdame* and she is usually formidable. There is no easy way of getting around her without literally mowing her down.

OFFICE ETIQUETTE

Assuming that you manage to convince her that your cause is good and that you will bring fame and/or fortune to her boss and/or the company (the Vorzimmerdame is immensely loyal and not bribable), and assuming that you get an appointment to see the boss (whom we can assume is a man, because statistically, any German boss is likely to be), keep in mind that while the Germans in general tend to be formal, German managers, especially in industry and banking, are formal to a tee. So be sure to stick to the rules:

The Formidable Vorzimmerdame

- Keep your appointment. Last-minute cancellations or postponements are unacceptable.
- Dress formally unless you are in an industry such as advertising or any of the high-tech sectors, which have their own dress code. German managers, even the very young, tend to wear suits and ties.
- Arrive punctually—early is even better. Shake hands and move back a few steps—if you don't, your host probably will.
- Sit wherever you are offered a seat. This is likely to be at the far side of a desk, or in a seating arrangement consisting of leather couches around a low table. Do not attempt to move your chair closer to your host. Do not get up and pace the room.
- Do not address your host by his first name.
- Do not slap him on the back, put your arm around him, or indulge in any other such expressions of camaraderie.
- Do not ask to use office equipment, such as a fax or copy machine, for your own (as opposed to directly visit-related) purposes. If you have to make a phone call, keep it short. It is not stinginess that

makes Germans less generous with their machines than, say, Americans, but rather their culturally imbued sense of possession.

- Never overstay your welcome; leave promptly when your host looks at his watch, or when the secretary comes in with an urgent (and almost always prearranged) message.
- Business lunches have caught on with a vengeance over the past decades, and the business breakfast is increasingly coming into fashion (see p. 36).
- Remember that it is still rare for a German to mix business and private life, so don't expect to be invited home to meet the wife and kiddies. If you are, it is an honor you should recognize with a small gift and due thanks.

GETTING AROUND 5

*Traffic on the motorways may often come to a standstill, train delays
are no longer unheard of, flights sometimes queue up on runways and
in landing patterns—but western Germany still has one of the world's
finest transportation networks.*

Susan Stern: *Meet United Germany*,
Volume 2: Handbook

*(Since I have just quoted myself—an unforgivable sin—I can also update myself: it's not
just western Germany that can boast an excellent transportation network, but the whole of
Germany, because the 1990s saw mega-progress in transportation infrastructure in the new
Länder.)*

SO NEAR, SO FAR

Since the Federal Republic is pretty small—even after unification it's
only 137,744 square miles—no place within the country is terribly far
from any place else. Hamburg to the north and München (Munich)
to the south are worlds apart to hear the locals tell it, but, in fact, they
are separated by a mere 500 or so miles. And these, and other, miles
are easy to cover, since the country is crisscrossed by autobahns (free-
ways as opposed to payways, although they may not continue to be
free for ever) and railroad tracks. Moreover, most major cities boast
an airport, so they are also interconnected by air.

TRAINS

A very good way to move about Germany is by train, courtesy of the
German federal railroad company, now partly privatized, Deutsche
Bahn (DB). There are all kinds of trains, from the village-to-village
and town-to-town type to the latest in city-sprinters. On some main
routes between major cities, there are superfast, streamlined, high-

tech trains which offer much of the luxury of a plane, including audio and visual entertainment, even in second class. Called ICEs (for Intercity Express), they can travel at well over 150 miles per hour, and do wherever tracks permit; they service the stops along their way at regular intervals, at least once an hour. The ICEs came into being in 1991 and since then have proliferated rapidly.

If your route doesn't happen to be an ICE route, it may well be an IC—an Intercity without the Express, but still pretty fast and comfortable. There are literally hundreds of ICs, and similar ECs, linking German cities reasonably efficiently and regularly. Note, however: German trains are not—repeat not—as punctual as they are reputed to be. Expect a delay, and you'll be pleasantly surprised if there isn't one.

All in all, if you're traveling relatively short distances, let's say under 400 miles, the ICE and the IC/EC systems are practical and convenient. From downtown locations it's always quicker to get to the main railway station, traditionally in the center of the city, than to the nearest airport—traditionally not. The ICE and IC/EC cars are easy and pleasant to work or relax in because they're laid out as in a plane, each seat with a table, two seats abreast, with an aisle down the middle. There are outlets to plug your laptops and portable cassette recorders and CD players into. You should specifically request a seat in a *Grossraumwagen* when you make an ICE or IC/EC advance reservation because the old-style, six-seat compartments still exist.

As far as reservations are concerned, the ICEs fill up fast, and you are well-advised to buy your ticket and reserve a seat in advance (at least 24 hours before departure), either at a train station or at a travel agency that sells train tickets. And therein lies a catch: small agencies don't! Look on the door for a sign saying DB. The IC/ECs too can be pretty crowded at peak times and throughout the summer, so the same advice applies. Advance seat reservations for ticket-holders are worth the couple of dollars they cost. If you don't buy-and-reserve in advance, make sure you arrive at the train station with plenty of time to spare; at peak times, getting your ticket can take ages, even though large stations have installed automatic ticket machines. If you board a train without a reservation, look for a seat that has no reserved card stuck in the holder above it (these days, digital signs on the ICEs)—otherwise, you may find yourself unseated by the rightful occupant with his reservation in hand. Tips: If the ticket line is so long that you risk missing your train, you can buy a ticket from the train conductor—but it will cost you more. If you have no seat reservation and there's standing room only, head for the restaurant or buffet car.

Special rates abound and change all the time, so what is true today may not still be true by the time you read these words. Be sure to check at a train station, or again, at a travel agency that sells train tickets, because you can often save up to 50 percent on the regular rate on both first and second class fares. For longer-term visitors to Germany, so-called train cards (*Bahn Cards*) can be interesting; they are valid for a year from date of purchase, and during that time, all train tickets can be bought at half price. This may change soon: there are rumors that the reduction may be reduced to 25 percent. Note too that there are a number of super-deal rail passes for visitors from outside Europe; you should check at a travel agency at home, because some such passes can't be purchased in Germany.

PLANES

As indicated above, travel by air within Germany doesn't always save much time, since airports are outside town and these days, with increased security measures, check-in procedures take forever. Moreover, domestic flights are frequently late . . . Still, for longer distances such as Munich-Bremen or Berlin-Frankfurt, it can make sense to fly, and scheduled flying time is rarely longer than 70 minutes. There are plenty of flights, some direct, some via a hub such as Frankfurt or Munich. Berlin, now once again seat of the federal government, is about to build a super airport, but until that comes into operation (scheduled date: 2007), the three existing airports are vastly overstretched, and most flights to destinations outside the country are via a hub. The German carrier Lufthansa is trying to compete with Deutsche Bahn for passengers and keeps introducing special fares for non-business passengers—that is, passengers who stay over Saturday night. Regular fares, however, remain horrendous—a weekday trip from Frankfurt to Berlin and back is about the same price as an inexpensive round-trip from Frankfurt to the United States.

A word about airports: Germany has some really nice ones, the sort of place you can visit on a Sunday excursion, especially if you want to go shopping, because shops there are allowed to stay open when shops elsewhere are required to be shut (see p. 203 on). The biggest and best airport is Frankfurt airport, which is a mini-city employing some 60,000 people and complete with boutiques, food stores (including Harrods of London), cafés, banks, an emergency clinic, a police station and a nondenominational church. The best way to get around the place is on Rollerblades because distances are huge.

CARS

Germans travel by train and they travel by plane—but most of all, they travel by car. They love their cars, which are even more extensions of themselves than most of their other possessions. Depriving a German of his car is an amputation. Thus, for all that the Germans are more ecologically-minded than their European neighbors—and

I just love cruising along at 125 m.p.h. early Sunday mornings...

Safe driving

the rest of the world for that matter—they are not readily inclined to turn in their private motor vehicles for environment-friendlier means of transportation. And while it is true that a lot of Germans have bicycles, it's a common sight to see their bikes perched on the top of their cars as they race down the highway to a distant bicycle path.

The way many Germans drive—like bats out of hell—is very hard for life-loving foreigners to understand. Do German drivers have a death wish? It would appear so. A ride on a German autobahn either as a driver or as a passenger requires nerves of steel. There is no speed limit on many stretches, and the "recommended" limit of 130 km/hr—around 80 mph—is generally ignored. Well, that's the impression most foreigners get. The federal transportation minister sees things differently: he recently announced that in his opinion, the Germans were not the speed freaks they were made out to be, and he saw no reason to impose the general speed limits demanded by the Greens. Slower traffic is supposed to keep to the right, and the left lane—there are frequently only two lanes in each direc-

Once a Driver . . .

Getting a driver's license in Germany is costly for the learner and lucrative for the teacher, since all learners are required by law to take a horrendously expensive driving course costing around $1,500 at an authorized school before they can attempt the written and practical tests. It always strikes me as curious that young Germans, most of whom take the driving course, accept the financial burden without a whimper of protest, while they object vehemently to the very idea of paying for their higher education (see p. 142 on). Be that as it may; once they've obtained their license anytime after they've turned 18, they can drive forever without renewing it. Ancient drivers are a common sight.

tion—is strictly for overtaking. Even when the traffic flow in the slow lane is a steady 130 km/hr, drivers will zig-zag and overtake like maniacs. The one thing that keeps (some) mad drivers alive is their respect for the powerful-car pecking order: in the fast lane, where tailgating is the rule, drivers know who, or rather, which car, has the right of way, and a VW will cede to a BMW, which will cede to a Mercedes and so on. King of the road is still the Porsche.

Aggressive drivers with their egos behind the wheel menace city streets as well as highways, but here's some good news: city traffic is usually so dense that speeding by those who ignore the limits is physically impossible.

To frustrate the hellbent and force drivers to slow down, many residential neighborhoods have introduced bumps and raised studs in the road, slalom-type obstacles and complicated one-way street systems. These mazes also frustrate tourists and other non-locals who find themselves driving in circles, unable to get to an address just a few streets away.

Not surprisingly, one of the strongest and most efficient interest groups in Germany is the car lobby. The leading automobile club, the ADAC, is steadfastly opposed to speed limits on the autobahn and sees no meaningful correlation between driving at a breakneck pace, air pollution and traffic accidents.

Wherever there are too many cars, there is a parking problem. This has gotten so bad in built-up areas that there are no longer illegal parking spots to be found, and many sidewalks have de facto ceased to exist. Apartment residents in inner cities sometimes find themselves parking several miles from home—an inconvenience which still doesn't get them to give up their cars.

Where, Oh Where

It doesn't take the American visitor to Germany (or to the rest of Europe for that matter) very long to figure out that city streets are not on a grid system, and that finding one's way around town is a game that requires patience. Longish streets can change their name without warning, or come to an abrupt end, only to restart somewhere else. House numbers, supposedly arranged with odd and even numbers on the different sides of the street, often play tricks; missing numbers may be tucked away in a courtyard behind the main street. There are historical reasons for this confusion; communities grew up over centuries, streets merged into one another and kept their old names, buildings were razed and replaced, but not always in the same slot. Sometimes, two buildings grew up where there had once been one, so the original number had to be split: 8a and 8b. But an understanding of history won't help you if you're lost. Carry a map. Taxi drivers are supposed to know their way around, but they very often don't, and frequently ask their passengers for directions. It's best to have some handy.

BICYCLES

The bicycle has always been a convenient way to move around a country as compact as Germany, but for a long time, the mad drivers mentioned above dissuaded many from trying to compete with motorized traffic. However, with an increase in concern for the environment and the need to get around town faster than you can in a car, the bicycle has revived in popularity, and bicycle paths now line a lot of city streets—either as part of the sidewalk, or as a bicycle-designated lane on the street itself. Unfortunately, a bicycle path is just too tempting a space for others—drivers, parkers and pedestrians pushed off the sidewalks—to leave to cyclists alone. Bicycle bells tingle furiously as cyclists try to navigate their way, and epithets often fly.

PUBLIC TRANSPORTATION

Public transportation is for the most part very good, often quite brilliant. In most urban areas, it gets you pretty well everywhere within a fairly wide radius of the city center efficiently, comfortably, and reliably from early morning to late night. The system is comprehensive and complex, and in many cities involves a network of mainly underground city trains (the *U-Bahn*), city-suburban under/over ground trains (the *S-Bahn*), streetcars and trams (these latter particularly in the eastern Länder, but they are becoming less frequent as tracks are being laid underground) and buses. The trouble—and not just for foreigners—is that the ticket-buying and ticket validation procedures differ from one city to the next and there is a truly bewildering range of fares, which depend on the zones to be covered, the time of day, the age of the traveler, the name of his dog and quite a few other significant factors. If you are caught on public transportation without a valid ticket, there's a fairly hefty fine to pay, so it's worth it to take the time to figure out the fare system. Note: Since city distances are often quite short, it is sometimes faster and cheaper to walk.

TAXIS

Taxis throughout the country are easy to identify. Usually beige or off-white Mercedes or Fords, they are clearly marked with an overhead taxi sign. Some of them look like London taxis (the increasing number that have been specially made in England for the German market). Taxi ranks are plentiful and so are taxis—except, of course, when you most desperately need one. At most times (other than during a trade fair or when it's raining), a phone reservation will reliably bring a taxi to your door within 10 minutes. In quite a few cities now, it is possible to arrange for a taxi to be waiting to pick you up at a subway station—for instructions, check the subway stations. It is not always very easy to hail a taxi from the street.

WALKING

Walking is advisable wherever possible, but remember: car drivers and cyclists do not like pedestrians. Remember too: German dog-owners do not clean up after their pets (see p. 53). When walking, keep your eyes fixed on the sidewalk, or scrape your shoes before entering a building.

6 HOTELS AND RESTAURANTS

> *But no matter where you travel, there are certain experiences you will bring home in your packet of memories which are typically "German:" down duvets fluffed high on the beds of every inn; breakfast buffets heaped with a tempting assortment of breads, salami, cheeses and jams; pretty barmaids carrying heavy steins of icy beer to laughing customers sitting at tables under chestnut trees; hearty meals of good "home cooking" always served in all-too-generous portions; chambermaids scrubbing floors until they glisten; wood stacked so neatly, so perfectly, that one wonders if any logs less than perfect were discarded.*
>
> Karen Brown: *German Country Inns and Castles*

HOTEL ACCOMMODATION

Frankly, I wonder if the above quote was written by someone who had actually traveled around Germany, or who had simply gotten hold of a some romantic propaganda. It's not that the individual observations could not be true at times, although I suspect that it might take a lifetime to spot a chambermaid scrubbing floors until they glisten; it's just that I can't imagine anyone going home with that particular packet of memories. But then, I'm a cynic.

Throughout Germany, hotels come in all shapes, sizes and price categories. Motels, on the other hand, hardly come at all. To get to your room wherever you are staying, you normally have to navigate a lobby and negotiate indoor corridors. Where you leave your car depends on the establishment and what you are willing to pay: luxury hotels often have their own parking facilities; modest hotels direct you to public parking or leave you to the street jungle.

ROOM AT THE INN

Planning and reserving ahead is always a good idea in Germany, since finding a place to stay is not always easy. Room shortages can become acute in urban areas during trade fairs, exhibitions and conventions, of which there are many throughout the business year; in resort areas during the vacations, and in other places at odd and unexpected times. But even when rooms are in plentiful supply—in cities in January, for example, and over weekends when business traffic is slow—an advance reservation can save you money, since you may be able to prearrange a surprisingly low rate in normally very expensive hotels. All of this (and much more) you should determine by contacting a good travel agent or by calling a toll-free number of the major hotel chains such as Hilton, Sheraton, Kempinski, Inter-Continental, etc. Always ask specifically about the special deals. Should you nevertheless arrive somewhere without a reservation, you can orient yourself by consulting a local hotel reservation center or a room referral agency, usually located at or near the main railway station and at the nearest airport. For a small fee (if any), you'll be directed to whatever is available that best matches your wishes and wallet. Again, keep in mind that during conventions and fairs, you may end up with literally nothing, or be given the choice of a room in a private home some 50 miles away or a suite in a luxury hotel for a small fortune.

Luxury hotels in Germany offer absolutely everything offered by their counterparts throughout the world, and at the other end of the scale, so do youth hostels, for which you need an international membership card. For the rest, middle-class hotels and guest houses are almost always spotlessly clean and adequate. Some rooms have private baths or showers and toilets, others don't, so if this is important to you, make sure to check. Breakfast German-style—bread, rolls, butter, jelly and often a boiled egg, cold cuts and cheese—is usually included in the price of the room, although this is not the case in luxury hotels, where a sumptuous buffet breakfast is offered for a sumptuous extra price. Note: this opulent buffet is often included in the special deals mentioned above.

HOTEL TIPS

Check-in: You are required to fill out a registration form to comply with the German bureaucrats' need to know who is where when. Public safety, they call it, and morals do not come in to it.

Singles and doubles: The older German hotels have a number of genuine single rooms equipped with one narrow bed. These rooms cost somewhat, but not very much, less than double rooms and tend to be pretty cramped.

Keys: Some room keys are heavy and cumbersome; you are supposed to leave them at the front desk whenever you go out, and pick them up again upon your return. Modern hotels provide you with flat security cards which are yours to carry around with you.

Payment: This is due when you check out. A service charge is included in your bill, so leave a gratuity only if you are particularly grateful to a member of the hotel personnel. Exceptions: the bellboy who helps you with your luggage and the doorman who gets you a taxi do expect a tip.

Single room

Help: The reception clerk (*Concierge*) is supposed to be a mine of useful information. Sometimes he is.

Meals: Some resort hotels insist on *Vollpension* (full board—break-fast plus two daily meals) or *Halbpension* (half board—breakfast plus one daily meal). This can be a convenience or a nuisance, but is often unavoidable. If you miss a meal, you'll pay for it anyway.

Baths and Soap: If you are likely to stay in very inexpensive hotels, bring your own soap. If you don't have a private bathroom, you'll find a "public" bath on each floor. There's usually a charge for using a public bathroom, but not for using the public toilets.

Bedding: Rooms in all but the international chain hotels come provided with a duvet or featherbed. If you'd prefer a top sheet and blankets, ask for a *Laken mit Wolldecken*.

RESTAURANTS

Germany is a prosperous country where people eat out and eat relatively well. Just about wherever you travel, you can find excellent restaurants offering international-type food at up-market prices; pizzerias galore; hamburger and other fast-food places, many of them familiar (McDonalds, for example)—and so on. Of course, there's nothing particularly German about this kind of dining experience, and if you're looking for plain, solid German food (*gutbürgerlich* or home cooking-type) in a more Germanic atmosphere, you'll probably end up spending a lot less at a place where you don't need a jacket and tie. Although the proliferation of fancy and foreign restaurants is making it harder and harder to find a restaurant in any price bracket that offers hearty German fare, don't despair! Genuine old-style German eateries still exist. A *Gasthof*, for example, is the kind of modest hotel which is likely to serve German food in so-called German (rustic) surroundings; and *Gasthaus*, *Gaststube*, and *Gastwirtschaft* are all labels for restaurants which regularly serve traditional and local dishes. A *Weinstube* (wine bar), a *Bierhalle*, *Bierkeller* or *Biergarten* (all specializing in beer) don't go in for food in a big way, but don't let their customers go hungry either. And even a *Lokal* or a *Kneipe* (both words for pubs) may have a few simple Germanic dishes or at least pretzels on offer. Important note: The more German the restaurant, the more likely you are to be smoked at. You'll have a hard time finding inexpensive eateries that have sections for nonsmokers, and rustic surroundings seem to encourage people to puff.

Restaurants in Germany are required to display a menu with inclusive prices for passers-by, so you get an idea what's in store before you go in. As a rule, in terms of quantity, you get a lot; Germans are used to big helpings. And in terms of quality, you generally get what you pay for.

Wherever or whatever you end up eating within the low-to-moderate price category, the restaurant culture—as opposed to the food itself—is likely to be German. You'll have to find your own way to a table, since there is rarely a host(ess) to seat you. If the restaurant is crowded, it's alright to ask if you can join people who are already sitting at a table with some space left. Beyond a friendly nod, you're not expected to chat with them during the meal. You'll order from a *Karte*: be sure not to ask for the *Menu*, because this is the word for a set meal of two or three courses. You're expected to order a beverage first while you're studying the Karte and making your food choice. You won't be served a glass of water, and should you want some, it'll come in a bottle and cost extra. Order tap water (*Leitungswasser*) and you'll get a funny look, although German tap water is perfectly okay to drink. And you can order coffee with your meal until you are blue in the face—it won't appear until after the dessert. Moreover, when it does come, it's not a bottomless cup; you pay for every refill.

The waiter or the waitress will bring out the dishes from the kitchen whenever they are ready—so the various people eating together get served at different times. There's no point in complaining—that's just the way it is. Service is often slow and not always friendly. This may be partly because customer-service-with-a-smile is neither expected nor provided in Germany as it (often) is in the United States, and partly because a service charge is always included in the price of each item, so the personnel is not dependent on tips. Nevertheless, you are expected to round off the final figure on the bill to a number with an zero or a five at the end, and in better restaurants, an extra 10 percent is customary. Payment is normally made directly at the table, and in smaller or family-run restaurants, credit cards are very rarely accepted. Even in expensive restaurants, you cannot depend on being able to pay with plastic. (This got me so mad recently—I was in one of Frankfurt's pricier restaurants, paying for a high bill for a dinner for six—that I insisted on being told what would happen if I refused to pay cash. The manager came to the table, and told me to go to a nearby bank and get some. Failing that, he would take my card to the restaurant next door, which does accept plastic, and slap a 10 percent surcharge on my bill—5 percent for his buddy next door, 5 percent for his trouble. So be warned—carry cash.)

RESTAURANT RESTROOMS

I've made this point earlier on: the Germans, direct in most of their behavior, don't go in for euphemisms. A toilet is a toilet, and any attempt to turn it into a restroom or powder room will be met with incomprehension or a smile. Just ask for the *Toilette, bitte*, and you'll be directed to the little girls' or little boys' room. Instead of the female or male silhouette indicating toilet segregation, you'll occasionally see the sign "OO." In families, the word for toilet is often *Klo*, a shortened form of "water closet."

Important note: The Germans borrow the French expression "restaurant" (pronounced res-tow-wrong) as freely as do the Anglo-Saxons. However, they also have a homegrown word, *Gaststätte*, and it is this word that you are likely to find in telephone books and the yellow pages.

SHOPPING 7

Germany produces some 200 kinds of bread, and almost as many sorts of Wurst.

John Ardagh: *Germany and the Germans*

PLENTY OF PRODUCTS . . .

Germany has plenty of shops with plenty of variety. Most items are international in nature, but if you search hard enough in touristy enough locations—the train station or airport, for example—you'll find local products such as cuckoo clocks (which are native to the Black Forest and not, as commonly believed, to Switzerland), beer mugs and other "Germano-phernalia." For the most part, and depending on the exchange rate, Germany is too expensive to be a shopper's paradise, but the quality is generally very good, so clothing items, for example, may be worth the extra.

. . . IN CLOSED SHOPS

Germany is a country in which only tourists and the wealthy unemployed find it easy to go shopping. For people with regular jobs, spending money is frustratingly difficult, because shopping hours are strictly regulated, and shops are not open when working people need them to be: late evenings, Saturday afternoons and Sundays.

The above betrays my position on an issue which has been hotly debated for years, and which the Germans simply can't agree on: whether shopkeepers should be allowed to freely choose their own opening hours, or whether the state should decide when shops must be closed. Current laws allow shops to stay open until 8 P.M. on weekdays and until 4 P.M. on Saturdays. On Sundays, shops are required to remain clam-closed, as they are on all of the many public holidays. This latter part of the law (the shop-closing law, or *Ladenschlussgesetz*) is based on a provision of the Basic Law, which declares Sundays and holidays as work-free days designed to regenerate the soul (or words to that effect). The Christian churches as well as the trade unions are all in favor of a narrow interpretation of the Basic Law, although there are many exceptions to the work-free Sunday rule (see below). As I write this, the debate is once again in full swing, and changes could be in the offing. I am skeptical. Moreover, even if shops were completely free to choose their hours, many would probably choose to be closed as much as possible: outside city centers, for example, smaller establishments open at 9 or 10 A.M., close for a two-hour lunch, close again at 6 P.M., and stay open only until noon on Saturdays. And only in large city centers do shops—some, not all—remain open until 8 P.M.

SHOPPING AFTER HOURS

However, here comes some good news: Those diehard consumers among you can go on limited sprees in the evening (at least until 9 or 10 P.M.) as well as on Sundays and holidays by taking yourselves to a decent-sized gas station, a major train station or airport, where the law allows emergency rations—essentially everything—to be sold. In these shoppers' oases, there are a range of offerings, sometimes fairly basic, sometimes quite exotic. The city of Leipzig has incorporated a large shopping center into its main station, thereby getting around the Ladenschlussgesetz. Convenience has its price, of course, and most items are more expensive than in a regular-hour shop. People like me are willing to pay more just to beat the system. For the rest, some shops do have special opening hours, depending on state laws; flower shops and cake shops may do business for a few hours on Sundays, and newspaper-and-sundry-item kiosks may be open at odd hours throughout the week. In touristy (spa, resort and "convalescent") areas, souvenir shops can usually keep exceptional hours. Some shops (including department stores) in some cities have taken to labeling all items "souvenirs," and remaining open at forbidden times. They then face legal procedures, but the battle continues. Progress in this area, as a recent economics minister said, is a snail.

WHERE TO SHOP

You'll find that most German cities and many larger towns have pedestrian shopping areas right in the city center. These attractively laid-out streets look remarkably similar throughout the country, either because the same architect designed them all (my personal theory) or simply because a lot of the shops lining them are nationwide chain stores, punctuated by Italian ice cream cafés, hamburger and other fast-food joints, flower stands and boutiques (everybody else's theory). At any rate, these pedestrian zones are both reliable and boring in their predictability.

Not all local shopping precincts are pedestrian zones, of course. Shopping streets dot the map of any community and you never need look far for convenience stores for household and hardware, for example, and fresh produce shops for bread and cakes, vegetables and fruit, meat and sausages, milk and cheeses. Some Germans still like to buy their provisions in small quantities daily, rather than in large quantities weekly—partly because they are hooked on the idea of freshness, partly because refrigerators are small boxes compared to the U.S. variety, and partly because there's no place to park in local shopping areas, so purchases have to be lugged home either by hand, or in a cumbersome tote-bag-on-wheels, or in a bicycle basket. And although freezers have become a common household appliance, they are used with discretion; not all Germans like to freeze bread, cakes or fresh vegetables. As a result of these frequent-shopping habits, the Germans are accustomed to buying produce in very small amounts. Cheeses and cold cuts are regularly bought in portions of 100 grams—less than a quarter pound. Bottles are often purchased individually rather than in crates and fruit is often bought by the piece. All in all, getting in household supplies can be a Sisyphean task. But it doesn't have to be. There are almost always large American-style shopping centers on the outskirts of town. These offer parking lots, covered walkways and other such shopper incentives; what you lose in local atmosphere, you gain in convenience. Some German shoppers, unwilling to completely abandon their familiar shopping routine, stock up on non-perishable goods at a shopping mall but still make the daily round of the local fresh produce shops and open markets.

Department stores, concentrated in very few corporate hands, have little specifically German about them. Many have a food market in the basement or on the top floor; more and more of them offer space to boutique chains, so a store may contain a number of franchises. The Bloomingdales of Germany is probably Berlin's KaDeWe, which covers a whole city block. It is perhaps best known for its remarkable food floor, where the shopper can purchase all manner of exotic produce and then linger at one of the many gourmet counters and corners to sample luxury edibles and sip champagne. Increasingly, you'll find fancy delis and snack bars in other department stores, but for sheer quantity and quality, KaDeWe is unbeatable.

Outdoor markets are popular throughout Germany, especially for food and flowers, with a few stalls selling cheap clothes and jewelry. Some of these markets, which can be quite large, are permanent, but most travel and appear in a particular place once or twice a week. In my city, I know exactly where my favorite market is every day of the week. Here again, prices are usually fixed, and they may actually be higher than in the local supermarket, but shoppers have the impression that the produce is fresher (and maybe it is). The disadvantage here is that touching the goods is often limited, and the cherries that looked so good on the stand don't seem to be the ones that end up in your bag. At other outdoor markets you can find arts and crafts, old books and antiques. Occasionally it is appropriate to bargain—play it by ear. Flea markets are permanent or regular institutions in many towns.

PRICING AND PAYING

The price on the label is the end-price—all taxes have already been included. Major credit cards are generally accepted in the larger department stores, but not always, so ask at the information counter before you attempt to spend a fortune; they are often not accepted in boutiques or supermarkets. Germans and other Europeans often pay with the increasingly popular Eurocard, but that's of no help to the visitor who doesn't have an account with a European bank. While I was doing research for this book, I happened to be at the brand new international newspaper and bookstore at the main railway station in Frankfurt. The person in front of me—an American—wanted to pay a sizeable bill with a Visa card. The saleslady told him that cards were not accepted. The man had no other means of payment, left the books on the counter and walked out. When I commented on this lost sale, the saleslady said it happened all the time, that she'd told her bosses, but nobody cared. Sales were apparently high enough . . .

Prices are fixed in Germany, so don't try to bargain except at flea markets or at used car dealerships. Moreover, German laws are strict on the subject of price-slashing. Sales (*Ausverkauf*) can take place only at certain preordained times, for example at the end of the summer and winter seasons—*Sommerschlussverkauf* starts on the last Monday in July and *Winterschlussverkauf* on the last Monday in January, with both sales limited to two weeks. When a shop has officially applied to go out of business, prices can be reduced by carefully supervised degrees. Note: Regulations on discounting and sales are being relaxed, so it may soon become easier to go bargain-hunting. Shops can, of course, have special offers (which sometimes are and sometimes aren't)—look for signs saying *reduziert*, *Sonderangebot* and *Sonderpreis*. Beware of any sign giving a figure after the word *ab* (from), because the word simply indicates the price of the cheapest item, which is never the one you are interested in. Some shops allow you to exchange items or they may give you a *Gutschein* (credit slip), but rarely can you get your money back for something you return.

CUSTOMERS UNWELCOME

I've said this before, and at the (high) risk of making myself unpopular with my German friends, I'll say it again: service in Germany is not always as pleasant as it should be, and it can be downright nasty. This applies particularly to supermarkets and department stores, where the sales personnel often give the impression they are doing the customer a favor. It is not uncommon that a customer has great trouble interrupting the conversation of two salespeople standing around chatting to each other. If you are treated badly, don't assume that you are being discriminated against as a foreigner—Germans are subjected to the same offhand manner. One reason good service is not a high priority is the lack of competition; almost all supermarkets and department stores, whatever name they carry, belong to one of very few mammoth chains which have divvied up the country. So although some customers still complain—most have given up—they continue to shop in the same place. Small, family-run mini-markets (called *Tante Emma Läden*—Aunt Emma shops) tend to be a lot friendlier— but they are correspondingly more expensive.

On the subject of supermarket service, or the lack thereof: for the convenience of the staff, and to remind the customer of his/her place, supermarket shelves are invariably loaded at peak shopping hours, which creates serious traffic jams in the very narrow aisles. It is always the customer who is expected to circumnavigate the obstruction. Traffic jams are also caused by two customers trying to pass each other, since aisles are not always wide enough for two shopping carts, but to be fair, this last has more to do with limited space in Germany than with intentional nastiness. And on the subject of shopping carts: these are usually chained together and can be released only by the insertion of a one-mark coin (refundable). Should you not have one handy, too bad—the check-out personnel will make you wait until a till is opened before grudgingly giving you the necessary change. When you've chosen your purchases and have waited for ages in one of the few open check-out lines, you'll discover that there are no check-out helpers to load your goodies into bags. This is something you have to learn to do yourself as speedily as possible, to avoid being hassled by the people waiting in line behind you. Moreover, there are no free paper sacks, only plastic bags that have to be purchased and are getting more expensive by the day. Supposedly, the idea is not so much to make money, but to encourage customers to bring along their own reusable carriers.

Some supermarkets are paying lip-service to the idea of customer service. My local monopoly has installed a bell for customers to ring when the lines at the only one or two open check-out registers are a mile long, and all the other registers are closed. The bell activates an automatic recording, "Thank you for letting us know that more registers should be opened. We will take care of the matter immediately." Nine times out of ten, nothing happens. I happen to know a lawyer on the board of this particular mammoth chain, and he agrees that service is the least of anybody's priorities. "Our customers have no real choice," he says with a grin, "there's nowhere else for them to go, so service, American-style, simply doesn't pay off."

CUSTOMERS WELCOME

Now a word of comfort. The times they are a-changing. Service is becoming a buzzword, even if many German enterprises are trying to figure out how to implement it without running up short-term costs. Customers are more likely to be treated well in small shops and boutiques, especially if these are run by the owners themselves—finding friendly staff is still one big headache. Some larger organizations are making a valiant effort to be nice(r) to their customers—even that most famously unfriendly of organizations, the German post office. You may have to wait in line for several hours to be served because there is only one open counter, but when your turn finally comes, you may be greeted with a smile. This is progress.

PART FOUR

Totally Miscellaneous Strange German Ways

KNIVES, FORKS AND FLOWERS 1

To Americans good manners are an indication of a good upbringing.
To Germans good manners are a necessity for everyone, regardless of
background or education. Germans realize that you are a foreigner
and do not expect you to know about their customs, but poor manners
will get you off to a bad start, which will be difficult if not impossible
to compensate for at a later time.
Nessa P. Loewenthal: *Update Federal Republic of Germany*

TO THE MANNER BRED

I heartily disagree with most of Nessa Loewenthal's words above—
which is why I have quoted them. I suppose that having good manners means behaving in a socially-approved or acceptable way, and
what is socially approved certainly varies from culture to culture. It
took me quite a while to realize that loud belching was considered
good manners in China—a sign of appreciation of a good meal. But
the assertion that only well-brought-up Americans have good manners, whereas all Germans do, is in my opinion pure nonsense. In
both societies, there are those who follow their prescribed conventions, and others who don't. I do agree that Germans don't expect
foreigners to "do the German thing." The Germans are pretty generous and indulgent, and forgive foreigners most cultural blunders;
even a truly horrendous contravention of German good manners
such as the American habit of eating while keeping one hand under
the table is unlikely to cause life-long enmity. My advice to non-Germans: when in Germany, go along with any unfamiliar ways of your
hosts, and try not to show surprise or amusement when they appear
oddly stiff and formal or just plain odd. Do what the Germans do—
but only if it comes naturally. I was never able to belch at the end of a
meal in China.

SOME SOCIAL NICETIES

Forms of Address: When Germans are introduced or introduce themselves, they shake hands and mutter their surnames. They tend to stick to the use of surnames prefaced by *Herr* or *Frau* (*Fräulein* only for pre-pubescent girls) or any appropriate title such as *Professor* or *Doktor* until their relationship with each other undergoes a quantum leap from acquaintanceship to friendship. This quantum leap may never happen in a lifetime (neighbors and colleagues tend to remain acquaintances), or it may happen fairly fast. When it does happen, the new friends move ceremoniously from surnames to first names, and almost always make a significant linguistic switch from the formal *Sie* (you) address to the informal *Du*. None of this should affect you, a non-German speaking foreigner, because most Germans you will encounter know that you are prone to use first names, and they are usually quite willing to accommodate you. In fact, as long as you are present and you are all communicating in English, the Germans are quite likely to address their fellow German colleagues and acquaintances by their first names, just to make you feel comfortable. The moment you are gone and they resume talking in German, they may revert to formality with each other. Then again, they may not. Young Germans are becoming noticeably less formal with each other, partly, I suspect, because of their constant interaction with the Anglo-Saxon, or at least English-speaking, world. I have observed the virus-like effect of one single English-speaker at a party: by the end of the evening, first names and Du are rampant.

Germans shake hands a lot, not just with strangers, but also with acquaintances, and often both at the beginning and at the end of an encounter. The hand-shaking is often replaced by kissing—or rather cheek-pecking—among opposite-sex friends and women. Male friends will occasionally exchange a short hug.

Some old-fashioned, but not necessarily old, German men have a startling way of greeting women acquaintances: in one flowing movement, they raise the hand proffered for a shake, and gently blow on it. This disconcerting ritual is called a "hand kiss." Only Germans can get away with it, so this is one custom you should not try to imitate.

Chivalry: When men and women walk along the street, men traditionally walk to the left of the woman. This medieval custom—it had to do with drawing swords to protect endangered damsels—belongs to the good-manners code of even the very young, and leads to a lot of side-switching.

Chivalry is not consistent in Germany. Men rarely open the car door for a women, but they do insist on helping women on and off with outer clothing, and they always walk into restaurants in front of the women they are with to clear the way and negotiate a table. That's one custom you should be aware of, since American women often consider men barging ahead to be rude. Men—even the fairly young—often (but not always) leap up to light the cigarettes of women present. This sometimes leads to several offered flames (in all senses) and the female has to make her choice.

Dinners and Parties: Invitations to people's homes are not dispensed lightly, and should be appreciated. Punctuality—which means arriving pretty well on the dot—is important, especially if you've been invited for a meal. There's no such thing as arriving fashionably late in Germany! You should take along a present such as a bottle of something alcoholic, chocolate or flowers. Apropos of flowers: the German way of presenting them is complicated. If the bouquet is wrapped in ordinary (as opposed to cellophane) paper, the paper must be removed on the doorstep, bundled into one hand, while the flowers are thrust at the hostess with the other. The savvy hostess will smile, and unobtrusively reach out for the balled paper as she takes the flowers. Never give an even number of any one type of flower (I have no idea why, that's just the way it is!). Red roses are an indication of love, white chrysanthemums are appropriate only at funerals. Anything else goes.

If your hosts are board-level/top management business acquaintances of the Old Economy sort, be prepared for considerably more formality than you would expect at home. It is quite common not to be invited to sit down for a cocktail before dinner, but to remain standing, glass of sparkling wine in hand, until all of the guest have arrived and been introduced to each other. Then everybody troops in for dinner—or rather, enters the dining room in an orderly manner and looks for his/her name-card at the table. The women can sit immediately, the men stand around until all the women are seated. This may all sound as stiff as the starched table cloths and napkins, but it has a lot of old-world charm that I personally have come to enjoy—admittedly though, it took a bit of getting used to.

The way Germans entertain varies a great deal, of course. At parties, people very often end up standing or sitting in awkward constellations from which there is little or no escape. Conversation can remain polite, superficial and sporadic. Silences often seem endless to those who perceive them as vacuums (most Germans apparently don't). Food is passed around the table accompanied by a chant of

Bitte sehr (the equivalent of here you are) and *Danke schön* (thanks) and the visitor often starts surreptitiously glancing at his/her watch before dessert. However, as I said above—this is not the way it always is or has to be. The degrees of formality have to do with age, occupation, position in the hierarchy, social class—let nobody tell you that Germany is a classless society—and a slew of other factors. I've been to countless completely laid-back gatherings and parties, even where the hosts and guests were neither particularly young nor particularly well acquainted with each other.

After being guests at someone's home, or after being entertained at someone else's expense, Germans express their thanks either with a phone call, fax or e-mail, or if they are more traditional, with a handwritten letter. You should remember to do the same.

Eating Etiquette: Germans tend to wait until everyone has been served before they start to eat, unless the hostess insists that the guests begin "while the food is still hot." The host will raise his glass and propose a toast (with or without accompanying clinking of glasses) to signal that it's okay to drink. The rules are slightly different in average, as opposed to fancy, restaurants, where the dishes are served as soon as they are prepared in the kitchen, so people eating together often get their food at different times. Then, the person who is served first is usually urged to start immediately.

Coffee is served after a meal, not with it. Milk with a meal is almost unheard of and few restaurants can rustle up fresh milk.

Water is not served automatically in restaurants (see p. 201). Ice water is completely unheard of.

An odd number, unwrapped ...

Germans often order water, but expect the bottled kind, which is often almost as expensive as the wine or the beer. There's a law which prevents it from being more expensive: the lowest priced beverage on the menu has to be non-alcoholic. Thus, mineral water is likely to cost the equivalent of, say, $2 and beer $2.10. Go figure. Germans are accustomed to sharing their table with strangers in non-fancy restaurants. However, other than saying hello and goodbye (*Guten Tag* and *Auf Wiedersehen*), they rarely talk to each other.

Wielding Cutlery: Germans, like other Europeans, tackle their food with a knife in one hand, a fork in the other, and don't play the American game of switching utensils every few minutes. If you don't know what I'm talking about, observe how Americans cut their food, lay down their knives, take up their fork in the hand that previously held the knife, eat with their fork while their other hand is presumably in their lap, then start all over again to cut up the next bit of food. In Germany, both hands—from the wrist up—must be visible above the table at all times. If a hand vanishes, it must be up to no good. Germans indicate that they are finished eating by putting their knives and forks together and laying them on the diagonal from 4-10 o'clock across their plate.

Compliments: Compliments are just as appreciated in Germany as they are in the United States, but the response is somewhat different. Instead of simply saying "thank you," the German is likely to downplay any praise. "What a delightful home you have," says the guest. "Thanks, but it really needs a lot done to it," replies the host. The guest perseveres. "But it's lovely just the way it is." "Do you really think so?" counters the host. And so on. Similarly, when a woman is complimented on something she is wearing, she almost inevitably points out how old or unfashionable it is, even when this is clearly not the case.

Germans don't gush. Gushing, or over-complimenting, is considered a superficial, insincere American habit.

Birthdays: These can turn out to be expensive for the birthday-person, who is expected to pay for birthday festivities. So if you invite friends out for a meal or afternoon coffee or a lunch or dinner, be prepared: the bill is yours. The giving of presents is much the same as in the United States. You must never ever ever wish somebody Happy Birthday in advance—that guarantees a German birthday person bad luck!

DIGITS AND DATES

Numbers: The Germans have a very confusing way of writing numbers—confusing, that is, for Anglo-Saxons. They put the dots and commas in odd places. They don't have decimal points, they have decimal commas; and to separate thousands they use dots. So the number five million five hundred and fifty five thousand five hundred and five point five is written as follows: 5.555.505,5 One and a quarter is written: 1,25. Fair enough, you might say. But the strange thing is that calculators used in Germany and throughout the world are all based on the Anglo-Saxon decimal dot principle. So everyone is confused.

More confusion. A million is a *Million*, but an American billion is a German *Milliarde*, whereas a German *Billion* is an American trillion.

The Metric System: Here again, the Germans and the rest of the world stubbornly insist on being different from the small but vociferous users of miles, yards and gallons. Germany is a land of meters, liters and grams, all calculated in multiples and divisions of tens, hundreds and thousands . . . and so on. We can end up with some pretty big and pretty small numbers. It's useful to memorize some of the more frequent measurements:

- A kilometer is roughly 0.6 miles, and an easy way to move from kilometers to miles is to divide by eight and multiply by five. Hence, 16 km is 10 miles. To go from miles to kilometers, divide by five and multiply by eight.
- A meter is 3.28 feet—close enough to a yard.
- A liter is roughly one-quarter of a gallon.
- A kilogram is 2.2 pounds.

Dates (the Calendar Kind): The Germans (and all other Europeans, including the Brits) start with the day, proceed to the month and end with the year; hence, the fifth of February 1993 is written 5.2.93. American officialdom has finally recognized that the month-day-year way of writing dates is peculiar to America, and it now requests that dates be written the rest-of-the-world-way on its immigration forms.

A Different Story: It's easy to end up in the wrong place when you're looking for a floor in a building, since the Germans (and all other Europeans) and Americans count stories differently. What for the Germans is the *Erdgeschoss or Parterre* (ground floor) is already the first floor in Americanese. From there on up, the two systems don't jibe; the *1. Etage* (or 1. Stock) is the second floor, and so on. Only the basement (*Keller*) and attic (*Dachboden*) are the same.

RECREATION 2

By the year 2000, Germans will be able to enjoy more than 2,800 hours of leisure time per year on average, 161 hours more than in 1991 and 876 hours more than 20 years ago.

Facts About Germany,
Federal Press and Information Service, 1996 Edition

WORKING AT PLAY

The Germans work very hard when they work, but compared to the populations of the rest of the western industrialized world, they don't work all that much—statistically, considerably less than anyone else (see p. 138). As a result, they have a lot of free time to organize during the year. This, of course, is a great responsibility and can even be considered as work in itself, since most Germans take the disposal of their leisure time very seriously and plan accordingly. There are basically three types of leisure periods: long ones, such as the five to seven weeks of paid vacation that all employees are entitled to each year; shorter ones, such as the long weekends built around a legal holiday; and, of course, the regular ones—evenings and normal weekends.

SCHOOL AND OTHER VACATIONS

For families with school-aged children, as well as for people in professions which are dependent on such families—teachers, doctors, many tradespeople—long leisure periods usually coincide with school holidays, which are staggered from *Land* to *Land* to avoid too much holiday congestion. Some Länder—Bavaria, for example—always schedule their six-week summer breaks in August and September, whereas other Länder have already packed up by the end of June. This means that if you or your kids have friends in another Land, you may never be able to go on vacation together. It also means that the

German summer vacation season, when business Germany hangs out a "Closed for the Duration" sign, stretches from mid-June to mid-September.

Summer time is going-away time, and the Germans are champion vacation-takers. They travel all over the place, within and without their own country, mostly to places with beaches, because most Germans are dedicated sun-worshippers. They don't necessarily spend the entire six weeks of the school break away from home, but obeying some mysterious lemming-like compulsion, they almost invariably take off for somewhere the moment that the school break begins, and return from somewhere on or during the night before school resumes. These mass population movements lead to predictable traffic chaos, which everybody complains about, but must, I figure, secretly enjoy. In fact, sitting in horrendous traffic jams for swelteringly hot days on end, or suffering interminable delays at overcrowded airports seems to be part and parcel of the vacation ritual.

Once on vacation, many Germans behave completely uncharacteristically. They abandon their usual predilection for privacy and space, and seek out the most jam-packed tourist areas they can find. The crowded bazaar atmosphere, the exuberant bustling, jostling, pushing and shoving that they so carefully avoid during the rest of the year turns out to be a desirable holiday feature. Which maybe all goes to show that people occasionally need to take time off from themselves.

Hardly is the summer vacation season over than the fall break season begins. Fall breaks are short school vacations of about a week which are also nationally staggered, so from the beginning of October to the beginning of November, you can count on some people, somewhere being on the go. This mid-term respite conveniently bridges the gap until . . .

. . . the start of the winter vacation season, which stretches from Christmas until Easter. Not that kids are home the entire time: school lets out a day or two before Christmas Eve and stays out for two to three weeks. This gives families the opportunity to dash off skiing, although it is not the best time of the year for domestic snow (Germany itself had only 17 significantly white Christmases in the 20th century, giving lie to a good many myths) and snow is not even guaranteed in neighboring Swiss, Austrian or Italian resorts. So those without children generally prefer to enjoy winter sports in February or March. Which brings us mercifully close to Easter, when kids get a two-week (or so) school break, and another mass exodus takes place.

Yet another one follows at Pentecost, when children have a one-day to two-week vacation depending on the particular Land. And scarcely has the last Land recalled its children to school after the Pentecost break when the first Land on the summer rotation schedule closes its doors for the long vacation—and the beat goes on.

One of the most agreeable aspects of German vacation habits is enjoyed by the non-vacationers. These fortunate few get to spread themselves out in their empty hometowns. Streets are pleasantly navigable, not just because there are practically no people around, there are also fewer cars, either cluttering the roads or parked on the sidewalks. There are no lines in shops—those few that have remained open—and shopping carts abound in supermarkets. Fortunately, the dedicated vacationers never get to discover how great things are at home in their absence, so these blissfully quiet periods are not endangered.

Postscript: In case you are still concerned that the Germans might not have enough time off, be reassured: there are around 15 legal holidays, secular or religious, dotted throughout the calendar. Not every Land enjoys all 15, but Bavaria has about 12 and Hesse has 11. These legal holidays can fall on any day of the week, and are not moved to the next convenient Monday as they are in the United States. If they happen to fall on a Monday or Friday, the weekend is conveniently long. If they fall on a Tuesday or Thursday, the weekend is often even longer: either a precious vacation day is sacrificed, or a mysterious illness becomes temporarily incapacitating. When a legal holiday falls on a Wednesday, a serious decision is called for.

SPORTS . . .

Germans love sports of all kinds, and they participate eagerly, either actively or passively. Since the country is so small and densely populated—don't forget, the 82 million residents live in an area roughly the size of Montana—there is relatively little space for "elite" sports the likes of golf or tennis, especially in urban areas. Golf and tennis players almost always have to belong to expensive private clubs, and even then, because of the high demand for courses and courts, they have to arrange their games well in advance. One way or another, "elite" sport enthusiasts are often forced to enjoy their passion vicariously on television. In recent times, the tennis-watching rage has affected the most unexpected public, and little old grannies sit glued to the TV screen for hours on end, shouting support for their chosen favorites.

But while Germans are tennis fans, they are football—the un-padded soccer variety—fanatics. No one single U.S. game can compete in popularity—you'd have to roll baseball, football, volleyball and ice-hockey together to come close. Football fever attacks the male more than the female population. Young and old, from the butcher and baker to the egghead and surgeon— few are immune to the excitement of the matches played among the *Fussball-Bundesliga* (Federal Soccer League), the German first division of the best 18 teams. During the football season—practically all year round but particularly from February through June, and from August through November—it is inadvisable to so much as phone a German fan on Saturdays between 6 p.m. and 8 p.m., for example, when the highlights of all the day's matches are shown. It used to be that public TV could broadcast Bundesliga games live; these days, viewers have to pay a private (pay) TV company if they want to watch the live action. The private company concerned is now planning to show all of the Bundesliga games live on different channels on Saturday afternoons, so it's likely that sports bars will become wildly popular. Public TV still has the right to transmit the European and World Cup games.

Note: German universities don't have sports teams in the way American colleges and universities do. This is perhaps one reason (among many) why German universities inspire less loyalty among their students and staff than do their counterparts in North America. (See section on Schools, p. 141)

Other German leisure activities of the physical sort include various forms of gymnastics, often organized by *Turn- und Sportvereine* (sports clubs), where healthy exercise is combined with social intercourse. Handball and volleyball are popular, as are swimming, jogging and hiking (*wandern*; now you can figure out where wanderlust comes from). The latter is particularly favored by senior citizens, who deck themselves out in leggings, long socks and sturdy boots and demonstrate amazing stamina. A really social (organized) hike of up to 42 kilometers or about 25 miles is called a *Volksmarsch*, and attracts large numbers of ambitious walkers who may receive an award (pin, certificate or medal) for their exertions. But such marathons are not for everybody. Many weaker-legged but strong-backed citizens prefer the German variation of nine-pin bowling (*Kegeln*).

. . . AND OTHER AMUSEMENTS

Germans play bridge, poker and rummy, just like everybody else. But their passion is *Skat*, a three-player, 32-card game which is not so much a hobby as an institution. Germans of all ilks, all professions, all walks of life get involved—often on a regular basis, often in clubs—in ordinary games, competitions and tournaments. Skat is fascinating, incredibly complicated (for the uninitiated) and incredibly fast. It can make even the bystanders nervous. I've seen fights break out over Skat among complete strangers in train cars.

THE ALMIGHTY BOX

When they are not watching football, stomping through the countryside or playing Skat, the Germans are often to be found relaxing in front of the idiot box. Since most of the rest of the civilized and uncivilized world does much the same, this is only interesting insofar as German television offers a pretty decent selection of capital "C" Culture in addition to all of the international sex-and-violence programs available throughout most of the country via cable and satellite. Germany has a number of "public" channels which, despite fierce competition from the commercial channels, have more freedom to occupy prime-time with lengthy news and commentary programs and documentaries. Film reruns and variety shows are quite generously interspersed with classical theater, music and satirical cabaret. But heading the list of serious programs are undoubtedly the ubiqui-

American Football—Here Today, Gone Tomorrow?

American football (football? As I understand it, only one guy is allowed to touch the ball with his foot) used to be almost unknown in Europe until the NFL—National Football League for the football illiterate—decided to use Europe as a summer training camp and bought up the existing World Football League, renaming it the NFL Europe. And although the game hasn't exactly been able to compete in popularity with European soccer, it's caught on nicely. Nowhere more so than in Frankfurt, home of Frankfurt Galaxy, winner of two World Bowl—the NFL's European Super Bowl—titles, where home games attract around 35,000 fans and are veritable happenings, complete with pre- and post-game parties, the most imaginative noisemakers ever, and Galaxy's very own cheerleaders. Minor league perhaps as far as American football goes, but major league fun. Well, the fun may be coming to an end. Word is that the NFL is thinking of establishing a new summer league in the United States and the future of American football in Europe is looking dim. Players will no longer have any reason to spend the summer in Europe. Galaxy fans are devastated.

tous talk shows. How the Germans love to talk! Only rarely, however, do they listen. The result, as far as talk shows go, is often a lively exchange of overlapping and non-related monologues or sermons. If the British are a nation of shopkeepers, the Germans are a nation of schoolteachers.

Of the public radio and TV networks, the two largest are ARD (First Program) and ZDF (Second Program) which are "cooperative rivals." Both ARD and ZDF have cultural offshoots and ARD is also in charge of regional stations, the so-called Third Programs. These networks are not directly government controlled, but run by public corporations supervised by boards (*Rundfunkräte*) made up of upstanding members of the community. The stations are financed partly through advertising, which is allowed only at certain times, never during the course of a program and never on Sunday, partly through sponsoring, but primarily through the monthly fee that every radio or TV owner in the country has to pay. It is up to the owners to register as such by filling in forms available at all banks; it would appear that most do. Occasional spot-checks exert a certain pressure . . .

A serious case of football fever

CULTURE

Capital "C" Culture is not everybody's cup of tea (or beer, as the Germans would say), but indirectly, every (tax-paying) body pays for it, since the promotion and development of culture is guaranteed by the constitution and heavily subsidized by federal, state and local government. As a result, Germany is very rich in cultural institutions, spread out throughout the country. Almost all of the major cities boast an opera house and many have their own symphony orchestra and ballet; most towns of any size at all have a selection of theaters, concert houses, museums and libraries. When times are good and public coffers are relatively full—this has not been the case in recent memory—the system works quite well, although the less highbrow are occasionally heard to complain about having their taxes pay for entertainment and exhibitions they neither enjoy nor frequent, and which could well be afforded by those who do both. When times are not so good and public coffers are not overflowing with distributable bounty, Culture is one of the first to feel the effect. Sponsoring, not long ago still considered as undesirable because of the influence sponsors might have on true Art, is now avidly sought after by cultural institutions.

SOCIAL LIFE

German social life takes on many different forms. Friends visit each other, go together to restaurants, shows, concerts, the theater. Younger Germans are great partyers, and parties, which are always open-ended, tend to continue into the wee, small hours. Germans are generally able to talk all night, regardless of—or perhaps enlivened by—the quantity of alcohol consumed.

Many Germans get together regularly—once a week or so—in their local watering-and-feeding hole, a pub or *Kneipe* which be-comes their *Stammlokal*, or favorite hangout. There, a table (often round) is re-served for the regulars with a notice which says *Stammtisch*, meaning a table reserved for their use. Knowing that a hard core of friends are always to be found at the Stammtisch at a certain time, the less faithful come and go. And the talk goes on and on, until closing time.

Social club life in

Clubs for everyone

Germany plays a major role in the lives of many Germans, and this is not too surprising, since the Germans are such good organizers. Still, the sheer number and diversity of the clubs (*Vereine*—see *Sports* above) can astound—there are clubs for just about everything. There are political clubs and religious clubs, clubs for business people and clubs for the housebound, clubs for employers and clubs for employees. Some clubs are organized around different occupations and trades, others around activities such as shooting, card-playing or bowling. There are clubs for book lovers and clubs for animal lovers, clubs for hikers and clubs for singers, clubs for singles and clubs for couples, clubs for the young and others for the old. The list is endless. Not all clubs are primarily social; many clubs are action groups or interest groups (lobbies), or protection groups, for example. But for many Germans, especially those over 45, social life revolves around a club (or two, or three or four) and the regular meetings or functions figure large on the calendar.

HUMOR

There are people who have a sense of humor and people who don't. Like all other nations, Germany has its share of both kinds. But since humor is an aspect of culture, it's not always understandable to foreigners—not even to foreigners who speak the language quite well. German humor is not as understated as the British, not as kidding and exaggerated as the American, not as graphic as the French. It tends towards the obvious. Let's say it has an elusive (not to be confused with light) quality, packaged in seriousness.

Peter Ustinov, the British humorist with German roots, likes to relate the following anecdote: At a Unicef gala given in Berlin on the occasion of his 75th birthday, he went up to Roman Herzog, then president of Germany, and thanked him for laughing so much at the speech that he, Ustinov, had just given. Roman Herzog replied, "Yes, as a matter of fact I really enjoy a good laugh. Of course, it always helps if there's something to laugh about." The English, says Ustinov, cannot figure out what's so funny about that story—the Germans, on the other hand, find it hilarious.

Funny?

TRADITIONS 3

In almost all societies that enforce severe restrictions upon eating and drinking and sexuality, "valve customs" develop along with the restrictions. These are occasions to "live it up," to satisfy bodily desires and thus restore a psychological balance among the population.
Dieter Kramer: *German Holidays And Folk Customs*

LETTING OFF STEAM

I've thrown in the quote above because I find it funny. The Germans may impose a lot of restrictions on themselves, but not noticeably when it comes to eating, drinking or sexuality. Be that as it may: The Germans are a tradition-minded folk who faithfully perpetuate a lot of customs handed down over generations. Since Germany is made up of so many regions that were once autonomous, a lot of the customs are purely local, while others are local variations of more widespread traditions. Some festivals have become internationally famous and are high on the list of tourist attractions – the Munich *Oktoberfest*, for example; others are simple village affairs. There are customs to celebrate milestones such as getting married and there are customs to bring good, or prevent bad, luck. Some customs involve the entire population (more or less), others just one individual. Indeed, there's probably not a German around who isn't caught up in some traditional practice or another, even if (s)he isn't aware of it.

With few, usually religious, exceptions, most traditional occasions, whether they are family feasts or gigantic folk festivals, include the consumption of huge amounts of alcohol. The Germans, normally so private and reserved in the earnest pursuit of their business, consider festive occasions the ideal excuse to let down their hair—and when they do, they go all the way. As in the case of mass-tourist vacations, it would seem that some Germans need to take periodic breaks from their otherwise sober selves.

THE BIGGEST ANNUAL BASH—
KARNEVAL OR *FASCHING*

Karneval, otherwise known down south as *Fasching*, is a major event in Catholic parts of the country, particularly in the Rhineland and throughout southern Germany. The festival season officially gets going at 11 minutes past 11 A.M. on the 11th day of the 11th month of the year (when nothing much happens), gathers momentum during the January doldrums and builds up to a frenzied crescendo of costume balls, parties and parades on the days immediately preceding Ash Wednesday and the start of Lent. The unsuspecting visitor who finds himself in Cologne, Mainz or Munich—the unrivaled carnival centers—during Shrovetide is in for a big surprise. The entire city (so it seems) is out in the streets in various degrees of fancy dress, dancing, swaying arm in arm, making a tremendous din, and generally playing the Fool—which is what Karneval is all about.

There is great method and planning to this carnival madness. In all three major cities, and in countless smaller communities, industrious citizens gather together in special societies or guilds and spend months organizing the Karneval events. These date all the way back to pre-Christian times and were originally designed to exorcise evil spirits. Later, the Catholic church considered the festivities a healthy way of getting rid of excess energy before Lent, and the customs prevailed. The societies hold *Sitzungen* (literally, meetings), at which no conventional business but much drinking, prescribed foolery and merriment dominate the agenda. In the more famous Sitzungen, notably the televised ones in Mainz, national figures have no compunction about dressing up and making clowns of themselves. Although each city and region has its own Karneval customs and traditions, most celebrations are presided over by a carnival "Prince," temporarily invested with the sovereignty of the city. There is usually an accompanying Princess; in Cologne, the Prince is joined by a Peasant and a Virgin. The latter is a man, since women were originally excluded from the Karneval festivities. As a reminder of the one day that women were admitted, women now reign over all Rhineland cites, including Bonn, on the Thursday before Ash Wednesday. The day is called *Weiberfastnacht* (*Weiber* meaning something like wench, although it comes from an old German word for woman or wife), and women have the dubious "right" to go around cutting off the ties of any males they can get hold of.

Oktoberfest — September madness

A highlight of the carnival events is the *Karneval Sonntag* or *Rosenmontag* (Shrove Sunday or Monday) parade of elaborate floats (often politically-inspired, particularly in Mainz), accompanied by masked jesters, bands of Fools, musicians, traditionally-costumed revelers and odd-assorted decorated vehicles. These long and loud processions, which can stretch for miles, move slowly through the streets, cheered on by thick crowds of spectators who grab for the candies thrown at them by the float-riders.

Karneval is not primarily a festival for children, but children are not left out either. During the whole of the last week, kids run around in fancy dress and have their own parties, some of them elaborate affairs organized by the community. On Shrove Monday and Tuesday, schools often close down earlier than usual and on Ash Wednesday, start later. And adults in automobiles are advised to carry some spare cash with them in case they are held up by vampires and cowboys at red lights and asked to pay a Karneval duty.

Abruptly at midnight on Shrove Tuesday, the festivities come to an end. Like Cinderella, the Germans shed their fancy clothes and don their normal habits, internal as well as external. Crazy-time is over until the next festival rolls around.

THE BEER BASH BONANZA—*OKTOBERFEST*

About six months after Fasching, the people of Munich have another excuse to cast aside their inhibitions and have a ball. This particular 16-day festival takes place in gigantic canvas beer tents erected on a meadow called the *Theresienwiese*; the time is late September and the festivities are called—surprise!—the *Oktoberfest*. There are a number of customs associated with this happening, which dates back to a royal marriage in the early 19th century. The most colorful event of the Oktoberfest is the *Trachtenfest* parade of thousands of people in local costume, with bands, floats and decorated beer wagons drawn by the brewery horses. But more dramatic than the organized events (at least in my opinion) is the sheer quantity of sausages and beer consumed to the beat of oom-pah-pah music by a vast, swaying sea of glazed-eyed participants. The noise is deafening, the beer fumes overwhelming, and hangovers are a thing of the morrow.

EPILOGUE:
THESE STRANGE AMERICAN WAYS

Back in 1990, a few months after the communist regime in East Germany had collapsed but before the unification of the two Germanys later that year in October, the Atlantik-Brücke, publisher of this book, set up a foundation in conjunction with the established exchange program, Youth for Understanding, to make it financially possible for 35 East German high school kids to spend a year in the United States. This was a revolutionary first, because East Germans had never before been allowed to participate in an 11th grade student exchange in the Wicked Capitalist West. It was also a curious last, because the following year, East Germany ceased to exist. By the time the 1990 group returned to Europe in the summer of 1991, their country had been absorbed into the Federal Republic of Germany. And while students from the eastern part of what is now united Germany have continued to participate in exchange programs ever since—and the Atlantik-Brücke Foundation continues to provide annual support—the 1990 pioneers remain special because they alone were raised exclusively in a communist culture and, when they embarked on their foreign adventure, had no first-hand familiarity with the West.

So off they went, those few fortunate East German award recipients. For a whole year, they lived with American host families, most of them in small communities in the Midwest and the Bible Belt. They learned English fast. They all went to school and many went to church, they were exposed to baseball, basketball and American football, as well as to proms, fast food and drive-ins. They dated and fêted and even lived through that peculiar phenomenon, "America At War Abroad"—in this particular case, the Gulf War. Inevitably, they formed their ideas about the American people, American culture and the "American Way of Life." When they returned, the Atlantik-

Brücke wanted to know what those ideas were, so the students were asked to incorporate them, along with their impressions, anecdotes and opinions, in an essay. The ten best essays were awarded prizes, and provided the material for a book, *Ten Went West—East German Students between Three Worlds.* Jim Neuger, a young American journalist, and I were responsible for putting the book together, and during the process, we spent some fascinating time interviewing the returnees.

Talk about unexpected opinions! America, land of the free? No way, said our East German friends. Americans, in their unanimous opinion, were free only if they conformed. That is, if they led "normal" heterosexual lives in "normal" nuclear families, went to church regularly, supported the community, including the local sports teams, approved of U.S. intervention abroad, rooted for "our fighting boys," and demonstrated true patriotic spirit at all times. Freedom to be different—homosexual, an unmarried parent, an atheist, a pacifist, a nudist—was not acceptable. Simply expressing solidarity with such so-called deviant behavior—most of it all perfectly acceptable behavior in East Germany—was considered not just weird but outright antisocial, and all of the students ran into trouble at some time or another for their dissenting opinions. Even their habit of closing their bedroom doors was considered bad form: what could they be doing behind closed doors? True, they were not thrown into jail or blacklisted; nevertheless, the young East Germans found it hard to understand why westerners were so critical of the former communist regimes. Admittedly, where they came from, there had been no freedom of speech when it came to politics and no freedom to travel beyond prescribed boundaries, but in other respects, they thought that communist society had been more open to and tolerant of the individual and his or her personal foibles. They saw little difference between communist and capitalist indoctrination—both systems were smug and self-righteous, convinced of their own superiority, and determined that everybody else they had dealings with should accept their values and beliefs as the only "true and correct" ones. They found the American "love us or leave us" attitude narrow-minded, American materialism overwhelming and detrimental to other more spiritual values, and the term "god-fearing" all too often synonymous with "bigoted."

They also found the Americans to be warm, friendly, generous and generally thoroughly decent people, despite what they perceived as their provincialism, prudishness, sexism and intolerance. They all wanted to return to the United States one day—to visit, but not necessarily to live there.

We—Jim and I—pointed out that their experiences may not have been "typical," that "Small Town USA" in no way resembled "Big City USA," and that in New York, Boston, Chicago, Los Angeles or San Francisco they would have found all the freedom and tolerance they missed. Or so we figured. After a while, we weren't so sure. The more we tried to pin down the notions, the more they eluded us. In other words, it took a group of East Germans to get us to question a lot of Strange American Ways that we hadn't given much thought to before.

A last note on Strange American Ways: the American humorist, Bill Bryson, spent twenty-plus years in England with his British wife. While there, he wrote marvelous books, such as *Notes From a Small Island*. After he returned to the United States in the mid-1990s, he wrote a regular column for a British newspaper on the strange ways of the Americans—strange, because after living abroad for so long, albeit in another Anglo-Saxon country, he found more or less everything he encountered in his homeland to be hilariously—well, "American." His columns, collected in such books as *Notes From a Big Country* and *I'm a Stranger Here Myself*, are not just stomach-clutchingly funny, they show just how relative "ways" are. In one column, for example, his anecdotes point out to what extent the Americans (as opposed to the Brits) are sticklers for rules, which they follow almost religiously no matter what. And I've been telling you in this book that that's what the Germans (as opposed to the Americans) do! In another, he talks about how "Americans these days find the most extraordinary things to worry about." Worry? The Americans? Hmm. Strange ways? They're all in the eye of the beholder.

REFERENCES AND FURTHER READINGS

Abdullah, Muhammad. *Was will der Islam in Deutschland?* Gütersloh, Germany: Gütersloher Verlagshaus Gerd Mohn, 1993.

Ardagh, John. *Germany and the Germans.* 3rd ed. Harmondsworth, England: Penguin Books, 1999.

Behal-Thomsen, Heinke and Lunquist-Mog, Angelika; Mog, Paul.(ed.) *Typisch deutsch? Arbeitsbuch zu Aspekten deutscher Mentalität.* Berlin: Langenscheidt, 1993.

Bissinger, Manfred; Kuhnt, Dietmar; Schweer, Dieter.(ed.) *Konsensus oder Konflikt? Wie Deutschland regiert werden soll.* Hamburg: Hoffmann und Campe Verlag. 1999.

Brown, Karen. *German Country Inns and Castles.* London: Harrap Columbus, 1987

Bryson, Bill. *Notes From A Big Country.* London: Transworld Publishers, 1999.

Craig, Gordon A. *The Germans.* Harmondsworth, England: Penguin Books, 1987.

Dahrendorf, Ralph. "Die Gefahr kommt aus der Mitte." Interview in *Wirtschaftswoche* No. 13, 20 March 1997.

Friedman, Thomas L. *The Lexus and the Olive Tree.* New York: Anchor Books, 2000.

Glouchevitch, Philip. *Juggernaut: The German Way of Business.* New York: Simon & Schuster, 1992.

Hall, Edward T.; Hall, Mildred Reed. *Understanding Cultural Differences.* Yarmouth, Maine: Intercultural Press, 1990.

Head, David. *Made in Germany: The Corporate Identity of a Nation.* London: Hodder & Stoughton, 1992.

Hill, Richard. *WeEuropeans.* Brussels: Europublications, 1997.

Hill, Richard. *EuroManagers & Martians: The Business Cultures of Europe's Trading Nations.* Brussels: Europublications, 1994.

Hofstede, Geert. *Cultures and Organizations: Software of the Mind.* London: McGraw-Hill International, 1991.

Joffe, Josef. "*Germany vs. The Scientologists*" in The New York Review, April 24, 1997.

Just, Dieter and Stern, Susan. *Steps on the Way to Modern Citizenship.* Bonn: I.N. Press, 1999.

Kalb, Rosalind; Welch, Penelope. *Moving Your Family Overseas.* Yarmouth, Maine: Intercultural Press, 1992.

Kempe, Frederick. *Father/Land: A Personal Search for the New Germany.* New York: G.P. Putnam's Sons, 1999.

Kielinger, Thomas. *Crossroads and Roundabouts: Junctions in German-British Relations.* Bonn: Bouvier Verlag, 1996.

Kramer, Dieter. *German Holidays and Folk Customs.* Bonn: Atlantik-Brücke, 1986.

Larson, Bob. *Getting along with the Germans*. Munich: Bechtle Verlag, 1983.

Lawrence, Peter A. *Managers and Management in West Germany*. New York: St. Martin's Press, 1980.

Lewis, Richard D. *When Cultures Collide: Managing Successfully Across Cultures*. London: Nicholas Brealey Publishing, 2000.

Lord, Richard. *Culture Shock Germany: A Guide to Customs and Etiquette*. Portland, OR: Graphic Arts Center Publishing, 1996.

Loewenthal, Nessa P. *Update Federal Republic of Germany*. Yarmouth, Maine: Intercultural Press, 1990.

Männle, Ursula. *"Frauen in der Politik—Strategie für eine bessere Zukünft?"* in Civis mit Sonde, Sinus Verlag, 3-4/95.

Marsh, David. *The Germans: Rich, Bothered and Divided*. London: Century Hutchison, 1989.

Mog, Paul. *Die Deutschen in ihrer Welt*. Berlin: Langenscheidt, 1992.

Mole, John. *Mind Your Manners*. London: Nicholas Brealey Publishing, 1995.

Nees, Greg. *Germany: Unraveling an Enigma*. Yarmouth, Maine: Intercultural Press, 2000.

Nietzsche, Friedrich (trans. Kaufmann, Walter). *Beyond Good & Evil: Prelude to a Philosophy of the Future*. New York: Random House, 1966.

Press and Information Office of the Federal Government. *Facts about Germany*. Frankfurt/Main: Societäts Verlag, 1999.

Seidel, Wolfgang. *Die Schwaben Pauschal*. Frankfurt/Main:Fischer Taschenbuch Verlag, 1999.

Smith, Gordon; Paterson, William; Padgett, Stephen. (ed.) *Developments in German Politics 2*. London: Macmillan Press, 1996

Stern, Susan. *Germany in Election Year 1998: One Foreigner's View*. Cherry Hill, New Jersey: American Association of Teachers of German, 1998.

Stern, Susan (ed.). *Meet United Germany*. Frankfurt/Main: Frankfurter Allgemeine Zeitung, 1992.

Stern, Susan (ed.). *Speaking Out: Jewish Voices From United Germany*. Chicago: edition q, 1995.

Stern, Susan and Neuger, James G. *Ten Went West*. Bonn: Atlantik-Brücke, 1992.

Stern, Susan. *The Financing of Culture in Germany*. Bonn: I.N. Press, 1995.

Stern, Susan. *Jews in Germany Today: 1995 and 1997*. Bonn: I.N. Press, 1997.

Stern, Susan. *The Social Integration of the Handicapped in Germany*. Bonn: I.N. Press 1996.

Stern, Susan. *Religions in Germany Today*. Bonn: I.N. Press, 1998.

Stern, Susan. *Working Women in Contemporary German Society*. Bonn: I.N. Press, 1997.

Steiner, Susan (ed.). *Federal Republic of Germany: Questions and Answers*. New York: German Information Center, 1996.

Wagner, Wolf. *Kulturschock Deutschland*. Hamburg: Rotbuch Verlag, 1996.

Watson, Alan. *The Germans: who are they now?* London: Thames Metheun, 1992.

Wünsch, Ulrich. *Die Rheinländer Pauschal*. Frankfurt/Main: Fischer Taschenbuch Verlag, 1999.

Zeidenitz, Stefan and Barkow, Ben. *The Xenophobe's Guide to the Germans*. West Sussex, England: Ravette Publishing, 1998.

The Author: Susan Stern is a British-born, U.S.-educated, decades-long resident of Frankfurt am Main. She teaches at the University of Frankfurt, although this may no longer remain the case if any of her colleagues read this book. Her field of expertise, for want of a better expression, is modern Germany; she imparts her very personal and sometimes irreverant wisdom through publications and lectures, and aims ("heaven knows why," she admits) to make the Germans understandable to others. She is sometimes the despair of the German government—the Press and Information Office, for instance—because she has trouble recognizing, or at least accepting, correct procedures. She occasionally takes outrageous advantage of being Jewish by saying things that non-Jews, especially in Germany, couldn't possibly say with impunity. She also takes advantage of being a woman (an older one at that) and a foreigner wherever she goes. "Being a token everything," she says "can be remarkably liberating." Some consider her a pest, others—at least her daughter, she hopes—love her.

The Illustrator: Hans Traxler is one of Germany's foremost cartoonists, a German with an eye for his country's foibles, which he appreciates as such by reading *The New Yorker.*

INDEX